Praise
Running the Show: Telev... ...nside
by Jeff Melvoin

"A wonderful ride through the raging waters of creating television. It's a book full of sharp insights, great advice, and legitimate wisdom." —**J.J. Abrams**, executive producer, director (*Star Wars, Star Trek, Mission Impossible, Alias*)

* * * * * * * * *

"An insightful, entertaining, insider's look at the entire process of showrunning written by one of the foremost practitioners of the craft. Jeff Melvoin's book is a gift to anyone who's ever considered pursuing a career in television or wondered what a showrunner actually does!" —**John Wells**, executive producer, director (*ER, The West Wing, Shameless*)

* * * * * * * * *

"'What's it like being a showrunner?' 'How do I break into writing television?' 'What are writing staffs like?' Doesn't matter what the question is—from now on, anyone asks, I'm just giving them a copy of Jeff's book. 'All television is personal' according to Jeff, so I'll get personal. I always knew Jeff was a great teacher—the appendix alone is more valuable than any class I ever took. I also know he's a great drama writer—just look at his credits. I find it annoying that he's so funny. It pains me to say, but it's rare that a book this educational is so damn entertaining.'" —**Bill Lawrence**, executive producer, director (*Ted Lasso, Cougar Town, Scrubs, Spin City*)

* * * * * * * * *

"*Running The Show* is as valuable to would-be showrunners as it is fascinating to veterans. Jeff Melvoin offers that rare combination: up-to-the-moment accuracy about a changing television landscape and an insightful historical perspective. There's great advice in every chapter." —**Michelle and Robert King**, executive producers (*The Good Wife, The Good Fight*)

* * * * * * * * *

"There's no one in the field who has mentored as many young writers and contributed more to this generation of showrunning than Jeff Melvoin. A powerful and necessary read." —**Veena Sud**, executive producer (*Seven Seconds, The Killing, Cold Case*)

* * * * * * * * *

"Whether you aspire to produce a television series or just want to know how it's done, there's finally a book with the answers. Invaluable! It's rare that a 'how-to' book is also a page-turner, but Melvoin has great stories to tell and invaluable skills to share. An essential book for anyone interested in the form. *Running the Show* is mandatory reading." —**Edward Saxon**, chair, Peter Stark Producing Program, USC School of Cinematic Arts; Academy Award-winning producer (*The Silence of the Lambs*)

* * * * * * * * *

"The best book on showrunning I've ever read. It's for anyone who wants to run shows or just know how they've been run across the years, even as the medium has changed greatly. It captures the many changes our business has gone through and the larger-than-life personalities and vast challenges one has to navigate and be successful at if you want the dream job of telling stories for tv." —**Greg Berlanti**, executive producer, director (*The Flight Attendant, All American, You, Supergirl,* and over twenty other television series)

* * * * * * * * *

"Melvoin has done pretty much everything in this business. And, more fundamentally, thought about everything. I recommend this book for any writer or aspiring writer." —**David Shore**, executive producer (*House, The Good Doctor*)

* * * * * * * * *

"I've spent the last twenty-three years of my life trying to understand all the tricks, nuances and pitfalls of being a television showrunner and Jeff Melvoin just goes and puts it all in a book for anyone to read? Where was this when I created my first show? Not only an indispensable guide to the mysterious art of creating, selling, staffing, casting, shooting, and posting a television show, but also a humorous and humble journey of one man's Hollywood career through some of your favorite shows. For any aspiring television writer, this is just about the most affordable grad level education you can get." —**Shawn Ryan**, executive producer (*The Shield, The Night Agent, S.W.A.T.*)

* * * * * * * * *

"Jeff Melvoin is the oracle and Yoda of showrunning, and this book demonstrates his decades of hard work and earned wisdom running award-winning one-hour drama series. Melvoin is also the founder of the Writers Guild Showrunner Training Program, guiding hundreds of writer-producers through the unique challenges and rewards of becoming a successful showrunner. Each compact chapter offers his experiences in the trenches, along with practical advice on developing, pitching, selling, getting staffed in a writers room, and, ultimately, running a show—all with candor, nuance, humility, and humor." —**Neil Landau**, executive director, MFA in Film, Television and Digital Media, Grady College of Journalism and Mass Communication, University of Georgia; author, *TV Writing on Demand: Creating Great Content in the Digital Era*

RUNNING THE SHOW

Television from the Inside

Jeff Melvoin

Essex, Connecticut

APPLAUSE
THEATRE & CINEMA BOOKS
An imprint of Globe Pequot, the trade division of
The Rowman & Littlefield Publishing Group, Inc.
4501 Forbes Boulevard, Suite 200, Lanham, Maryland 20706
www.rowman.com

86-90 Paul Street, London EC2A 4NE, United Kingdom

British Library Cataloguing in Publication Information Available

Library of Congress Cataloging-in-Publication Data

Names: Melvoin, Jeff, author.
Title: Running the show : television from the inside / Jeff Melvoin.
Description: Essex, Connecticut : Applause, [2023]
Identifiers: LCCN 2022059924 (print) | LCCN 2022059925 (ebook) | ISBN 9781493075294 (paperback) | ISBN 9781493075300 (ebook)
Subjects: LCSH: Television—Production and direction—Vocational guidance—United States. | Television authorship—Vocational guidance—United States. | Melvoin, Jeff | Television producers and directors—United States—Biography.
Classification: LCC PN1992.75 .M425 2023 (print) | LCC PN1992.75 (ebook) | DDC 791.4502/32—dc23/eng/20230316
LC record available at https://lccn.loc.gov/2022059924
LC ebook record available at https://lccn.loc.gov/2022059925

∞™ The paper used in this publication meets the minimum requirements of American National Standard for Information Sciences—Permanence of Paper for Printed Library Materials, ANSI/NISO Z39.48-1992.

CONTENTS

PART II
BREAKING IN

PART III
RUNNING THE SHOW

FADE IN

WHY THIS BOOK?

If all politics is local, all television is personal. Although there are plenty of books about the industry, I don't know any that convey what it's actually like to write and produce television from the inside—straight talk about what it takes to break in, get to the top, and stay there. Despite hunger for such knowledge from writers, students, and curious viewers, the goods are hard to find, especially in one place. This book, based on my forty years' experience in the business, is my attempt to fill the gap.

As a writer-producer, I've worked on more than a dozen series, contributing to more than 450 hours of one-hour drama, mostly as a showrunner. I've worked in every platform, on Emmy Award–winning shows and shows you've never heard of, but what matters most is that I've worked—and continue to. As a teacher, I've led semester courses at USC, UCLA, and Harvard; taught workshops at the Sundance Institute, the Film Institute of Cologne, and Northwestern, among others; and spoken at professional conferences around the world. For the past eighteen years, I've chaired the Writers Guild of America's Showrunner Training Program (SRTP), a six-week master class I founded for emerging writer-producers. So in addition to making television, I've spent a good deal of my career talking about it. In the many conversations I've had with colleagues, students, friends, and total strangers in that time, two questions often arise: "How did you . . . ?" and "How can I . . . ?" I've organized this book to answer both.

Part I traces my professional odyssey from the Stone Age of broadcast television through the explosion of Peak TV—the chaotic era we're living in today. It's a story of occasional triumphs and intermittent disasters and is the overture for all that follows, introducing motifs and themes to be fully developed in succeeding chapters. Part II tackles what it takes to make the climb from unproduced writer to writer-producer, covering everything from the rudiments of writing to tips on pitching series. Part III is essentially a distillation of the SRTP, providing not only my advice but also wisdom gleaned from the many guest instructors—showrunners, directors, producers, executives, and actors—and class members who have shared their stories over the years.

A caveat: this book is about one-hour television, where I've spent all my career. The worlds of one-hour and half-hour television overlap, but there are significant differences—particularly with traditional half-hour comedy. If you're looking for the inside track on half-hour, I suggest you seek out books specifically on that subject.

And a question: should we still be using the word "television" to define a medium in which many viewers watch series on computers, tablets, smartphones—anything but a TV set? To this I emphatically say, "Yes." I've yet to hear an alternative that could replace it. My friends at the Sundance Institute call their television workshop "The Episodic Content Lab," but I can't see that catching on—"Hey, hon, let's watch some episodic content tonight." If it ain't broke . . .

Finally, for those considering a career in television writing, a word of encouragement. Some TV veterans, either out of cynicism or a sense of moral obligation, do all they can to discourage new writers from entering the business. I'm not one of them, obviously, but if someone can talk you out of it, they've probably done you a favor. Television is a tough trade, and if you can't commit to it blood, bone, and sinew, you're likely better off pursuing something else. Nevertheless, I believe the right combination of persistence, resilience, and that elusive thing called talent will find its way. It might take longer than it used to, but there's simply too much demand for good writing for Hollywood to ignore anyone who can carry the load. When asked why my sons didn't go into the business, my standard reply is, "Just lucky, I guess." But had they chosen to follow in their father's footsteps, this is the book I'd want them to have on their bookshelves—and even look at occasionally. I hope it helps.

I

ADVENTURES IN THE SMALL-SCREEN TRADE

1

"STOP THAT CARROT!"

REMINGTON STEELE

In 1983, dinosaurs ruled the earth. Three dinosaurs, to be exact: NBC, CBS, and ABC. These behemoths were headed for near extinction, but no one knew it at the time. I certainly didn't. I'd been working as a *Time* magazine correspondent in Los Angeles when I jumped ship. Journalism had been a great way to get started as a writer, but I'd promised myself that I'd quit when I was thirty to try my hand at show business. Two months shy of that birthday, I resigned, then called a friend working at MTM Enterprises and told him I wanted to write scripts.

"Movies or television?" he asked.

"What's the difference?" I replied.

The difference, he said, was that nobody tells Paramount how many movies it has to make every year, but television needs three hours of prime time every night. That sounded like a better bet.

"How do you get a job writing for television?" I asked. And he told me.

You wrote a spec script—"on speculation," that is, your own dime—and got it to studio and network executives. Back then, a spec script meant a sample episode of an existing show, not an original pilot. A new writer submitting a pilot would have been laughed out of town. Originality was not what TV execs were looking for; Nielsen ratings were. And you didn't get Nielsen ratings by being original; you got them by being conventional. Before you could write like nobody else, you had to prove you could write like everybody else. And the truth was, the networks didn't *want* you to write like nobody else. The system worked. In 1980, the "Who Shot J.R.?" episode of *Dallas*, a prime-time soap on CBS, drew ninety million viewers, more than half of all US households. Why rock the boat?

Based on the industry's stunning success, the pattern for new writers was fixed: You started by writing on others' shows, learning the ropes for years before you were deemed ready to pitch your own series. This de facto apprenticeship had two major benefits for the networks. First, should the execs buy your idea, they had a reasonable expectation that you'd know how to run a show. Second, by the time you pitched an idea, the system had leached so much creativity from your weary soul that you were only capable of suggesting pallid variations on existing themes—which is all the networks wanted: fresh, but not too fresh; different, but not too different. "My detectives are a father and daughter." "My detectives live on a houseboat." "My detectives are married." "My detective's blind."

I didn't care. I just wanted a job. After leaving *Time*, I'd spent $5,200—my entire life savings—on the first IBM home computer and a Brother daisy wheel printer the size and weight of a boat anchor. I was all in. If I didn't sell a script in the next few months, I'd be looking for freelance journalism assignments. I needed a show to spec.

Back then, a sample for any one-hour series in a particular genre would serve as a calling card for all in that genre because, let's face it, they were pretty much the same show. But there were always series that stood out—they were better written, better produced, just . . . better. And one of them had recently appeared on NBC, produced by MTM, where my friend worked.

Remington Steele was a witty take on the private eye genre with a whiff of cultural relevance in its gender-bending premise: a female detective invents a fictitious male superior to get work; when a con man assumes the role, she has to play along to stay in business. Actors Stephanie Zimbalist and Pierce Brosnan lent the series a light, romantic touch reminiscent of Grace Kelly and

Cary Grant in Hitchcock's *To Catch a Thief*, making the proceedings fun to watch even when things got a bit silly, which they often did.

Mystery was a genre I knew something about (I'd written my college thesis on American detective fiction), so I had my friend sneak me some *Remington* scripts to study. This was a rare gift: unlike today, television scripts were hard to come by, and there was actually a black market for them. With my friend's help, I wrote a spec *Remington*, which was pretty awful but contained one line that changed my life. It appeared in the opening scene, a Beverly Hills costume party where our heroes have been hired to look out for a jewel thief. Remington comes dressed as Sherlock Holmes. Laura Holt (Stephanie's character) comes as a bunny rabbit. She's irate because Remington picked the costumes without consulting her. (It was a different era.) The jewel thief, it turns out, comes dressed as a giant carrot. I have no explanation other than writer's need. When the thief makes off with a diamond necklace, Remington turns to Laura and shouts, "Stop that carrot!" That was the need: a bunny chasing a carrot.

As I said, it was pretty awful. But kind of funny. Maybe. At least Michael Gleason thought so, and that was all that mattered because he was the cocreator and showrunner of *Remington Steele*. Michael invited me in for a meeting and explained that he wasn't interested in the script but had to meet the person who wrote, "Stop that carrot!" In an under-the-table arrangement that would have appalled the Writers Guild, he actually bought that opening scene for $300, my first money in show business. With it, however, came something more valuable: the promise that if *Remington* were picked up for a second season, I'd get a script. Michael subsequently grafted my idea onto a pending episode. The Beverly Hills costume party turned into an "old California" costume party. "Stop that carrot!" became "Stop that Zorro!"

Fine with me. *Remington* was renewed for a second season, and I got a freelance assignment. Midway through writing it, I was offered a job as staff writer, the lowest notch on the totem pole. It was an amazing opportunity but was complicated by a competing offer I'd received to write a freelance episode of the Emmy Award–winning police drama *Hill Street Blues*, also produced by MTM. I'd met *Hill Street* showrunner Steven Bochco a year earlier when I interviewed him for *Time*. After leaving the magazine, I sent him some pages of a *Hill Street* script I'd written. Bochco set up a meeting for me in the show's writers room, presided over by writer-producers Jeffrey Lewis and David Milch.

My recollection of that meeting mostly involves throwing a football around with David, Jeffrey, and other writers until the ball exited through an open second-story window. When a staffer went to retrieve it in the parking lot below, David mooned him. Later, a chocolate cake was brought in for a staffer's birthday and David smashed a piece in his own face. Not quite what I'd expected, but if there had been some sort of test involved, I must have passed it. I got the offer to write an episode.

So now I had a choice. *Hill Street* was clearly the more prestigious show, but it was only a script assignment—and that locker room of a meeting made me wonder where I was likely to learn most. I went with *Remington*. It was the right call. Over the next three years, Michael Gleason became my Irish Catholic rabbi, tutoring me in the craft of episodic writing and the art of being a mensch in a brutal business. I wrote fifteen scripts and contributed to the writing of some fifty others. I was paid to go to school. Such apprenticeships were common then but are increasingly rare today.

I found the demands of TV staff work not dissimilar to being a *Time* correspondent: you were surrounded by bright colleagues in a deadline-driven environment, doing the best you could with the time you had before moving on to the next assignment. Episodes fell into a handful of templates—not formulas, per se, but patterns that challenged you to innovate within familiar guidelines. When writing my college thesis on detective fiction, I'd corresponded with mystery writer John D. MacDonald, author of the Travis McGee series, who likened series work to composing sonatas. I found it an apt analogy: if you're Mozart, the results are brilliant; if you're Salieri, you can still make a living.

Michael prodded us to keep every episode fresh, funny, and unpredictable. He had two ironclad rules for villains: no mobsters and no psychos. Mobsters were a cliché, and psychos led to sloppy plotting—they could do anything *because they're crazy*.

I actually did write one episode featuring a mobster, but since it also involved boxing and a baby left in a gym locker (echoes of Damon Runyon), Michael let me get away with it. I'd originally pitched boxing, a baby, and Christmas, but Michael frowned: "I'll give you two out of three." I dropped Santa.

During my three years at *Remington,* I rose from staff writer to story editor to executive story editor to supervising producer. Sounds impressive, but (as I'll explain more fully in later sections of this book) writers' titles in television are relatively meaningless. On most TV shows, most writers are mostly doing the same thing: breaking stories and grinding out scripts. This was never better illustrated than on the day Michael burst into the writers room toward the end of my second season and proceeded to ask everyone their titles; he had to let the studio know his lineup for next year. "You're staff writer? Next year, you're story editor. You're story editor? Next year, you're executive story editor." He turned to me: "You're executive story editor? Next year, you're supervising producer." Then he left as abruptly as he came. There was a long silence, finally broken when a writer asked, "What was that?" That was television in the 1980s.

It was a much different business than it is today, more carefree for a host of reasons, not the least of which is that the networks were making money hand over fist with no competition in sight. Furthermore, the average content wasn't that good, which made it easy to feel special working on a clever show being watched by twenty million people each week. Although the country had suffered through assassinations, Vietnam, and Watergate, broadcast was still largely an escapist medium where viewers went to be entertained, not challenged. I wouldn't say it was a more innocent time, because the darker truths of the American story were always there to be mined, but it was a more sheltered time, an era when mass media spoke with a singular, powerful voice, providing a daily dose of reassurance for most viewers. One consequence of this cultural subtext was that we didn't come to work on *Remington* feeling the weight of the world on our shoulders, just the weight of the next episode. We were young and cocky, having a ball playing in the world's greatest sandbox. Although I knew better, there were days I felt like it would never end. But of course, it did.

2

TOUGH BEAT

HILL STREET BLUES

NBC canceled *Remington Steele* for the first time in the spring of 1986. After four years of on-screen flirtation, the sparkle between Remington and Laura had faded for many viewers—and for the writers, too, if I'm honest. But interest in the show suddenly revived when it was rumored that Pierce Brosnan would become the next James Bond. Banking on that possibility, MTM entered feverish negotiations with NBC, exercising its options on Pierce and Stephanie Zimbalist the day before the ninety-day option period in their contracts expired. Unfortunately, the gamble backfired when Timothy Dalton was named 007. It would be seven years before Pierce received his license to kill. In the meantime, NBC was unwilling to pay for a full fifth season of *Remington* with the actor who *might have been* James Bond and settled on three two-hour movies instead. The results, to be charitable, were uninspired, and when filming was done, NBC killed the series again, this time for good.

I watched this scenario play out from across the studio lot, because when NBC canceled *Remington* the first time, I'd accepted MTM's offer to join *Hill Street Blues* as a co-executive producer. *Hill Street*, one of television's landmark shows, was entering its seventh, and almost certainly final, season. The ratings were down and the actors' contracts were up. (At the time, seven years was the standard length of actors' commitments in broadcast; today, it's five or less.) My job was to help steer the proud ship to the scrapyard. It turned out to be a rocky voyage.

Showrunner Steven Bochco had been fired off the series after season 5, allegedly for refusing to cut costs, but friction had been building with the studio for some time. In Steven's stead, lieutenants Jeffrey Lewis and David Milch, the guys I'd tossed a football with three years earlier, had taken over. Both were brilliant but burned-out after six years of pounding the same beat. When I showed up in Jeffrey's office that May, he groaned, "I don't want to be here." And I think he meant it.

Hill Street turned out to be a decidedly mixed bag. I'd assumed that a long-running show, especially a hit like *Hill Street*, would be running like a Swiss watch after six years, so I was amazed—appalled might be a better word—to discover what a shambles it was behind the scenes. To begin with, David and Jeffrey had decided to divide the season in two and work independently of each other, a questionable move almost certain to cause dysfunction. Sure enough, we started the season behind on scripts and never caught up—you never do in broadcast television; you just circle the drain in accelerating cycles of despair. Making matters worse, part of my job became patching up writers' psyches after they'd gone ten rounds with David, who could be brutal on scripts and the poor souls responsible for them. I found myself losing sleep; I'd wake up in cold sweats, wondering how I was going to get through the next day, much less the next week.

This downward spiral continued to a point deep in the season when I felt like I was losing my mind, literally. I decided to quit. My agent persuaded me to step away for a week to think things over, using illness as a pretext. With the benefit of some rest, I changed my mind; I didn't want to wonder for the rest of my life whether I could have stayed the course. I told the studio I had only one condition: I be allowed to produce the remaining episodes I was responsible for alone. Under those terms, I finished the season.

On the final night of filming, I was the only producer on set. Lead actor Daniel Travanti and I took a long walk along Ventura Boulevard, chatting about the show and show business. When the last take was done, there was no fanfare, no speeches, just a few handshakes and hugs. *So this is how one of the greatest shows on television ends,* I thought. There'd be an official party later, well attended by network and studio brass, but on this last night of actual work, we simply turned out the lights and went home. *Hill Street* slipped beneath the waves without a sound.

3

STARDUST

OVERALLS, NORTHERN EXPOSURE, *AND THE SUNDANCE KID*

When you're part of a hit show, you're covered with stardust for a while, regardless of what your actual contribution might have been. Coming off *Hill Street*, I had one of the best credits in town and was ready for the next rung of the television ladder: development. If you've never heard of "development hell," the short strokes go like this: a writer comes up with an idea that executives love to death with notes that stretch on forever, ultimately resulting in a script the writer disowns and the studio discards. Development can be far more palatable, however, when the word "deal" is attached to it.

When *Hill Street* ended in 1987, "overall" development deals were the rage, tying a writer to a studio for a set period of time rather than to a specific project. Recognizing the rising value of showrunners, studio execs were throwing extravagant sums at promising writers in what often amounted to little more than raw speculation. Minimally, by signing a hot prospect, a studio took that player off the market, preventing competitors from capitalizing on their potential. It was Hollywood's version of tulip mania (the financial world's first speculative bubble, which burst in Holland in 1634). Lucky me. I happily indentured myself to Columbia-TriStar, where I was given an office, an assistant, a personalized parking space, and more time than I knew what to do with. A colleague told me the key to enjoying an overall was finding the best shopping and dining near the studio. He wasn't joking.

I wrote four pilots over the next two years; two were produced, both based on ideas the studio suggested. One was a spy thriller filmed in what was then Yugoslavia and the other a "space western" produced at Pinewood Studios in England. Neither was picked up to series, but Columbia-TriStar reupped me for another two years. I subsequently wrote several more pilots. This time only one was produced, however, and when it didn't get picked up, the studio couldn't find a reason to keep paying me, and I couldn't blame them. I was thinking maybe I'd be better off writing movies, which is when the last unproduced pilot I'd written (a police drama intended for Harry Belafonte) unexpectedly became my ticket to the best new series on the air.

Northern Exposure was the story of a Jewish doctor from New York City unhappily working off his med school debts in the remote hamlet of Cicely, Alaska. It premiered on CBS in July 1990 as a summer replacement series, the network euphemism for commitments that get burned off when no one's watching. But *Northern Exposure* didn't die. It attracted enough viewers during its initial eight-episode run to warrant another eight-episode order. To CBS's surprise, the audience grew, so the network picked it up for a full season of twenty-two episodes, which is when my agent submitted my Belafonte script to land me an interview. And it worked—almost too well. When I sat down with series cocreator Joshua Brand, he said that based on my material, he thought I'd be better off on another show that he and his writing partner, John Falsey, had created: *I'll Fly Away,* a civil rights drama set in the 1950s. No, no, I insisted. *Northern Exposure* was the right fit for me. Josh relented and hired me in the spring of 1991 as a supervising producer. (John effectively departed *Northern* shortly after I came on board to supervise yet another Brand-Falsey series, *Going to Extremes,* about a med school in the Caribbean.)

Josh and John had cut their teeth at MTM, so they knew what they wanted—and it wasn't conventional television. For *Northern Exposure,* they drew inspiration from films like *Local Hero* and *My Life As a Dog* and from authors as diverse as Herman

Melville and Eudora Welty. Theirs was an Alaska of the mind, where virtually anything was possible; the show eschewed usual broadcast fare like car chases and mayhem in favor of dream sequences and magical realism.

For writers, it was an oasis—provided you could survive. Operationally, there are two types of television shows: teaching hospitals and private hospitals. *Remington Steele* had been a teaching hospital. Showrunner Michael Gleason took us on rounds and let us treat patients, but stepped in before we could kill anyone. *Northern Exposure* was a private hospital. Josh wanted surgeons who could operate without supervision. He wouldn't intercede. If the patient died, you were fired. A lot of excellent writers washed out at *Northern* because they couldn't get on Josh's wavelength quickly enough to stick around. At the age of thirty, I'd been the youngest writer on the *Remington Steele* staff. At forty, I was the youngest on the *Northern Exposure* staff; it was veterans only. My first decade in the business had prepared me well—and if I ever needed justification for my liberal arts education, this was it: everything on *Northern Exposure* was grist for the mill.

My baptism by fire was a page-one (total) rewrite of a script about the town's discovery of a Napoleonic soldier in a block of ice; the dead Frenchman carried a diary revealing that Napoleon hadn't been at the Battle of Waterloo but was actually across the Siberian ice bridge in Alaska at the time, having an affair with an Aleutian woman. When CBS president Jeff Sagansky read the script, he offered Josh $100,000 to stop production. Josh refused. The episode was shot as written, and when it was broadcast in November 1991, CBS cultural critic John Leonard appeared on the network's *Sunday Morning* to exult, "*Northern Exposure* is back."

That script established my bona fides with the other four writers on staff, made up of two teams: husband and wife Andy Schneider and Diane Frolov and partners (and eventual husband and wife) Robin Green and Mitch Burgess. The five of us wrote—or rewrote—most of the scripts over the next four years. What was unique in my experience was how different yet complementary we were as writers. I would marvel when the others' scripts came out. *How'd they do that?* I'd wonder. Then my next script would appear, and they'd ask the same thing. It made for a collegially competitive environment in which we pushed ourselves to outdo one another.

The ratings climbed. At the end of my first season, the network ordered fifty more episodes. Two twenty-five-episode seasons. It was unprecedented. We were nominated for numerous awards. I bought a tux and a Fender Stratocaster. *Northern Exposure* won the Emmy for best drama in 1992. The entire writing staff was nominated individually for best writing; Andy and Diane won. The next year I was nominated again for best writing. I lost (to an episode of *Homicide* written by Tom Fontana), but shrugged. We'd all be going to the Emmys for a long time, I thought. Two years later, *Northern Exposure* was gone. What happened?

After the fifty-episode order was satisfied, CBS ordered a fifth season, at which point Josh Brand stepped away to develop new material. Andy and Diane were tapped to take the reins with veteran writer-producer David Chase, who was reluctantly available because, despite critical raves, *I'll Fly Away*, the show he'd been running for Josh and John, had been canceled. *Northern Exposure* was an odd fit for David; whimsy and warmth aren't exactly the first words that come to mind with him. In fact, in Brett Martin's 2013 book *Difficult Men*, David reveals his contempt for *Northern Exposure.* He'd kept it well hidden from me; I thought David's mordant wit led to some brilliant episodes.

With this new triumvirate in charge, *Northern* was subsequently renewed for a sixth season, which is when things went south in a hurry. Lead actor Rob Morrow, who had grown increasingly unhappy, was written out, his character replaced by a married couple who didn't catch on with the audience. When the network began to tinker with the time slot, the end came quickly.

To consumers today, time slots may seem a quaint notion, but in the second half of the twentieth century they were a matter of life and death for broadcast shows. If viewers couldn't find a program at its usual day and time, they were lost—and so was the program. When *Northern*'s time slot was moved the first time, almost a quarter of our audience disappeared overnight. As the network continued to play with the schedule, ratings plummeted to the point that CBS pulled the plug in the spring of 1995, giving us little time to write a suitable finale. The final insult was the network's decision to burn off the last three episodes in July, when no one was watching. What had begun as a summer replacement series died the death of a summer replacement series.

I recall telling friends at the time that once you understand how broadcast works, what amazes you isn't how much bad television there is, but how anything good gets on the air at all. *Northern* had been a happy accident. Initially, CBS execs thought they'd bought a conventional doctor show set in Alaska; when it turned out to be something else, they did their best to bury it. It was only viewer and critical response that kept the show alive until it became too big to kill.

I'd hoped *Northern Exposure* might teach broadcast how quality drama can succeed with a mass audience and so was thrilled when Robert Redford's company approached me to write a pilot based on *The Milagro Beanfield War*, the John Nichols novel that Redford had directed as a movie in 1988. I saw *Milagro* as the natural successor to *Northern*—similarly philosophical and humane, but specifically grounded in its New Mexico setting, a tragicomic context teeming with magic, myth, and mystery. Between seasons of *Northern*, I visited the villages Nichols had used as the basis for his fictional town of Milagro. In Los Angeles, I interviewed Mexican American students at UCLA to flesh out a character I was introducing. After I hammered out an outline, the day came for me to meet Redford at his beach house north of Malibu. His girlfriend let me in. The Sundance Kid was eating breakfast at the kitchen table; I found myself standing over him, starstruck. All I could think was, "Wow—great hair." Redford invited me to sit down, and minutes later, we were just two guys talking story.

I'm not the kind of writer who immediately falls in love with his material; I tend to pick up my first drafts with tongs, but from the beginning I felt I was on to something special with *Milagro*—with full credit to author John Nichols, of course. I wrote and rewrote, then submitted the pilot script. Redford's development exec told me it was the best first draft she'd ever read. She had notes, of course, but they were easily accommodated. A few days later, we met with ABC. The execs were exceedingly polite—never a good start. They said the material was "high quality," but *Milagro* was competing with another high-quality pilot they'd commissioned, a high school drama called *My So-Called Life*, and they were going to go with that instead. I blinked. The network only had room for one high-quality show on their schedule? They wouldn't even commission the pilot? It made no sense. Because it was a lie.

This became clear when Redford subsequently floated the offer to direct the pilot himself. What network wouldn't want a pilot directed by the guy who, in 1980, had won three Oscars for *Ordinary People*, including best director and best picture? ABC, apparently—because their decision had nothing to do with quality. It had to do with too many brown-skinned people in the cast. Nobody would say that out loud, of course, but that was the explanation I got years later from a former ABC executive who'd been involved. The network brass didn't think *Milagro* would draw a mass audience, so they killed it in the cradle.

I was crushed. Which is why it's particularly painful to concede that ABC probably made the right decision. For them. At the time. The show *wasn't* suited for the mass American audience of 1994. The fate of *My So-Called Life* proved that. Created by Winnie Holzman (who would go on to write the book for the Broadway musical *Wicked*), produced by TV veterans Ed Zwick and Marshall Herskovitz (*Thirtysomething*), and featuring a cast led by a thirteen-year-old unknown named Claire Danes (*Homeland*), it was an outstanding series that earned critical raves—and sank like a stone, canceled after nineteen episodes. Clearly, reserving even one prime-time slot for a "high-quality" show was a risk for ABC. In retrospect, *Northern Exposure* was even more of a miracle than I knew at the time.

Had niche programming existed back then, perhaps both *My So-Called Life* and *Milagro* would have enjoyed healthy runs. But those weren't the rules; it was the tyranny of the majority with no court of appeal. So after *Northern Exposure* folded, I found myself holding few cards. Then I got a call from David E. Kelley.

4

"THEY'VE RUINED MY FAVORITE SHOW"

PICKET FENCES

Picket Fences premiered in 1992, two years after *Northern Exposure*, and was a critical smash. It was also a major pain in our side at *Northern*. In 1993, *Northern Exposure*'s fourth season, we were nominated for sixteen Emmys (a record) and didn't win a single one (also a record). We lost the best series award to *Picket* that year—and the next—and weren't even nominated in our final season. Adding insult to injury, critics tended to lump the two shows together as "quirky" dramas, which did both a disservice. Although *Picket* bore superficial resemblance to *Northern* as an ensemble drama set in a small town, it was very much its own show, reflecting the unique talent and tastes of its creator, David E. Kelley, a former attorney with a flair for wrapping controversial subjects in seriocomic stories that resolved in the courtroom.

A critical favorite if not a ratings champ, *Picket* was renewed for a fourth season in 1995 as an enticement by CBS to keep David tied to the network. It didn't work. He signed with ABC instead. While playing out his CBS commitment, however, he wanted someone to take over the reins at *Picket* for what would almost certainly be its final season due to declining numbers. Although we didn't know each other, David called to ask if I might be interested. I was—with reservations. I wasn't sure I could replicate his signature style and thought it would be a mistake to try. I'd have to come up with stories that reflected my *Northern Exposure* sensibility, leaning on character more than ripped-from-the-headlines issues. David was encouraging; we agreed to talk further.

That week, I also had a meeting with Les Moonves, then president and CEO of Warner Bros. Television, who wanted me to sign a development deal there. When I told him about the situation at *Picket*, he flicked his hand dismissively. "I don't get that show," he said, adding some disparaging remarks. "Come to Warner Bros."

Signing with Warner Bros. meant going back to development. *Picket* would be my first showrunning job, a major step up the ladder. Considering the series' sagging ratings, I felt there was little to lose and perhaps much to gain by making a course adjustment. That was criminally naive on my part, but David was willing to go along, so I signed on. I called the cast to let them know what I had in mind, put together a writing staff, and went to work. All seemed to be going well as we approached the September premiere, which is when the first drop of blood hit the water.

The Television Critics Association reception was an annual industry event where members of the press had the chance to preview the coming season and interview execs, writers, and actors. Important fact: some weeks after my meeting with Les at Warner Bros., he left the studio to become president of CBS, home to *Picket Fences*. When I arrived at the TCA reception, I was immediately collared by a pair of his assistants, who said that Les was so sorry, he didn't mean it, and he wanted to see me. Sorry about what? It turns out that during the CBS press conference, a critic had asked if Les thought the quality of *Picket Fences* was the same as it had been under David E. Kelley. And Les, who'd denigrated the series to my face only months before, answered slyly: "What do you think?"

That critic did the CBS president a huge favor. In *Picket*, Les had inherited a critical darling that was a ratings loser. If the press bailed on the show, he could kill it without any stink sticking to him. All that was required was to throw the new showrunner under the bus, which he'd just done—and subsequently denied.

"Not what I meant," Les said apologetically when we sat down in a half-empty cocktail tent. "I don't even know what

I said." It was all a bit surreal, the network president assuring me he had my back after sticking a knife in it. I merely nodded. What else could I do? The damage had been done; it wasn't like Les was going to reconvene the critics to correct the record. All I wanted to do at that moment was get back to the office to keep working on the next script. Which I did.

Two months later, in late October 1995, our sixth episode, "Heart of Saturday Night," was broadcast. It had been my idea. Inspired by the Tom Waits song of the same name, I wanted to center an episode around a few hours in the lives of the show's main characters. There were no headline issues, simply a series of small moments well observed, exactly the kind of episode I'd wanted to bring to the series. Ellie Herman wrote a beautiful script; director Jeremy Kagan and the cast brought it to life. I loved it.

TV Guide hated it. "They've ruined my favorite television show" was how "Couch Critic" Jeff Jarvis led off his column after the episode aired. He then proceeded to catalogue how thoroughly I had desecrated the church of David E. Kelley. For readers born after the Reagan administration, *TV Guide* was the bible of the TV-watching public, a weekly digest the size and heft of a paperback novel listing the week's complete TV schedule in detail (when such a thing was possible). It also featured articles and reviews that were a major influence on viewers. I couldn't imagine a worse start to my showrunning career. What surprised me was my reaction—or more accurately, my lack of reaction. *Guess he didn't like it,* I thought. This was an act of neither supreme self-confidence nor delusional denial, but a reflection of the workload I was managing. I couldn't waste time worrying about what Jeff Jarvis or anyone else thought; I had a season to finish.

I don't know if the ratings declined after that *TV Guide* column. Truth is, I've never paid much attention to ratings one way or the other because I've always felt you can't do much about them. What the audience is reacting to is something you worked on months before, so altering course after getting bad numbers is like telling the *Titanic* to turn left after hitting the iceberg. I knew the numbers for season 4 weren't great, but I don't recall getting any worried calls from Les or other CBS execs—which, by the way, is not a good sign. The opposite of love in television isn't hate; it's apathy. When the network stops giving notes, it's time to update your résumé.

I'd known *Picket* was doomed since the TCA debacle, but we soldiered on, eventually finding a comfortable balance between a *Northern Exposure* sensibility and David's issue-driven style. Of course, by then, the critics had abandoned us, along with a sizable chunk of the audience. When *Picket* was canceled at the end of the season, the received wisdom was that the show had declined in quality and the ratings had followed. The truth is more nuanced. The show was nominated for five Emmys during my season—more than the previous year—and won two: outstanding lead actress for Kathy Baker and outstanding lead actor for Ray Walston. (Louise Fletcher was also nominated for outstanding guest actress, and the other nominations were for casting and costumes). Actors don't win Emmys without good material to deliver.

Nevertheless, I'd taken a pretty good beating. Like Rocky Balboa in his first outing, I had stayed on my feet until the final bell, but I certainly hadn't won on points. What I've subsequently concluded is that the key to your first showrunning job is to survive it. Anything else is gravy. But there was a final twist in the tale. In its June 28, 1997, issue, *TV Guide* ran a cover story called "The 100 Greatest Episodes of All Time." They chose one *Picket Fences* episode: "Heart of Saturday Night." (Clearly, Jeff Jarvis had not been part of that jury.) The accompanying description read:

> What happens when you explore the "Heart of Saturday Night" in Rome, Wisconsin? Nothing much . . . just love and death and friendship and stars. Just life . . . boring, sad, frustrating, ethereal—a miracle. And based on the marvelously subtle, sweet, and profound episode—which has the strength and integrity of TV's Golden Age dramas—it's hard to imagine a better place to spend an evening.

Admittedly, such judgments are subjective and quickly forgotten, but it was gratifying to know that at least one person understood what we'd set out to do so many months before. It meant a lot to me then; it still does today.

5

HOBSON'S CHOICE

SHOWVERALLS, EARLY EDITION

After *Picket Fences,* I was no longer such a hot prospect. The show had been canceled on my watch, which is all that matters to casual observers—which is to say, most of Hollywood. So I was extremely grateful when my old benefactor Columbia-TriStar took me in again, although I discovered that the development business had changed since I'd left it. The extravagance I'd known a decade earlier during the peak of overall deals had been the result of a market bubble. When it burst under the weight of too many failed pilots, the studios sobered up. Now, in 1996, rather than let unsuccessful pilot writers simply ride out overalls doing nothing, execs assigned idle hands to existing shows. The hope was that these shotgun marriages would produce beautiful children, but at the very least, studios could charge off an overall writer's salary against services rendered. These new deals, sardonically referred to by writers as "showveralls," generated resentment on both sides of the showrunner's desk: pilot writers bristled at having to work on someone else's show, and showrunners disliked having to accommodate grumpy veterans they hadn't hired. No matter. There had been a market correction, and this was the new reality. So be it. I was happy to have a home.

Eric Tannenbaum, president of Columbia-TriStar's TV division, had offered me a variation on a showverall: if I consulted on one of two shows on his slate, I could use the rest of my time to develop pilots. I chose *Early Edition*, a rookie series starring newcomer Kyle Chandler as Gary Hobson, a Chicagoan who gets tomorrow's newspaper a day early. The idea had been hatched by two unproduced writers; they shared the concept with a screenwriter, who wrote the pilot and was subsequently replaced by veteran showrunner Bob Brush. The show was written and edited in Los Angeles but shot in Chicago. Not surprisingly with such a pedigree and corresponding logistical challenges, chaos reigned behind the scenes. When I asked a beleaguered Bob Brush what he wanted from me, he smiled wearily and said, "A script."

So I wrote an episode and was about to go to work on my own development when Columbia-TriStar exec Sarah Timberman asked me to look at a pilot script, a teen drama written by a feature writer. If the pilot turned out well, she said, the studio wanted an experienced writer-producer to assist with the first season. I thought the script was very well written, but I couldn't relate to it; it didn't reflect my sensibility. It was called *Dawson's Creek*.

After the pilot was shot, Sarah asked me to watch it, and she actually sat in the room with me to guarantee that I did. I could see why she thought she had a hit on her hands. It was a well-produced hour with a stellar cast, but I still didn't respond to it, and because you can't write well for something you don't believe in, I passed again. *Dawson's Creek* went on to become a smash, running for six years. Sarah went on to become a highly successful independent producer, and I went back to my desk, where, after a few weeks, I got a call from Bob Brush asking me to help steer *Early Edition* through its second season. The studio sweetened the pot with a heftier deal. I liked Bob, I liked the show, I liked the money. Done.

Shortly after that, Bob essentially disappeared, content to leave me in charge. I reassured the trio of writer-producers who remained that I wasn't coming in with a broom. Even if I'd wanted to replace them—which I didn't—I had no time to make new hires. We got through the season. When the show was renewed, I was able to expand the staff. The series ran for two more years, providing me with a laboratory in which I was able to develop my showrunning skills in all departments.

It also provided a bruising lesson in power politics from Les Moonves. *Early Edition* was a CBS show, so it was his baby. When the network renewed it for a third season, Les had an idea for two new characters: a single mom and her young son. I thought it was a decent idea, so we wrote them in. When it came time for casting, Les had a suggestion for the mom: Kristy Swanson, who'd played Buffy in the 1992 movie *Buffy the Vampire Slayer* (which preceded the TV show by five years). I honestly don't know why Les suggested Kristy—and I'm not being coy. I assumed he thought a movie star would be good for ratings, and maybe that's all there was to it. Regardless, Kristy was "offer only," meaning she wouldn't read for the part; we'd have to offer it to her. But she wasn't sure she wanted it, so she asked for a meeting.

While that was being set up, we proceeded with the normal casting process, which is when I got a look at the CBS corporate culture that would ultimately bring Les down two decades later. In a casting discussion with a CBS executive, I mentioned an actor who'd been the costar of a hit sitcom a few years earlier. She was at the upper end of the age range of actors we were considering, but I found her appealing in a wholesome way. The exec tilted his head, genuinely puzzled: "Would you want to fuck her?" I blinked, stunned—and confused. Did he mean fuck her as a character on-screen or in her trailer between takes? Based on subsequent disclosures, I'm inclined to believe the latter. At the time, however, I merely stammered that I thought she'd be good for the part.

That night, I met Kristy Swanson for drinks in Hollywood. She was as glamorous as advertised. We had a pleasant conversation during which I did my best to sell her on the part. A day later, she passed, which was fine with me. I didn't think she was right for the role, and considering her reputation for being difficult on set, I felt we'd dodged a bullet.

We subsequently brought three actors to CBS. "Taking an actor to the network" is a ritual that oozes executive power. The prospects are led individually into a small theater with raked seating to read before the network president, like a gladiator competing before the emperor (or empress) and a retinue of courtiers. When the auditions were done and the last of our three combatants had been escorted out, Les turned to me and asked, "So, what do you think?" All heads swiveled in my direction—network sessions aren't just stressful for actors; they can be hard on showrunners, too. I swallowed and said the actor I liked most was a former model named Leslie Bibb. Les asked, "You don't think she's too young?" She was younger than I'd originally envisioned, I admitted, but I thought she'd play well opposite Kyle; I believed in her. Les considered, then nodded. We cast Leslie Bibb.

That was on a Friday. On Monday, Leslie was on an airplane from LA to Chicago when I got a call from Nina Tassler, VP of drama at CBS. "Are you sitting down?" she asked. Not a good start. "Les talked to Kristy Swanson over the weekend. She's going to do the part."

"No, she's not," I said. "Kristy had her shot and passed. Leslie Bibb's on a plane to Chicago right now." Nina said she understood, but this was what Les wanted and that was the way it was going to be. "Then I quit," I said, and I hung up.

Minutes later, my agent called. "What did you just do?" I explained that Les Moonves couldn't just step in after the fact and change things. My agent proceeded to school me in the ways of Hollywood. "Quitting won't do anything except hurt your career," he said. "Les is network president. He's going to get his way. If you quit, you're going to let down the two hundred people who work for you, the show will shut down until they find your replacement, Kristy Swanson will still do that part, and you'll be out on your ass."

There are few moments in life when one has a genuine epiphany. This was one of them. The light suddenly dawned for me as vividly as it does for wayward newscaster Peter Finch in Paddy Chayefsky's movie *Network* when corporate chairman Ned Beatty rails: "You have meddled with the primal forces of nature, and YOU WILL ATONE!"

I didn't want to let people down, and I certainly didn't want to ruin my career for nothing. Fuck. I mentioned that I'd already quit. I could hear my agent exhale: "Oh, Nina's fine with that.

She said she admires your integrity." Right. The integrity I was about to sell out. Okay. Fine. I was back in. Now I had to do damage control. When Leslie landed at O'Hare, the line producer apologized profusely and gave her the choice of staying in Chicago overnight or getting on the next plane back to LA. She decided to turn around. I sent her a boatload of flowers and an anguished apology. I'm not sure anything could have improved the situation, but life—and the series—went on.

It turned out Kristy Swanson never felt comfortable with the part or the show. She and Kyle had zero chemistry onscreen—and it showed. Eventually, CBS conceded that the arrangement wasn't working. We wrote Kristy out. Fortunately, ratings remained high enough to warrant a fourth season, but we started the year with lower numbers and never recovered. When CBS called it quits in spring of 2000, we had completed ninety episodes, ten shy of the coveted number for syndication but enough to give the studio a profitable run in secondary markets. Instead of the guy who'd killed *Picket Fences,* I was now the guy who'd saved *Early Edition.* It gave me more options, which proved a blessing—because the world of television had just changed forever.

6

CRACKS IN THE FOUNDATION

GOING TO CALIFORNIA

On January 10, 1999, *The Sopranos* debuted on HBO. It was the beginning of the end of the broadcast empire. Ironically, creator David Chase had first tried to sell the show to the big three networks, but they had all passed. HBO was a last resort; few writers at the time would have considered the subscription cable channel a desirable home. HBO had flirted with original series for a decade without making a dent in public awareness (despite some innovative programming). A major hurdle was Americans' reluctance to pay for programs of unproven provenance when they'd always gotten their television for free. HBO catered to a select audience primarily interested in exclusive sporting events, comedy specials, and uncensored movies.

So when *The Sopranos* appeared, critics were astonished. The *New York Times* said it "may be the greatest work of American popular culture in the last quarter century." It became the first cable series to receive an Emmy nomination for outstanding drama. Not long after the premiere, I called to congratulate David, whom I'd worked with on *Northern Exposure*. He asked if I thought the broadcast networks would learn anything from the show's success. "Yes," I said. "All the wrong things." Rather than look for original material with a deeply personal point of view, they were going to commission a lot of gangster shows and amp up the sex and violence as much as the FCC would allow. Which is pretty much what happened.

But the revolution had begun. Before *The Sopranos,* no one expected TV to compete with the movies in content, sophistication, or production value. *The Sopranos* flipped the script. Even if broadcast executives had been prescient enough to perceive the threat, however, there was little they could have done to stop it. Not only was HBO unbound by government strictures on language, sex, and violence, but the channel also had a radically different economic model than broadcast, relying on subscribers rather than advertisers for revenue, which freed HBO execs from fear of Madison Avenue. In fact, where broadcast shunned controversy, HBO courted it, targeting viewers tired of the same old stuff. It was the opposite of broadcasting; it was narrowcasting.

The Sopranos had an immediate impact on me. Before the series appeared, my colleagues and I might have boasted among ourselves that we were making little movies every week, but we didn't mean it—not really. The fact is, we weren't making movies; we were making *television,* which was its own thing, something we could be proud of at its best, but not to be confused with movies. Now, television could aspire to cinematic heights—or at least shows on premium cable could. Broadcast suddenly found itself crippled by what traditionally had been its strength: its business model. And HBO knew it, hammering their advantage home with the marketing mantra: "It's not television, it's HBO."

No kidding. Broadcast had been a great training ground for me, but clearly it was time to move on. Opportunity soon presented itself at Showtime, HBO's emerging rival. Though the channel had enjoyed some success with original programming, they hadn't come up with a breakout hit on par with *The Sopranos.* They thought they might have found it, however, in *Going to California,* a pilot written by screenwriter Scott Rosenberg (*Beautiful Girls, Con Air*). Broadcast still demanded years of TV experience from writers before they could pitch series, but premium cable welcomed outsiders like Scott. Being new to television, however, Scott needed a creative partner to produce the show—and the studio execs insisted on one to protect their investment. Because that studio happened to be my old benefactor Columbia-TriStar, *Going to California* landed on my desk. I loved it. It was *Route 66* for the MTV generation, the picaresque adventures of two small-town Massachusetts dudes who hit the road to retrieve a buddy gone missing after a romantic calamity. Scott and I hit it off from the start. If nothing else, I thought, this would be fun.

The pay at Showtime was not on par with broadcast—cable series were still in their infancy and money was accordingly tight—but I was in it for the creative opportunity, as were others who signed on, including the pilot director, Peter Howitt (*Sliding Doors*), and other feature directors who committed to individual episodes. The stars were unknowns, but many of the guest cast were drawn from Scott's orbit of movie colleagues, including Vince Vaughn and Rosanna Arquette. Adding to the novelty, Showtime agreed to shoot all twenty episodes on the road, which allowed us to write locations as characters in themselves. For example, Scott was driving through North Carolina one day when he noticed roadside advertising for a nudist colony. On the spot, he decided to set an episode there. As he later told the *Los Angeles Times*: "The difference (between features and TV) is that I came up with the nudist colony idea three weeks ago and now we are shooting it. . . . That's amazing, because even the best-case scenario for features is a year from page to stage, so you just can't beat it."

The scripts for *Going to California* were fresh, funny, and often oddly moving. When the show was previewed for critics, *Newsday* raved, saying the series would do for Showtime what *The Sopranos* had done for HBO. It didn't.

There were several reasons. First, we premiered in August, when nobody in America was looking for a new series. Second, by the time the *Newsday* review appeared, we were told that Showtime had exhausted its marketing budget—on what I'm not sure, but apparently there was no money left to trumpet the *Newsday* review. The real show-killer, however, was distribution. Back then, Showtime lacked a truly national subscriber base, which became painfully clear when we held our wrap party in Austin, Texas. We'd just finished filming there on the very day the series premiered, so naturally we wanted to hoist margaritas with cast and crew while watching the show. Trouble was, we couldn't find a single bar or hotel in Austin that carried Showtime. Not one. This was not a good omen. Subsequently, *Going to California* was enjoyed by dozens of viewers around the country before driving off a cliff à la *Thelma and Louise*. Showtime would find its breakout hit a few years later with *Dexter*, but by then our show was long gone.

Nevertheless, I had few complaints. Premium cable had lived up to its reputation for no-holds-barred storytelling. And despite squabbles over budget, disappointment over marketing, and the hysteria of producing twenty episodes on the road, the studio and the network had stood behind the show to the best of their abilities. We were ahead of our time—at least that's my story, and I'm sticking to it. We weren't *The Sopranos*, but we were good. And different. And I'd been right about one thing: we had fun.

7

ONE AND DONE

LINE OF FIRE

Going to California was my first "one and done," a series canceled after just one season. Before that, every show I'd worked on had run for at least four years. I didn't realize how unusual that was until colleagues told me they'd never returned to the same show from one year to the next. That floored me. A long-running series is a learning factory. Of course, as *Hill Street Blues* demonstrated, not every hit is an oasis of stability—in fact, many successful shows are total shitstorms behind the scenes, but even so, there's usually a modicum of established protocol to learn from. By contrast, first-year shows are a constant fire drill; you might never get your bearings before you find yourself back on the street.

Historically, being part of a failed series made you damaged goods, if only temporarily. After *Going to California* went down, I thought my career would hit a lull. But winds of change were blowing. The operating ethos for broadcast had always been "Don't rock the boat." Now the boat was taking on water. The first torpedo had been *The Sopranos* in 1999; the second came in 2002, when actor Michael Chiklis won the Emmy for best actor for his performance in *The Shield,* Shawn Ryan's incendiary cop show on FX. The impact of that victory was stunning. *The Sopranos* aired on subscription cable, reserved for those willing to pay for it, and so could be dismissed as marginal damage—and more to broadcast's prestige than to the bottom line. But *The Shield* was shown on basic cable, available to a much wider audience, and thus represented a greater economic threat. It was time to man the pumps.

To this point, broadcast's response to cable had been tepid at best. Now the networks found themselves up against a growing number of original cable series exploring creative terrain that broadcast feared to tread—and critics and viewers were celebrating. What's astonishing in retrospect is how successful the networks had been in ignoring the wave of popular dissent sweeping the country since the mid-1960s. An undercurrent of social criticism had long been represented on the big screen, but on network television it was still John Wayne's America. That was about to change. Because of cable's success with controversial material, the fissure in the cultural firmament could no longer be ignored. The question was, how would the networks respond? And the answer soon came back: poorly.

Faced with a nuanced, genuinely complex problem, broadcast execs responded with simplistic, monolithic solutions. Essentially, they did a one-eighty: convention was out; originality was in. Before, television experience had been considered an asset for a writer; now, it was a contagion. Broadcast execs were looking for anyone *but* veteran TV writers. Screenwriters, playwrights, journalists, short-story writers, and even poets suddenly found themselves hunted like big game. A recent college grad with a short film at Sundance could land a lucrative pilot deal.

This convulsion had an obvious upside: broadcast was finally pursuing fresh ideas. But the strategic flaws were quickly revealed as shows created by rookie TV writers crashed and burned, not for lack of talent, necessarily, but lack of experience. The networks realized that their promising neophytes needed veteran guidance. It was this logic that had led Columbia-TriStar to pair me with Scott Rosenberg (and several years later would prompt me to create the WGA's Showrunner Training Program to compensate for the lack of apprenticeship opportunities as the industry expanded).

I soon found myself assisting rookie creators on several series. One venture involved feature director-writer Rod Lurie (*The Contender*), who'd sold *Line of Fire*, an FBI show, to ABC.

Rod was one of the first feature directors to come to broadcast, and he personified the best and, on occasion, the worst of that trend. He knew how to load up a movie with excitement but had little feel for the broader canvas of a television season. Like many writer-directors I've subsequently worked with, Rod wrote scenes he wanted to direct, which made for good moments but not necessarily good stories—and series television depends on good stories. It devours good stories. What happens next, and why? These are the questions writers are constantly asking in the writers room. Directors tend not to care so much about things like that; once a big idea surfaces, they're quickly downstream contemplating what crane they want to use. I told Rod, "You keep dropping big rocks in the pond. But television isn't just about the splash. It's about playing the ripples." Rod didn't like the ripples. When *Line of Fire* was canceled after only nine episodes, there were no eulogies in the press.

But there was at least one bright spot for me personally. The fine cast included Leslie Bibb, last seen in this narrative arriving at Chicago O'Hare International Airport with a leading role in *Early Edition*, only to be put on a plane back to Los Angeles without that role because CBS president Les Moonves had given it to another actor. After that injustice, I wouldn't have been surprised if Leslie never spoke to me again, but she was extremely gracious during our time together on *Line of Fire*, which provided a nice coda to what had been a disgraceful incident.

After *Line of Fire* went down, ABC asked me to look at an outline written by Damon Lindelof and J. J. Abrams for a series called *Lost*. I did—and passed. Now, before I appear to be the worst literary judge of all time, let me restate something I said earlier when passing on *Dawson's Creek*: you can't contribute meaningfully to a show you don't have a feel for, and I didn't have a feel for *Lost*. Also (he says a bit defensively), the outline I read was significantly different from the pilot that was eventually filmed. For example, Jack, the lead character played by Matthew Fox, got sucked into a jet engine at the end of the pilot and died. And there were no flashbacks revealing the characters' backstories, no indication of what was to follow. To me, the outline read like a combination of the Tom Hanks movie *Castaway* and a haunted house thriller. I still have my notes: *Can we stay interested in this group of survivors on an island for three years? I wonder.*

Okay, clearly, I wasn't the right guy for the job.

But one door closes and another opens.

8

TAKE THE J. J. TRAIN

ALIAS, *SHOWVERALLS—THE SEQUEL*

When *Line of Fire* ended in spring of 2004, ABC offered me a showverall, which led to a phone call from J. J. Abrams: Would I be interested in taking over the fourth season of *Alias*, his spy drama starring Jennifer Garner? Under the terms of a showverall, I knew it was better to jump than be pushed. I added it up: *Alias* was a hot show; I found J. J. to be funny, whip-smart, and charming as hell; and finally, it's not often a fifty-year-old father gets to be a hero to his teenage sons, and mine loved *Alias*. I jumped.

Broadcast had been ripe for a new breed of television creator when J. J. came along. A true Hollywood wunderkind raised on *Star Wars* and *Indiana Jones*, J. J. knew how to push TV's cinematic boundaries—and did. His signature style on *Alias* was to tantalize the audience with jaw-dropping twists, fantastical backstories, and relentless action. Should things ever slow down, the go-to move was kill off a series regular. After three years of breakneck storytelling, however, there were few regulars left to kill, and the plotlines had become such a confusing tangle that even the most die-hard fans had trouble untying them. My mission was to help straighten things out and get the show a fifth season.

J. J. and I cowrote the opening two-parter, but as production approached, he disappeared with the script and added an entirely new opening: a fight sequence on a train involving heavy use of green screen and visual effects. It was an eye-opener for me; I'd never worked with VFX before. J. J. was a wiz with the latest technology. He sensed the sequence would be a real grabber—and it was. I'm not sure it made a whole lot of sense, but it launched the season with a bang. Cinematic stunts like that had traditionally been too time-consuming and expensive for television, but J. J. was one of the pioneers demonstrating how new cameras and software could make spectacle accessible to the small screen. It was one of several innovations that *Alias* helped introduce to the medium.

Less flashy but no less significant, J. J. changed the way viewers actually watched television. Before *Alias* debuted in 2001, the standard broadcast template for a one-hour script was a teaser and four acts. Teasers—the short sequences that lead to main titles—allowed viewers with remote controls to sample shows at the top of the hour before settling on a choice. (This was in the early days of DVR technology, before time-shifting—the ability to record a show for later viewing—was a thing for consumers.) Recognizing this, J. J. deliberately lengthened the teasers on *Alias,* so that by the time viewers could tell where an episode was going, it was too late to switch channels. He essentially turned the teaser into act one, transforming the template from a teaser and four acts into no teaser and five acts. Over time, with the networks' active encouragement, this template would morph into six acts on most broadcast dramas, with the final act being little more than a punctuation point. Neither writers nor consumers would argue that six acts make for better television, necessarily, but once J. J. stretched the form, the money people realized they could cram in advertising more frequently if they had more acts—and so they did. *Alias* deserves a footnote (albeit of dubious distinction) for its part in this "evolution."

Another unintended ramification of *Alias* was the death of reruns. Previously, networks reran every hour of a twenty-two-episode order to fill out the season. But that proved problematic with *Alias* because viewers had to watch every episode to keep up. This led to cultlike devotion among fans but simultaneously diminished the value of reruns. Die-hard viewers didn't need or want reruns; they wanted fresh episodes every week and complained when they didn't get them. So ABC stopped using reruns on *Alias*. Over time, all three networks would drop reruns on serialized dramas, ending a source of incremental revenue for writers, actors, and directors.

As for my season on *Alias*, after the opening two-parter, J. J. was only an intermittent presence because he was being pulled in so many directions, particularly prep for *Mission Impossible Three*, his first feature assignment as a director. Subsequently, the writing staff and I managed to untangle most—if not all—of the knots plaguing the series, while tying a few of our own. Benefiting from a time slot change, *Alias* received its highest ratings ever, winning renewal for a fifth season.

Having satisfied ABC's corporate goal, I was given license to leave the show to pursue my own development with ABC. Excited to get going, I met with former NBC president Warren Littlefield, now an independent producer under contract to ABC, who pitched me a captivating family drama based on a true story about a bookie in suburban Cleveland. I happily wrote the pilot, thinking that with Warren's participation we had an excellent shot at getting on the air.

New Yorker movie critic Pauline Kael once wrote that Hollywood is the only place where a person can die of encouragement. Well, we got plenty of encouragement. Unfortunately, it all came from midlevel development execs at ABC, not the upper-tier decision makers. A few days after I turned in my script for formal network approval, Warren called: "It's real quiet over there." We were done, but we didn't know why. You rarely do in this business. It's only when the band starts packing up for the night and you're still sitting in your folding chair that you realize you're not going to be asked to dance. I suspect the reason for such bad manners is that most midlevel execs don't really know themselves why your show didn't make it. Or they do know—their bosses overruled them—and are equally embarrassed to admit that. Regardless, after six months of work . . . crickets.

Because I was still on a showverall, the piper now had to be paid, so when ABC suggested I join a midseason replacement series created by feature writers Michelle and Robert King, I readily agreed. It was an ensemble drama called *Injustice* about a group of lawyers and investigators working on behalf of the wrongfully convicted.

Despite a powerful pilot and strong cast, the show failed; among other factors, I don't think the broadcast audience was willing to embrace the idea that there are a lot of wrongfully accused people behind bars. Regardless, Michelle and Robert learned from the experience. Their next series, *The Good Wife*, would run on CBS for seven years, proving it was still possible to mount an outstanding broadcast drama in the face of cable competition. For me, however, it was another one and done. My ABC contract expired soon after *Injustice* did, so I was pondering next moves when I got a call that would change the next seven years of my life.

9

TOUR OF DUTY

ARMY WIVES

"There's this new Lifetime series that's in trouble," my agent said.

"I'm not interested in a Lifetime series," I said.

"It's called *Army Wives*."

I said I *really* wasn't interested in a Lifetime series called *Army Wives*, which sounded like a rip-off of the hit ABC show *Desperate Housewives*. And Lifetime, a self-styled "women's network" known for soapy melodramas, was about the last place I'd want to work. My agent suggested that out of courtesy to my recent employer ABC Studios, which coproduced *Army Wives*, I should at least take a look. Besides, he said, there were some pluses to consider: The show was picked up; the cast and crew were in place in Charleston, South Carolina; and it would be a chance to work in basic cable. He had a point.

Basic cable occupied creative territory somewhere between broadcast and subscription cable. Fueled by both advertising revenue and license fees from distributors, it could be more adventurous than broadcast, though not as bold as HBO or Showtime. There were still advertisers' sensibilities to consider, and scripts still had to be written with act breaks for commercials. Budgets were tighter and pay scales lower than broadcast, but I'd heard the trade-off was broader creative scope and streamlined bureaucracy. So I took a look at the pilot—and was astounded.

The writing was terrific, the acting first-rate, and production values high. Although the plot could get a bit operatic, the show put a spotlight on an important slice of American society during the Afghanistan and Iraq wars that broadcast series had failed to capture. Despite this, however, the production was in a deep hole. Series creator Katherine Fugate, a screenwriter with limited television experience, had been paired with a first-time showrunner, and the two didn't get along. After filming just one episode beyond the pilot, production had shut down for lack of scripts, and the showrunner was fired. Nevertheless, the studio wanted to be back up and running within ten days.

Walking into a crisis like that is like pulling up to an accident scene on the interstate. It's triage; you have to assess what needs to be done and in what order. I didn't know if the patient could be saved, but I'd performed enough emergency surgery to believe that I was as well-equipped as anyone to try. And I wanted to try. I had an immediate feel for the show, and with only a thirteen-episode order instead of the twenty-two I was used to in broadcast, I figured it would all be over in less than four months one way or the other. What the hell?

I sat down with Katherine and assured her I wasn't there to take her show away from her, which is the biggest fear of inexperienced creators. I said I was there to get her show on its feet. I next called the actors to introduce myself and let them know that filming would resume soon. Then I had to make good on that. Utilizing Katherine's writing to the fullest while supervising a small staff and a handful of freelancers, I got us back into production in ten days and we didn't shut down for the rest of the season. *Army Wives* went on to become the biggest one-hour hit in Lifetime's history to that point.

As the show rebounded from its initial trauma over the course of the season, however, so did Katherine, who became increasingly vocal about where she wanted the series to go. That was only natural—it was her show. The problem was that we disagreed. Although individual episodes of *Army Wives* could slip into melodrama, I felt the show's greatest strength was small moments well observed, a particular preference of mine. Influenced by other series' finales, however, Katherine felt the first season needed to end with a bang. Literally. She wrote a concluding episode in which a deranged soldier blows himself up on our army base, leaving the audience to wonder who in our regular cast had been killed. I thought it was ill-advised. For one thing, it seemed inappropriate to have the show's first fatality be a family member at home while the soldiers in our series were risking their lives abroad. For another, I thought such a finale would shroud the second season in an oppressive veil of grief. Based on these truly creative differences, it was clear to me that one of us had to go, and I thought it should be me. Only a few months earlier, I'd looked Katherine in the eye and told her I'd never take over her show; I wasn't about to change my tune now that the series was a hit. I shared my thoughts with the execs at Lifetime, who reluctantly agreed. I left on good terms—with no inkling I'd end up working on the series for another five years.

On my own again and facing the prospect of more development, I changed agents. For most of my career, I'd been with the same agent, a thorough professional I liked and respected who ran his own shop. Although I'd been courted by the big agencies at regular intervals, I'd never seen reason to change—until recently. The large firms had come to dominate TV development through "packaging," the practice of offering studios an alluring, if extortionary, combination of an agency's writers, actors, and directors in an all-in-one deal. Writers liked packaging not only because it created work but also because agencies would waive their normal 10 percent fee for writers (which seemed like a great deal at the time but was eventually revealed to benefit agents far more than writers).

Seeing friends prosper through package deals and discouraged by my track record of failed pilots, I felt like I was swimming upstream; no matter how much I liked my agent, a one-man shop couldn't compete with where the market had gone. My agent had paled when I expressed this a year earlier, but he hadn't disagreed. Instead, he'd asked for time to merge with a big agency, which I freely granted. The company he eventually joined, however, was not one of the major players, so now I felt I had to move on—though not without pangs. I'm a loyal person, but I reluctantly concluded that I owed greater loyalty to myself and my family. I'd been impressed by a young agent who'd reached out to me from Endeavor, the feisty firm that would soon merge with William Morris to become the powerhouse WME, so I signed there. In the short term, nothing changed. In the long term, nothing did, either. But I'm getting ahead of myself.

Shortly after leaving *Army Wives*, I got a call from Harvard University, where I'd gone to college, to teach an undergraduate writing seminar I'd proposed months before. The timing was fortuitous considering that the Writers Guild was about to go on strike. So in the winter of 2008 I found myself teaching in Cambridge, Massachusetts, rather than walking a picket line in Burbank, California. (I was a strong supporter of the strike, which was largely about securing writers' rights in the new digital age, and so felt some guilt about being gainfully employed on the opposite coast—but not enough to turn around and come home.) The strike lasted a hundred days. When it was over and my semester done, I got a call from Lifetime.

Although *Army Wives* had enjoyed a successful second season in the ratings, it had been a bloodbath behind the scenes. Katherine had been fired early on, and the show subsequently burned through three showrunners. When I met with JoAnn Alfano, the new head of Lifetime, I told her I felt fundamental creative mistakes had been made in season 2. I laid out my suggestions to correct them and told her not to hire me if she disagreed, because this was the only way I knew how to guide the show. Joann paused, then said, "How soon can you start?"

Army Wives turned out to be the longest job I've held in the business, six years in all. After making a few personnel adjustments over the next two seasons (a painful but necessary task for the health of the show), I had a dream team of collaborators. Of all the casts, crews, and writing staffs I've worked with, I remain friends with more members of that group than any other. In June 2013, the series was canceled after seven years and 117 episodes; I felt it could have gone on longer, but JoAnn had left the network and her successor showed little interest in renewing a series she hadn't developed herself. *C'est la guerre.*

I remain immensely proud of *Army Wives.* At the time, I wanted the world to take more notice, which led to a disturbing discovery: in the shifting television landscape, it was possible to be a hit on your own platform and yet not be part of the national conversation. That wasn't possible when I started in broadcast. If you were a hit, everyone knew it. Increasingly, however, the audience was watching more shows in decreasing numbers. The common language of broadcast was splintering into a host of dialects. It felt like the end of something. And it was.

10

BRAVE NEW WORLD

AMAZON

On February 1, 2013, *House of Cards* dropped on Netflix, the first "bingeable" series in TV history: an entire season of episodes available to subscribers all at once. This event would eventually transform the industry, but the implications at the time were surprisingly easy to ignore—at least for me. I was skeptical that viewers would rather gorge on an entire season than dine out on one episode per week, the custom since the birth of prime time. Even prestige leader HBO abided by the once-a-week diet.

So when I sat down to write a pilot after *Army Wives* was canceled, I wasn't worried about streaming so much as what to write. Critical taste had gone decidedly darker in recent years, as represented by *Mad Men* and *Breaking Bad,* two AMC series that dominated the Emmys. Much as I admired those shows, my temperament ran to more uplifting material. Thinking a period piece might provide a suitable setting, I was going over World War II material when I stumbled across a story I'd never seen before. Shortly after Pearl Harbor, some twenty-five female American pilots crossed the Atlantic to fly for the British Air Transport Auxiliary, piloting everything from fighters to bombers. I wrote a script and showed it to my agent at WME. (In typical Hollywood fashion, the junior agent who'd brought me to Endeavor had left shortly after I'd signed, leaving me with a notoriously hard-nosed senior agent who displayed the sensitivity of a sledgehammer). Our conversation went something like this:

> Sledgehammer: "Why didn't you talk to me before you wrote this?"
>
> Me: "Because I knew you'd tell me not to write it."
>
> Sledgehammer: "You're right. I can't sell this. Nobody's looking for this."

That tells you everything you need to know about my relationship with WME. Looking for new representation, I approached an agent-turned-manager I'd admired for years who'd recently returned to the agency business with Creative Artists Agency. I expected her to greet me with open arms but found her surprisingly cool. She deemed my pilot out of touch; I needed to write something that would "make noise" and "rise above the clutter." This was the first time I'd encountered these new watchwords of the day. To make noise, I needed "edge." "Edge" was the opposite of "soft," and coming off *Army Wives*, I was definitely "soft." She said I needed to reinvent myself, a phrase I've always detested, implying that you can somehow swap out your sensibility as easily as changing the oil in your car. But I got it. I had to reintroduce myself to a new generation of execs for whom "edgy" meant a beheading or kinky sex act in a broom closet—preferably both—within the first two pages of a script. I wasn't going to do that, so I had to find an edgy premise I could get behind.

It arrived in the form of a book that movie producer Janet Zucker brought to my attention: *The Bubble Gum Thief*, a first novel by Jeff Miller about an anorexic FBI agent on the trail of a serial killer. The book had edge, but it also had a heart and a brain. Janet and I pitched the project around town but didn't get a sale. My agent encouraged me to write the pilot anyway, emphasizing that I still needed a sample script, and because I knew the book well, I had a leg up. I agreed. My agent was delighted with the results and used the script as a calling card, which is how I ended up working with screenwriter-director Shane Black (*Lethal Weapon, Iron Man 3*) at Amazon.

Amazon czar Jeff Bezos had recently become what I called "the Stalin of streaming," willing to sacrifice millions of dollars to halt the advance of the Netflix hordes. To do so, Amazon was using a sweepstakes approach to development, producing a slate of pilots available to Amazon Prime subscribers, who could subsequently vote on which projects should move forward. It was a wasteful and not totally honest idea—Amazon ultimately made its own decisions regardless of audience feedback. But the company had money to burn, and burn it they did.

In that spirit, they'd bought a pitch from Shane Black and writing partner Fred Dekker for a spaghetti western called, appropriately enough, *Edge* (based on sixty-one paperback novels written by British author Terry Harknett under the pen name George C. Gilman, a series the publisher branded as "The Most Violent Westerns in Print"). Shane had directed the pilot in New Mexico, where production challenges had ratcheted the price tag from $9 million to $12 million. This gave Amazon pause. *Edge* drew the largest audience of that season's pilots, but viewer reviews were decidedly mixed, which gave Amazon further pause. It was at this point that I was brought in.

The tune was familiar: a pair of TV outsiders looking for help getting a series on its feet. What made this different was the elevated nature of the players. Shane and Fred knew writing and production. What they didn't know was how to satisfy what Amazon was looking for. I don't think Amazon knew, either; the sweepstakes approach amounted to little more than throwing spaghetti—western or otherwise—against the wall. But the one thing Amazon insisted on was that *Edge* had to be bingeable: it had to feature cliffhangers that forced viewers to watch the next episode without a break. Shane and Fred's original bible had included plenty of stand-alone episodes. That had to change.

So, after working on a revised bible to make the series more binge-worthy, we found ourselves sitting in Amazon's outer offices awaiting a meeting with studio head Roy Price. I was wearing my usual work outfit of slacks, button-down shirt, and sport coat; Shane and Fred were in the standard Hollywood writer's uniform: flannels and jeans. David Greenblatt, Shane's manager, told me I was overdressed. Only half-joking, I told David my job was to look like the adult in the room. At that moment, a short guy with a tuft of spiky hair, wearing black denims, white V-neck T-shirt, and leather motorcycle jacket, exited the elevator and scurried past, looking like an extra from a *Mad Max* movie. "That's Roy Price," David said. Reassessing, I said, "David, you're right."

Our meeting turned out to be as odd as Roy's appearance. The studio head was curt to the point of rudeness, chiding Shane and Fred for the mixed reviews. I got the distinct impression he didn't like this runaway train but didn't know how to stop it without admitting he'd burned $12 million on a nonstarter. With barely an encouraging word, Roy ended the meeting by ordering three scripts for further review. Right then I knew the project was dead, but we had our marching orders.

We wrote outlines, which were approved, and then each of us wrote a script. A few days after they were submitted, Amazon passed. That didn't surprise me. What bothered me was that the execs cited problems with storylines they'd explicitly vetted in outline—and this after I'd insisted to Shane and Fred that we go through the outline process precisely to avoid this kind of setback, which made me feel like a schmuck. It also made me suspect that compared to their broadcast and cable counterparts, Amazon execs had little accountability. Insulated from the culture and protocols I'd grown up with in the business, they could spend and spend until they came up with that rare strand of spaghetti that finally stuck to the wall.

So that was the end of *Edge*, but not the end of my Amazon tenure, which continued when the studio asked me to work with yet another pair of inexperienced TV writers, a husband-and-wife team working on a pilot about the famous Tropicana nightclub in Havana on the eve of the Cuban revolution. Once again, a promising topic; once again, an engaging team of collaborators. What could possibly go wrong? Pretty much everything, as it turned out.

The project had a troubled history including an earlier writer, producer, and script that no one at the studio wanted to talk about. All I was told was that the current script needed work, which the studio wanted me to supervise. What the studio failed to tell me is that they hadn't relayed this news to the writers, who had been led to believe that Amazon loved their latest draft. Meanwhile, despite the lack of a script, Amazon instructed us to start interviewing directors. To me, it was a clear case of putting the cart before the horse. Nevertheless, we'd all settled on a well-regarded feature director with a James Bond film under his belt when the execs ditched him for another hot director who had just helmed *The Night Manager*, the John le Carré miniseries that looked to be a sure Emmy winner (and eventually was). Unfortunately, when this director took the job, she failed to tell the studio that she hated the current script and wanted to bring in her own writer. While this may be common practice in the feature world, it simply wasn't done in television. Further complicating matters, with neither a shooting script nor the slightest assurance that we could shoot in Cuba, the director traveled to the island to scout locations with a production designer and line producer in tow. In the midst of this, a new fly appeared in the ointment—literally. The Zika virus, a mosquito-borne disease, was sweeping the tropics, making production anywhere in the region extremely uncertain.

Once again, Amazon had a runaway train on its hands, but the only folks who seemed to realize it were the company's production execs, whom I found exceptionally sharp. I laid things out for them in the hope they could impose some coherence on the chaos. They smiled; they'd seen it all before. Confirming my earlier suspicions, they intimated that Amazon's creative execs had license to make major decisions with little regard for fiscal discipline or practical reality, leaving the production to tear up budget after budget and write bigger and bigger checks. I found it all more than a bit bizarre, but there was nothing I could do except let events play out to their inevitable end. Which they did.

When the director returned from Cuba, I encouraged her to share her feelings about the writers and script with the studio. She did—and quietly left the production shortly after. The studio then reapproached the original director, but, not surprisingly, he'd soured on the project and taken on other work. In a last-ditch effort, the studio asked me to talk to him, which I did. We had a pleasant meeting in which the director told me he'd like to work together on something else, but it wouldn't be this. That ship had sailed.

After this turn of events, the execs suddenly announced that they had more script notes. Big notes. This came as a surprise to the long-suffering writers, who asked me later if I thought this was still a green-light project. No, I told them, this was now a yellow-light project. And we all know what follows yellow. I felt for them, but seeing little upside at this juncture, I settled out my deal and walked away.

As I did, I recalled that meeting with the production execs. When I'd asked their advice, they'd done a quick, clinical analysis: on the one hand, you have a pair of unknown, relatively inexpensive writers who weren't even the first ones on the project; on the other, you have a hot director with considerable momentum. There's no question about the right corporate move: you jettison the writers and go with the director.

I shook my head. This flew in the face of everything I knew. Yet I had a flicker of doubt. The director had strong ideas and the moxie to make them happen; the writers were confused and demoralized. If I were in charge, I'd go with the director, too. Wait—what was I thinking? I dismissed the thought as soon as it formed. It was heresy. This was television. Wasn't it?

11

BRAVE OLD WORLD

DESIGNATED SURVIVOR

If I'd had any doubts, Amazon removed them: television was changing—exploding, shape-shifting, moving too quickly and in too many directions for any one set of assumptions to apply. Correspondingly, showrunning was no longer a one-size-fits-all job. Streaming and subscription cable were rewriting the rules, and showrunners would have to adjust, fighting to preserve the power that came freely in broadcast—which, as it turns out, is where my next offer came from. I hadn't been pursuing it, but I was happy to be returning to a business with clearly defined parameters

Nevertheless, broadcast was facing its own critical challenges. Shackled by a rigid creative format of linear programming with commercial breaks and further impeded by federal regulation of content and language, broadcast faced a choice with its scripted dramas: go old or go bold. Industry leader CBS had stayed in front by going old, catering to its aging audience with familiar fare. Floundering in third place in 2016, ABC had gone bold with *Designated Survivor,* a high-concept thriller starring Kiefer Sutherland. The premise could have been lifted from a Tom Clancy novel—and in fact, some claim it was (check out *Executive Action,* Clancy's 1998 entry in the Jack Ryan saga). When the US Capitol is blown up during the State of the Union address, the only cabinet member left alive, the "designated survivor" sequestered in a secure location, is mild-mannered Secretary of Housing and Urban Development Tom Kirkman. Catapulted into the Oval Office in the wake of incalculable tragedy, Kirkman must lead the country back to normalcy while figuring out who was behind the worst act of political assassination in national history—and proving himself a good husband and father at the same time. With Kiefer as Kirkman, the show was guaranteed to draw eyeballs, so ABC went all in, skipping the usual pilot process to order thirteen episodes up front.

The show premiered to glowing reviews and an audience of more than ten million, a smash by contemporary standards. ABC immediately upped its order to a full twenty-two. Then reality reared its ugly head. High-concept shows walk a tightrope, often unable to sustain the excitement of the pilot for more than a few episodes before plunging to an untimely death. *Designated Survivor* quickly began to wobble. By the time ABC called me halfway through the season, the audience had shrunk to less than six million and the show had gone through two showrunners, the first fired after the pilot.

Once again, it was triage. I flew to Toronto to get Kiefer's blessing. As an executive producer, he had showrunner approval, another first for me. In the past, television stars had enjoyed a certain amount of clout, but any producer title they might have held was largely a vanity credit; the star didn't play an active role in the creative direction of a series. Now, however, with the growing migration of movie talent into television, star power was increasingly being written into contracts, which meant showrunners had to make time for another layer of notes and discussion.

Kiefer was thoughtful and polite during our first meeting. Over the next eighteen months, I'd be involved in some less pleasant conversations, but even in the worst of those, I always felt he was trying to do what he genuinely thought was best for the show. That said, he wanted the series to conform to his notion of what he'd signed on for, which didn't necessarily coincide with what the network, studio, or writers thought he'd signed on for. Kiefer wanted the scripts to be more *West Wing* and less Tom Clancy. I think he saw Tom Kirkman as the antidote to Jack Bauer, the violent hero of *24* (Kiefer's last megahit), who'd become a right-wing icon for his violent pursuit of justice by any means. In real life, I found Kiefer to be a liberal thinker with genuine passion for social change, so I could understand why he'd want Kirkman to be more of a vehicle for his personal philosophy—but I also felt you couldn't drop the thriller aspect without sacrificing a good part of the show's appeal.

Yielding to his request, however, the writing staff and I concluded the initial conspiracy story at the end of the season and were working on ideas for season 2 when a new showrunner was abruptly brought in to shepherd the show in a more political, less thriller direction. A studio executive—I'll call him Malfoy—had engineered the coup without letting me know what was going on. I was outraged, but after being told that my option was going to be picked up as an executive producer for season 2, I got over it. Mostly. My job for season 2 would be to assist the new showrunner with scripts as needed but principally to take charge of editing. Fine. I loved editing. Looking at it positively, I was going to be paid more to do less.

Despite these changes, however, ratings continued to decline. We finished the season with about three and a half million viewers, which is when ABC killed the show. So ended what had been heralded as the most promising new broadcast series of the 2016 season. Two things happened in the final days, however, that redeemed much of what had gone before. First, Kiefer called. I'd barely spoken to him during the second season, so I was surprised—and a bit wary. "Hey, man," he said, "I just heard you've been supervising all the cuts this year. Is that true?" When I conceded that it was, he continued, "Great job, man. Awesome work. Thank you." Stunned, I thanked him and hung up. That would have been a nice note to end on, but what happened next was even more surprising.

Malfoy called to tell me he'd just been fired by the studio; he didn't know if I'd heard. I hadn't. That was impressive enough, but he proceeded to thank me for my work and apologized for the way things had gone down. He should have handled it differently, he said; he was sorry. I told him there were no hard feelings—and I meant it. In that moment, I realized Malfoy was just another guy trying to do the best he could in a brutal business. There was nothing more behind his actions than a momentary excess of ambition, perhaps—and if that were a crime, most of Hollywood would be behind bars.

A year later, *Designated Survivor* was resuscitated for a third season under a fifth showrunner for a ten-episode run on Netflix, where it finally gave up the ghost. By that time, however, I was in London.

12

INTERNATIONAL INTRIGUE

KILLING EVE

Killing Eve had been the sleeper hit of the 2018 season. With fiendish wit and wicked plotting, writer Phoebe Waller-Bridge had transformed a series of novellas by Luke Jennings into a subversive take on the espionage genre, an erotic game of cat and mouse between arch assassin Villanelle, played by Jodie Comer, and unlikely MI5 agent Eve Polastri, played by Sandra Oh. Phoebe left after season 1 to write and star in her own series, *Fleabag*, which would launch her into the critical stratosphere. Another writer-actress, Emerald Fennell, was brought in as lead writer for season 2, but she subsequently left, too, to play Camilla Parker Bowles in the Netflix series *The Crown* and to write and direct *Promising Young Woman*, the movie that would win her an Oscar for best screenplay. Heading into season 3, the London studio behind *Killing Eve* handed the baton to Suzanne Heathcote, a British playwright who'd been working in American television, most prominently as a writer on *Fear the Walking Dead*.

The execs thought a more American approach to running the show might provide more stability behind the scenes, which is how I found myself sitting down with Suzanne over coffee at Soho House in West Hollywood. I'd read one of her plays, so I knew how talented she was, but I hadn't expected her to be so charming and funny. When I stood up two hours later, I felt we'd already begun a productive collaboration—and we had, although as events would prove, the "more American" approach was doomed from the start. Which requires some explanation.

The typical British television production doesn't employ a showrunner as we know the position in the States, preferring a "head writer" or "lead writer," responsible for scripts only and with little influence over production or editing. As a seasoned British television colleague told me, "They let you play in the sandbox, then pat you on the head and send you home with nothing to say about directors, casting, or anything else, including post." There are many reasons for this—historical, economic, cultural—all traceable to the dramatically different ways in which mass media developed on opposite sides of the Atlantic. The celebrated success of the showrunner in the United States, however, has made some British studios wonder whether it's time to consider a change—not a complete makeover, perhaps, but something of a hybrid in which the "lead writer" might enjoy more autonomy.

It was in this spirit, with the best of intentions on all sides, that Suzanne and I flew from Los Angeles to London in February 2019 to hire a writing staff. Not one writer from either of the first two seasons had returned. (Phoebe and Emerald had done the lion's share of writing during their respective seasons, but other writers had contributed scripts.) Some of the turnover could be attributed to the British system, in which writers are accustomed to scrambling from job to job, even medium to medium—television, movies, theater, radio plays—without long-term commitments to any. Some of it, however, could also be linked to a healthy amount of chaos behind the scenes at *Killing Eve*—nothing uncommon, but precisely the situation execs hoped we might improve upon.

As soon as we landed, I got the first hint that this hybrid approach was going to be tougher than advertised. American showrunners are used to hiring their own staffs, but the studio immediately handed us a list of ten writers to choose from. I bristled—until I read their sample material, which was outstanding. We ended up hiring three writers from the studio's list and a fourth whom Suzanne had recommended. Although the Brits don't normally use the American writers room approach to break episodes, the studio agreed to give it a go and rented office space for us in central London. We went to work in early March. So far, so good.

Unlike the American broadcast system, in which scripts are written serially throughout the season, the British model favors a practice closer to the movies, in which virtually all scripts are written in advance of production. It's an approach that many streaming platforms have adopted, which allows for significant economizing in preproduction while subsequently conferring more power on the director and the studio at the showrunner's expense. We were given eight weeks to break the season of eight episodes, ridiculously tight by American standards. Because filming wasn't slated to begin until August, however, I felt that if all stories were broken before the room dissolved (a big "if," as it turned out), writers could continue to work with Suzanne one-on-one to finish outlines and drafts. Accordingly, I created a schedule that projected all written material being delivered with plenty of opportunity for notes and revisions before production began. It didn't work out that way.

The fundamental problem was that the studio wouldn't let us out of the gate. Although Suzanne had been hired on the basis of her ideas for season 3, for a long time we couldn't get approval of the initial episode, which backed everything up. The writers room was extended by two weeks, but progress remained glacial. I think the conflict was as much cultural as creative; the studio just couldn't relinquish the control it was used to exercising as part of the British tradition.

Eventually, we found our way. The production team kept the cameras turning across a taxing schedule that included location shoots in Spain and Romania, maintaining momentum until December, when at last we had to shut down to allow the final two scripts to catch up. It was an unfortunate turn of events—the only shutdown in my career—and it forced cast and crew to work six-day weeks after the Christmas break to finish the season. But the job got done—and done well. Season 3 of *Killing Eve* would go on to be nominated for eight Emmy awards, including outstanding drama series. The cast, crew, and studio all deserve full marks, and I reserve special praise for Suzanne, who prevailed under tremendous pressure. By the time filming ended with an all-night shoot at Liverpool Street Station, however, she was more than ready to hand the baton to the next head writer for season 4. Because my job was tied to Suzanne, I left the show when she did, with good memories but some regret that we hadn't been able to better realize our managerial goals.

Perhaps future efforts to combine the American and British approaches to production will be more successful, but the players will have to overcome a fundamental barrier: in the States, the writer-producer is both labor and management; in the UK, the writer is traditionally perceived as labor only, which creates a very different working environment. For example, in America, editors traditionally report to the showrunner, who has final cut on all episodes. On *Killing Eve*, the directors hired their own editors and exercised considerable influence in the editing room, where neither Suzanne nor I ever set foot. So, when it comes to ways of making television, "East is East and West is West, and never the twain shall meet." At least for now.

This was confirmed by British writer Jed Mercurio, the creator of *Line of Duty* and *Bodyguard* (the most-watched drama in BBC history when it premiered in 2018). I met Jed toward the end of my stay, when we were both speakers at a seminar for the Writers Guild of Great Britain. Although Jed is one of the few writers in England to have achieved the status of showrunner, I was astounded to hear him tell the audience of his ongoing battles with the BBC to get series launched. His listeners had no trouble understanding, however, clucking in sympathy as Jed freely mentioned execs by name.

I followed up with him over a pint. Surely the BBC would roll out the red carpet for someone who'd done so well by them? No, he said. He still had to claw for every ounce of influence he could get. Rather than being revered for his achievements, Jed said he more often found himself resented by execs because he was a threat to the established order. No amount of success was going to make a BBC commissioner kowtow to a writer-producer. So, I asked, what would he do next? Go to Hollywood, he said. He had a few projects in development there. Of course.

When I returned to Los Angeles in January 2020, I felt ready to write the book I'd been making notes on for years. Then the COVID-19 pandemic hit, providing an unexpected dose of enforced discipline and a built-in excuse for prolonged periods of antisocial behavior. I proceeded to do what all professional writers do: sat down and stared at the computer screen for a while. Then I got to work.

II

BREAKING IN

13

SIX RULES

THE MAKING OF A TELEVISION WRITER

Some people may be born to write, but no one's born to write television. There's too much involved. Assuming you've developed sufficient craft to be hired on a writing staff, you must subsequently harness your sensibility to the wagon of someone else's star and pull to the point of exhaustion, dismissal, or cancellation, subordinating your own raging insecurities to help fellow writers overcome theirs in creating episodes for which you will receive neither credit nor thanks while losing sleep, friends, and composure under crushing deadline pressure. To succeed, you must not only accept this, you must embrace it.

I occasionally meet aspiring television writers who introduce themselves with a beatific smile, declaring, "I'm a storyteller," which tells me they're most likely recent English majors who have somehow confused television with shamanism—too much Joseph Campbell can be a dangerous thing. I wish them luck, but fear for their reentry into earth orbit.

When I knew him in our younger days, Dick Wolf, the hugely successful writer-producer responsible for the *Law and Order* and *Chicago* franchises, wore a suit and tie to work. When interviewing writers, he'd ask, "You want to know why I dress like this?" Without waiting, Dick would thunder, "BECAUSE IT'S A BUSINESS!" Indeed, it is. A tough business.

Success in television writing results from a number of factors, of which talent is one. But persistence and resilience are equally important, arguably more so. Luck and a sense of humor also help. Talent, to the degree it can be defined or quantified, is relatively meaningless in the absence of these other qualities.

Television writers come in all shapes and sizes and enter the business through an equally varied number of routes. Though many students head for Hollywood right after college or grad school, I have particular fondness for those sturdy souls who arrive after collision with what is generally regarded as the real world. No doubt this predilection can be attributed to my own path, which included seven years as a journalist before I wrote my first produced script. Regardless of how you get to Hollywood, however, your journey will be uniquely your own. Consequently, you must filter all advice—including mine—through your own sensibility, tempered by appropriate doses of skepticism. In that spirit, here are six "rules" to becoming a television writer. Three are mandatory, two my own prejudices, the last utterly beyond your control.

Love Television and Movies with a Passion

And I mean a burning, all-consuming passion, because only that fervor will get you past the rough spots along the way, of which there will be many. Watch everything, including black-and-white movies from Hollywood's Golden Age. When a showrunner friend of mine recently asked his staff to name their favorite classic film, one writer immediately responded with *The 40-Year-Old Virgin*. With no disrespect to Judd Apatow, please take a deeper dive.

Read

Not just scripts, but plays, novels, poems, nonfiction, newspapers, periodicals, everything. Follow your gut—and curiosity. Read not just for content, but for forms of expression. Oscar-winning screenwriter Waldo Salt (*Midnight Cowboy*, *Coming*

Home) once said the closest literary form to screenwriting is poetry, which renders more than it can describe. Nothing's wasted; it's all grist for your mill.

Write

Seems obvious, but many aspiring writers never get past the "wannabe" phase. Desire is no substitute for effort. A writer I know landed an interview right out of college with a major television producer and told him she wanted to be a television writer. He asked what she'd written. Nothing, she responded. The producer said that was like wanting to be a concert pianist without knowing how to play the piano. Reddening, the young woman fled. Subsequently, she began writing, went to grad school, wrote more, and eventually got her break. We all start by wanting to write, but if you want a career, you need to do it. Now.

Do Theater

Nothing is better training for television than theater, whether in high school, college, or beyond. Theater is performance stripped to its bare bones: text, actors, audience. It instills respect for the production process and everyone involved, from lead actor to prop manager. It also offers a group experience that Hollywood rarely provides. Everything I know of lasting value in this business comes from my high school drama teacher Barbara Patterson, who inspired generations of students in Highland Park, Illinois, including my fellow thespians Gary Sinise and Jeff Perry, who went on to distinguished careers as actors and directors. Mrs. Patterson literally changed our lives.

Major in Liberal Arts

Assuming you go to college. Not all writers do; a few don't make it past high school. You play the cards you're dealt. If you do attend college, however, I recommend spending your undergrad years majoring in something other than television, film, or theater. I know it's counterintuitive—and it's certainly a minority view—but if you're serious about becoming a writer, you can pick up the bulk of the job training you need after college. Take classes in the arts, certainly, but consume everything you won't get the chance to study later: history, literature, art, language, music, social studies, anthropology, economics, astronomy, whatever. Dig your well as deep as you can and fill it with as much as you can because you'll draw upon it for the rest of your life. I recognize that majoring in liberal arts involves a leap of faith because it doesn't offer a clear path to employment, but if you must think about college as trade school, consider that writing takes the world as its subject.

Have an Unhappy Childhood

This is the rule you can't do anything about, obviously, but many writers have found it beneficial. Not only does an unhappy childhood provide fodder for a lifetime of writing, but it also fuels the drive to succeed, a need to prove something to the world. You don't have to endure Dickensian horrors; a narcissistic parent will do. Director-producer Paris Barclay, past president of the Directors Guild of America, says most people come to Hollywood seeking a second family, their "real" family. I think there's a lot of truth to that. If you had a happy childhood, however, don't despair. All writing is a form of protest, and the world provides plenty of targets. Scratch the surface of any writer, and you'll find complaints about something, if only the inescapable fact that we're all born to die in a world we'll never fully understand.

* * * * * * * *

So that's it. Six rules. And one request: Don't just want to be a writer. Want to be a good writer, a truthful writer. You can want fame and fortune, too, of course, but want them as the result of writing well.

14

DUMBO'S FEATHER

FILM SCHOOL

Aspiring writers often ask whether they should go to film school. My answer is always the same: maybe. First, a clarification: "Film school" remains the predominant term to describe graduate programs covering both movies and television. For a long time, academia's dim view of television was reflected in a paucity of television courses. No more. All reputable film schools now offer plenty of classes in TV. With that out of the way, let's state a simple truth: Hollywood doesn't care whether you went to film school or not. Nobody checks your credentials at the door; all that matters is whether you can do the work. And do you need film school to do the work? No. Plenty of successful television writers skip film school; I'm one of them. So why bother? Reasons abound.

Content

Film school will expose you to a universe of resources you might not be aware of otherwise. Beyond introduction to such materials, film school provides the time, motivation, and enforced discipline to actually study them. On the other hand, if all you're going to do is watch a lot of movies and television, there are cheaper alternatives—like your parents' couch.

Instruction

As a journalist, I had the opportunity to interview Boston crime novelist George V. Higgins (*The Friends of Eddie Coyle*) in the late 1970s; out of self-interest, I slipped in a question about how to become a writer. Higgins said, "I don't believe writing can be taught, but it can be learned." I've come to agree. The knowledge is available, but it can't be given, it must be earned.

Does that mean writing classes are a waste of time? Not at all. A good writing teacher creates an environment in which learning can take place. And nothing is more valuable than constructive criticism from an instructor who cares enough to go over your work in detail. There are plenty of such teachers out there. As in any academic field, however, especially one undergoing such rapid expansion, there are also some less-than-stellar instructors, so let the buyer beware.

I can't leave this topic without mentioning a form of teaching I've found problematic in film school: the workshop. In theory, workshops are great—your work is critiqued in an open forum by your peers. In practice, however, I've found workshops are often intellectually lazy sessions that devolve into rounds of mutual admiration: "I loved your script." "I loved *your* script more!" Such logrolling would be okay if the instructor stepped in occasionally to interject some reality. But I've seen too many teachers simply go with the flow, which strikes me as an abdication of responsibility. I'm not suggesting classmates go at one another like feral dogs—sensitivity is required, but there must be honest criticism or nobody learns anything. In fact, knowing how to accept and deliver criticism are necessary survival skills in the business. Students may emerge from poorly run workshops feeling better about their work, but I doubt they come out better writers.

Classmates

Some of the greatest assets of film school are your fellow students, who will turn out to be future collaborators, colleagues, competitors, and employers. Being surrounded by motivated peers is a source of constant stimulation and provides a readily available pool of actors, directors, camera operators, and volunteers to get pizza at all hours. Although you can find educational materials and mentors elsewhere, you find classmates only on campus.

Writing Time

Film school enforces discipline, so if you're one of those dilatory souls who needs deadlines to make your fingers dance, film school may be just what the doctor ordered, albeit at concierge prices. At the other extreme, if you're a compulsive writer constantly stealing time to write, film school will feed your habit without guilt. Both situations are relative luxuries, of course. Unlike most Hollywood crafts, writing is a skill you can practice by yourself. Although writing while holding down a day job can be taxing, writers have done it for centuries, long before film school was a thing.

Production

Before the digital revolution, if you wanted to make a student film, you had to go to film school to get your hands on the cameras, film, editing equipment, lab processing, and personnel needed for even a modest effort. Today, a sixth grader with a smartphone can make a good-looking movie on a shoestring. As for collaborators, there are plenty of people out there willing to help for little more than a slice of pepperoni. Check the internet. Of course, film schools still offer assets most folks can't afford—like studio space, lights, state-of-the-art editing bays, and qualified instructors to show you how to use all those shiny toys—but the point is that you don't need film school to make a movie.

Jobs

Here's where the rubber meets the road for many prospective students. Every film school boasts about its successful alums, regardless of the institution's role in their success. The posters in campus hallways promoting the work of prominent grads can make it appear that fame and fortune are merely a diploma away. The reality, of course, is more sobering. Even the most well-connected film school can promise only the opportunity to network with working professionals; employment is a crapshoot for everyone. Film schools in Los Angeles and New York enjoy an advantage because working pros in both cities often drop in on classes. (Many institutions located away from production hubs still manage to bring in their share of distinguished guests; it's a matter of relative numbers.)

But intense networking can have a downside. I've found proximity to Hollywood can produce a distinctive strain of gold fever among students, a contagious lust for immediate success that can overwhelm a deeper commitment to substantive learning. Be forewarned. When I taught a television writing class at USC, one of my students told me he was thinking of joining Teach for America after graduation. Great idea, I said; the experience would expand his horizons and get him out in the world. He frowned. "But it's a two-year program, Mr. Melvoin," he said. "Do you think I'd be able to get back into the business?" When I realized he wasn't joking, I said as gently as I could, "Let me explain something, Mike. You're not in the business. You're a senior at USC." I assured him there'd be plenty of time to start his Hollywood career two years on. But I could see he wasn't convinced. Hats off to USC for making students believe admittance is tantamount to being part of Hollywood, but caution to anyone who doesn't understand that film school is just one means to an end, not the end itself.

Confidence

For some writers, the most valuable aspect of film school is the most intangible: confidence. A writer can't get out of bed without confidence, and if film school can give you that, it's a powerful argument in its favor. I learned this decades ago when I was working on *Hill Street Blues*. Laurie, a highly capable production assistant, asked if I'd write her a recommendation to USC's Professional Writing program (a now-defunct cousin of the film school). Sure, I said, but I wondered why she was applying, considering she already had her foot in the industry's door. "Yeah," she said shyly, "I just feel I need it. I'd always think I was missing something if I didn't go."

"Dumbo's feather," I said. She looked at me, confused. "You don't remember Dumbo's feather?" Clearly she didn't, so I gave her a quick rundown of the Disney classic. Dumbo, the young elephant with oversized ears, has one friend in the circus, Timothy, the mouse. After a drunken misadventure, Timothy realizes Dumbo can fly, using his ears as wings, but Dumbo can't remember what happened, so doesn't believe it. With the help of some friendly crows, Timothy gives Dumbo a "magic feather," convincing him it has the power to make him soar. With the feather clutched in his trunk, Dumbo flies.

Subsequently, Timothy arranges for Dumbo to headline a spectacular circus act, but when the moment comes for Dumbo to jump from the highest perch of the big top with Timothy as his passenger, the feather slips from his grasp. Dumbo and Timothy start plummeting earthward, which is when Timothy frantically yells in the elephant's ear that the feather isn't really magic; Dumbo can fly on his own. Willing himself to believe, Dumbo spreads his ears and flies. It's a wonderful moment.

What I realized was that for writers like Laurie, film school is Dumbo's feather. She might have been able to write without it, but she didn't believe it, which is all that mattered. She got into the USC program and went on to a successful career in comedy writing. When I ran into her years later, she told me she'd learned more about writing in her first two weeks as a writers assistant on the hit comedy *Golden Girls* than in two years at USC. But she had no regrets. "I needed to give myself the space and time to get what I thought I needed," she said. "It's about knowing yourself." Hard to argue with that.

15

ANDERSON'S YARDSTICK

TIMING

If you're serious about a career in television writing, at some point you're going to have to put on your parachute and jump out of the airplane—that is, devote yourself wholeheartedly to finding work as a writer. This almost certainly means landing in Los Angeles or New York. Los Angeles is the larger market, but New York remains an important hub (just ask any New Yorker). Despite Zoom and other video platforms, getting a writing job requires networking that is best achieved through face-to-face meetings and the serendipity of being in the right place at the right time.

So the leap is mandatory; the question is when to take it. Jump too soon and you sabotage your best shot at success. Delay too long and life grabs you by the ankles, making it difficult to wriggle free. I took a college seminar from playwright and screenwriter Robert Anderson (*Tea and Sympathy*, *I Never Sang for My Father*), who provided this rule of thumb: "A young poet is sixteen, a young novelist is twenty-six, a young playwright is thirty-six."

Anderson was talking about the relationship between form, content, and maturity. Poems tend to be short, utilize prescribed structures, and express the poet's immediate experience of the world, and so are well suited for young souls. Which is why a young poet is sixteen. By contrast, novels are longer, employ no fixed structure, and typically encompass a wider world of characters and events, and so require a broader level of experience. Which is why a young novelist is twenty-six.

Unlike either a poem or a novel, however, a play—and by extrapolation a screenplay or teleplay—is meant to be performed, not read. The audience only knows what it knows in the order in which it knows it; there's no flipping back or jumping ahead. Because of this, scriptwriting puts a premium on structure—and structure is hard. Which is why a young playwright is thirty-six.

Since I heard Anderson lay out his yardstick some fifty years ago, writing students have become far more sophisticated, exposed to a vast range of resources unimaginable back then. Consequently, the pace of a young writer's education has accelerated to such a degree that I suspect thirty-six is too high for a young playwright, but I still believe there's wisdom in Anderson's words. It takes time for a scriptwriter to develop the requisite maturity to recognize the difference between intent and execution—and the discipline to bridge the gap between what you're saying and what you *think* you're saying.

The gospel on many college and film school campuses today is: get to Hollywood immediately upon graduation to grab the lowest rung of the hiring ladder as an assistant or unpaid intern. I even heard a "seasoned" writers' assistant insist that recent grads must start on the desk of a major talent agency like CAA or WME, an experience guaranteed to suck the soul from any sensitive creature, in my opinion. Nevertheless, some people swear by it.

Any of these positions will provide opportunities to observe various aspects of the business, read scripts, and network with like-minded colleagues, all of which can be valuable. But these experiences won't necessarily broaden your understanding of the world beyond Hollywood or make you a better writer. Which brings me to what I consider the biggest rookie mistake in Hollywood: reading "show business" backward.

Many aspiring writers put too much emphasis on "the business" and too little on "the show." You can network like a champ, but if your writing doesn't shine, you're not going anywhere other than the next party. Admittedly, networking is more fun than figuring out why your second act doesn't work, but that's where your future lies.

Every generation produces a handful of writers who can create compelling material from the crucible of their own imaginations, and perhaps you're one of them, but most of us have to do some living—and struggling—before we're ready to take on Hollywood. Personally, I experienced some serious depression after college and found myself living at home, where I got some therapy for the first (but not last) time. It was a tremendous help. Once back on my feet, I decided to try my hand at journalism to see if I could make a living as a writer. It took me seven years to work my way to Hollywood.

I suspect more writers' dreams have been shattered by premature commitment to Hollywood than by prudent delay. Fortune may favor the bold, but it devours the unready. As a teacher, I've seen promising students head to the West Coast upon graduation only to hit a wall, lose heart, and leave after a year or two. I imagine they're happier doing something else today. I certainly hope so, but I'm not sure they gave themselves the best shot at making it. There's risk at every turn, of course, but don't put unnecessary pressure on yourself. You don't have to be famous by Friday. Be ambitious enough to be patient.

16

CARPENTER'S APPRENTICE

CRAFT

There are plenty of books about how to write scripts. This isn't one of them, but I do want to talk briefly about craft because the subject so often gets left behind in the race to get ahead. Your success as a television writer will depend foremost not on your personality or connections, but—wait for it . . . on your writing. If that sounds obvious, you'd be surprised how many would-be writers forget it once they hit town. And good writing involves craft, the means by which you communicate effectively with an audience.

Craft gives form to feeling. Knowing what you want to achieve and achieving it are two very different things; the failure to recognize this distinction is the biggest stumbling block I've seen with beginning writers. Barbara Patterson, my high school drama teacher mentioned earlier, used to drill it into us as actors: "You can feel it till hell freezes over, but if the person in the back row doesn't feel it, you haven't done your job." That's about as pithy a summation of craft as I can imagine.

It's no coincidence that Oscar-winning screenwriter William Goldman (*Butch Cassidy and the Sundance Kid, All the President's Men*) likened screenwriting to carpentry. Both require a set of skills to create something useful. As Goldman wrote in *Adventures in the Screen Trade*: "If you take some wood and nails and glue and make a bookcase, only to find when you're done that it topples over when you try to stand it upright, you may have created something really beautiful, but it won't work as a bookcase." Goldman's famous rule about Hollywood is still quoted all over town: "Nobody knows anything." But most people don't remember—if they ever knew—that it's only the first of two rules he postulated in his book. The second? "Structure is everything." On this point, Goldman is emphatic: "Yes, nifty dialogue helps one hell of a lot; sure, it's nice if you can bring your characters to life. But you can have terrific characters spouting just swell talk to each other, and if the structure is unsound, forget it."

Structure is a by-product of craft. How to develop craft? There are no shortcuts; you have to read and write. Read scripts—not just teleplays, but screenplays and stage plays. Reverse engineer them; take them apart like a clock to understand what makes them tick. John Ciardi wrote a book about poetry called *How Does a Poem Mean?* You need to figure out how a script means. Of course, you can also read books about writing, of which there are an impressive number, but be wary. Some authors make it appear that scriptwriting is no more complicated than following a recipe: prepare ingredients in this order, combine accordingly, bake, and serve. In my experience, screenwriting is closer to mud wrestling than cooking. There's a lot of messy back-and-forth before you can pin your opponent to the earth.

In addition to reading, write. Regularly and often. Be your harshest critic. Ernest Hemingway famously said, "The most essential gift for a good writer is a built-in, shockproof, shit detector." True enough. If you're constantly falling in love with your first drafts, read them again. Read them aloud. Then put them in a drawer for a day or two before reading them one more time. (The classical Roman poet Horace recommended putting poetry aside for nine years before publishing, but the writer in me doubts that even Horace ever went that far; poets have to eat, too, after all.) Michael Gleason, my boss on *Remington Steele*, once told me, "As you write more, the good writing doesn't come any easier, but knowing when it doesn't work does."

Follow the rules of good storytelling until they've become second nature. I'm talking about the basic elements that you ignore at your peril: a beginning, middle, and end; an identifiable protagonist with a conflict that escalates over time; stakes that make us care. You learn these rules by putting them into practice. Familiar as they are, you'd be amazed how many scripts fail because writers don't observe them—and I'm talking about scripts that are paid for, even produced. It might be fun to experiment with form, but know the rules before you go breaking them. And don't worry that following the rules will somehow stifle your creativity. As painter Auguste Renoir said, "Be a good craftsman. It won't stop you from being a genius."

Concentrate on the work. When *Northern Exposure* was at the height of its fame, a friend asked me what it felt like to be influencing American culture. That was flattering, but honestly, what was most on my mind was getting the next script out on time. Oscar-winning screenwriter Paddy Chayefsky (*Network, The Hospital, Marty*) put it this way: "Artists don't talk about art. Artists talk about work. If I have anything to say to young writers, it's stop thinking of writing as art. Think of it as work. If you're an artist, whatever you do is going to be art. If you're not an artist, at least you can do a good day's work."

Of course, effective scripts need to be more than well crafted; they need to be well felt. Craft without feeling is as impoverished as feeling without craft. In his book, *Into the Woods: How Stories Work and Why We Tell Them*, former BBC exec John Yorke quotes a Chinese proverb: "You need the eye, the hand, and the heart. Two won't do." To which I add that you must apply those essentials in service of a theme, which screenwriter Budd Schulberg (*On the Waterfront*) defined this way: "Beyond the structure that holds it all together, there should be something more, the reason you're telling this tale. If characters-in-action equals plot, then plot-to-a-purpose equals theme. Take the theme away and we're just out there juggling for the hell of it."

As a television staff writer, you won't always have the luxury of choosing what you write about, but you should always find a why, a reason for what you're doing. As a staffer, I would put blinders on when necessary, convincing myself that whatever I was working on right then was the most important thing I could possibly be doing. Your reason doesn't have to be lofty or "important"; it can be light and silly. But it should represent something genuine for you. Don't find yourself juggling for the hell of it.

17

THE ARROWS IN YOUR QUIVER

SPEC SCRIPTS

As an unproduced writer, your goal is to get a script in front of someone who can hire you to write. All the strategizing, networking, and pleading in the world has that one object in mind: read my stuff. Which means your stuff had better be good, better than most stuff out there—something that makes the reader sit up and ask, "Who wrote this?" And you do that with spec scripts, material you've written "on speculation," for free. What type of scripts should you write? It depends on your sensibility and goals, of course, but the general answer is as much as you can and as varied as you can. The more arrows in your quiver, the better. Having a variety of scripts demonstrates your versatility and commitment to the business—and it gives you a better chance of hitting whatever targets might appear in front of you.

A spec script is advertising for yourself. Because nobody asked you to write it, everything about it reflects on you as a writer: subject, characters, plot, dialogue, spelling, formatting. And because nobody gave you a deadline, it should represent the best you can possibly do. You get only one shot with most readers, so make it count. The most realistic hope is not to sell your spec (which rarely happens) but to get an interview with a showrunner or a meeting with someone who can introduce you to a showrunner.

Spec scripts fall into two categories: spec episodes of existing series and spec pilots. When I broke in, all anyone wanted to see were spec episodes. Pilots were the exclusive province of veteran writers. Since then, the spec market has done a one-eighty. Spec pilots are in and spec episodes out, a change largely attributable to the rise of Peak TV, which has made it impossible for even the most obsessed television watcher to know every series that's out there. Consequently, it's hard for a writer to pick an existing series that will be familiar to most readers and stay on the air long enough to remain relevant. The only exceptions, perhaps, are the long-running broadcast series that trod familiar ground: crime shows, lawyer shows, doctor shows, and action shows of one sort or another.

Nevertheless, I encourage you to write at least one spec of an existing series, both for the discipline it imposes and the learning that results. And there are still showrunners who welcome spec episodes, believing they're better predictors of a writer's potential on staff than spec pilots. I'm one of them.

But spec pilots are preferred by most showrunners and execs, which sets the bar at a considerable height because spec pilots are harder to write (and read) than spec episodes. A spec episode is like playing a game of tennis: the challenge is how well you play within the lines. By contrast, a spec pilot asks you to play a new game while inventing it. The pilot writer must craft a compelling hour while simultaneously creating a framework for six to twenty-two episodes per season. Many seasoned pros have trouble doing that. What makes it particularly tough for rookies is that their pilots are judged with the same scrutiny applied to veterans. That's unavoidable, but I think the more appropriate standard for first-timers should be the potential the script suggests rather than its readiness to be put in front of the cameras tomorrow.

When I read a spec pilot—or any script, for that matter—the acid test is: do I want to keep turning the page? Do I want to know what happens next? Beyond that, I look to see whether a script is well crafted: does it show familiarity with the form? If craftsmanship falters, is there enough life in the writing—subject, characters, humor, imagination—to make me want to meet the writer behind it? Showrunner Nkechi Carrol emphasizes the importance of a unique point of view in spec material. "I can teach structure," she tells members of the WGA Showrunner Training Program. "I can't teach voice."

Conversely, any number of things can stop me from turning the page. My two most common complaints: (1) I immediately know where a script is going, so there's no surprise or delight; and (2) I don't know where it's going, but I don't care because I'm bored, confused, or don't recognize the characters' behavior as identifiably human. Typos, incorrect grammar, and bad formatting are further annoyances that make it easy to put a script down. There's no excuse for sloppiness; it suggests the writer didn't have enough respect for the reader or the business to do a professional job. Don't bank on your brilliance to compensate for poor workmanship. Remember, showrunners are not reading your material to make you a better writer; they're reading it in hopes of making their lives easier.

I once asked Chris Carter, creator of *The X-Files*, what he looked for in a spec. Three things, he said: originality, honesty, and intensity. I think that's spot on. Originality speaks to the freshness of ideas and manner of expression. Honesty demands that the writer keep things real, truthful; it also means playing fair with the audience—not torturing logic or unreasonably withholding information to manipulate the viewer. Intensity describes the skill with which the writer conveys tension, passion, and excitement.

With these qualities in mind, I suggest you only write specs that you have a feeling for. Not only will this bring out your best, but it will also provide the fuel required to get through the rewriting that all good scripts demand. Let your sensibility lead. Do not chase the market, writing something because it's what you think buyers are looking for. If you do, by the time you've finished, it's likely the market will have shifted. Furthermore, chasing the market leads to dishonest writing—surrendering your better instincts to baser influences. This doesn't mean be unmindful of the market; just keep it in its proper place.

Think about what form of pilot best suits your idea. I've found pilots fall into three general templates: the premise pilot, the "typical episode" pilot, and the "chapter one" pilot. There's some overlap, naturally, but each has unique characteristics.

A premise pilot explains how your lead characters get together to provide the basis for a series or how Peter Parker becomes Spiderman. A potential problem with premise pilots is that they fail to show what the series will look like from week to week. But if you can get the reader to the end of your script with an engaging story, you've likely earned an interview.

The "typical episode" drops you into a fully realized world: a law office, police station, hospital, or the like. You don't have to worry about how the characters got there because they're already in place. It's not uncommon for writers using this template to introduce a new member of the team or an outsider to act as the audience's surrogate in exploring the creative landscape.

The "chapter one" pilot is the beginning of a wholly serialized story. This variation has become quite popular in the wake of successful streaming and premium cable series, but it's also quite a challenge, requiring the writer to envision an entire world and enough of a seasonal arc to find the proper balance in the pilot between too much exposition and too little.

Any of these templates can be used as calling cards everywhere—good writing is good writing, after all—but each skews a certain way. The first two are particularly well-suited for broadcast and basic cable series that employ act breaks and combine self-contained stories with ongoing character development. The third is more calibrated to streaming and subscription cable services that emphasize serialized stories without act breaks.

To maximize your versatility, I suggest you have some specs with act breaks and some without. You can never have too much spec material, but you can have too little. Showrunners will be reassured if they can read scripts that align with their show—and they'll be impressed that you have an array of choices.

What else belongs in your quiver? Screenplays can be effective samples, but they aren't as practical, largely because they take twice as long to read as a typical pilot and don't necessarily reflect an affinity for or commitment to series television. Nevertheless, a screenplay can show off an aspect of your talent that your teleplays might not cover; if you have appropriate material, bring it along.

Similarly, stage plays can be useful, especially plays that have been produced. (Anything that shows you've been paid to write is to your advantage.) The downside of plays is that they don't use the language of film and are restricted in scope. Some showrunners may be fine with that, but others might lack the patience or understanding to relate to a play. Novels, short stories, journalism, and even poetry can find their way into your arsenal, but unless you're already a working pro in those fields, they shouldn't be your priority. The key, of course, is what showrunners or execs want to read, a question you should ask before submitting anywhere. Tastes can run the gamut, so keep those arrows coming.

Finally, I suggest you bear in mind two signs that writer Robert Anderson kept at his desk. The first: "Nobody asked you to be a writer." The second: "Don't despair. But if you must, write in despair."

18

WHY AGENTS DON'T MATTER

REPRESENTATION

Having written a spec script, many writers believe the next step is to find an agent, which is understandable. Understandable, but wrong. Odds are you're going to have to find your first job—and your second—yourself. Yes, theoretically, an agent can provide your first break, but it happens so rarely that you're better off acting as if it never does. Does this mean agents—and by extension, managers—are worthless? Not at all. What it does mean, however, is that most of them won't be interested in you until you've demonstrated you can make money for *them*, which means selling something on your own. We'll explore how to do that over the next three chapters. First, however, it's important to dispel some illusions about representation. Let's begin with an overview.

There are three layers to representation in Hollywood: agents, managers, and lawyers. Each takes a cut from your paycheck. Typically, agents and managers get 10 percent and lawyers get 5, meaning if you use all three, a quarter of your gross pay is gone before you see a dime. Consequently, it's good to know what you're allegedly paying for.

Agents are licensed by the state of California to negotiate contracts for writers but are prohibited from becoming producers on projects. Conversely, managers are not licensed to negotiate contracts but can become producers. Lawyers run the gaps, scrutinizing—and sometimes negotiating—contracts. If that sounds confusing, it is. I'm still not sure what managers do—and I have one.

Agents

The agency business was stunned in 2019 by a WGA job action that eventually forced agencies to abandon television packaging fees and curtail investment in production companies. At their worst, these and related practices had generated clear conflicts of interest for agencies, resulting in suppressed wages and limited job opportunities for all but the very top tier of writer-producers. The campaign began when all WGA members voluntarily fired their agents to compel compliance with a new set of WGA standards. Before the last agency signed on twenty months later, many writers had gotten by without agents. Managers, lawyers, the WGA, and individual initiative had filled the gap.

So, if you can get work without an agent, why do you need one? Good question. Some veterans would argue you don't, but for most writers, agents still perform valuable functions. They remain the front line in finding job opportunities and advocating on your behalf. The best agents keep working for you when you already have a job, lining up future possibilities and keeping options in front of you. And agents can still help put together your projects with actors and directors, even if they can't profit from the practice as they once did through packaging fees.

Some writers genuinely love their agents. That said, most agents aren't Jerry Maguire; they're strictly business, interested only in knowing how to peddle your services. Consequently, don't expect much handholding or genuine career guidance. As Oscar Wilde said of cynics, the stereotypical agent knows the price of everything and the value of nothing.

Because it's extremely time-consuming to help an unproduced writer get established, most agents would rather represent veterans. I heard one agent tell an audience of rookies, "When you're ready, we'll find you." Thanks for nothing. Yes, there are agents who seek out unproduced talent—and of these, some are genuinely devoted to launching careers. There are even agency assistants who will knock themselves out to help new writers get their start. (Of course, there's some enlightened self-interest here; a junior employee who can bring in a productive new client is going to rise.) Many agents looking for new writers, however, are in that position because they lack the experience or clout to sign anyone else. In all cases, if you sign with an agent before you've sold anything, resist feeling so gratified that you end up writing for the agent as if they're a producer. They're not, although some would love to be treated that way.

Should you sell something without an agent, you'll find many established agencies will then be happy to take 10 percent of your future income now that you've done the hard work of getting your foot in Hollywood's door. Use your leverage. Interview potential agents; don't simply let them interview you. Ask how they'd handle your career moving forward. Don't forget: the agent works for you, not the other way around. They're not doing you a favor; they're not your friend. They make money off you. And if they do a lousy job, find a new agent.

Managers

Managers have long been an asset for actors, who characteristically require steady encouragement and support. Agents have only limited time and patience for such humanity. So in addition to whatever career guidance a manager might provide, they often take on the role of professional friend. I get that. What I didn't get for a long time is why writers need managers, but it's gotten to the point where it's become standard practice. Why? The most common response: "My manager returns my calls." It's a shocking commentary on how shoddy the service of many agencies has become, but it's my answer, too. My manager persuaded me to hire him when he said, "My job is to poke the bear." He then explained that the bear wasn't the greater world of Hollywood; it was CAA. So I reluctantly agreed to pay a manager 10 percent to get an agency I was already paying 10 percent to do their job.

The results? Well, I've kept working, but I can't tell you exactly who's done what on my behalf. I know that my agent (whom I'm personally fond of) has found me work, but was that because my manager poked her to do it? Does it matter?

Overall, managers tend to have fewer clients than agents and thus more time to spend on them; I certainly talk far more with my manager than with my agent. By legal definition, managers can act as producers on their client's projects, including profit participation, which means many of the management companies aggressively pursue packages of their own, albeit without the packaging fees or monopolistic leverage that corroded the agency business. Because managers are prohibited from negotiating contracts, they avoid the obvious conflicts of interest that infested the big agencies. If you have only a manager, however, you need someone else to negotiate your contract, which brings us to the final player in the game.

Lawyers

The need for a lawyer to negotiate in the absence of an agent is clear. What's less clear is why writers retain lawyers when they have agents, whose firms have their own legal departments. The reason generally given is that due to the explosion of platforms, business models, international markets, distribution channels, and the like, writers' contracts have become so complex that you need your own expert to make sure you're not getting screwed. I understand the complexities (profit definition alone can consume pages of a contract), but I still think agencies should do the legal work as part of their 10 percent fee. But that horse left the barn years ago. The big agencies will be happy to refer you to entertainment law firms they're cozy with, who, in turn, will be happy to take you on for an additional 5 percent of your earnings.

It wasn't always this way. Attorneys used to work on a fee-for-service basis, billing by the hour. Shortly after I entered the business, however, some top lawyers began charging clients 5 percent of whatever contract they were working on, and others quickly followed suit. I employed a leading entertainment firm at the time and remember my attorney telling me they were switching to the 5 percent model. I asked, why should I pay 5 percent in perpetuity for a contract that took him a matter of hours to execute? He seemed uncomfortable with the question, explaining that for my 5 percent, the firm would also help with any other legal matters I might have, like taxes or real estate. I said, thanks, but I'd be happy to pay for those services on an hourly basis if I needed them. I subsequently left the firm and found perhaps the only attorney in Hollywood who would agree to a fee-for-service arrangement—but with the stipulation I never tell anyone.

Although I continue to find the 5 percent arrangement questionable (to say the least), I recognize it's partially because my experience began on long-running broadcast shows that produced twenty-two episodes a year. Once a contract was done, typically, I'd go to work for the next two, three, or four years without need of further legal involvement. Under such circumstances, it seemed outrageous to give an attorney an ongoing part of my income.

Today, however, in a television universe dominated by shows of shorter duration, I've been told that the 5 percent fee can actually work to a young writer's advantage. For example, if the overall value of your contract is relatively low, as most contracts are for beginning writers, the 5 percent legal fee can come out to less than it would have cost you on an hourly basis. In such cases, the attorney is banking on your future success.

In all cases, a good attorney can protect you and may actually get you more money during negotiations. A young writer recently told me his attorney saved him from an open-ended development deal that would have kept him working for months for nothing. And a showrunner told me her lawyer's work on a recent contract resulted in substantial additional earnings that more than compensated for her legal fees. May it happen to you.

* * * * * * * *

So ultimately, agents do matter, as do managers and lawyers. The question is, how much? As I've said, once you have multiple reps, things can become so hazy it's hard to know just who does what. All that's clear is you're shelling out 20 to 25 percent of your earnings. But should you find yourself troubled by such issues, it means you're sufficiently successful that no one's going to want to listen to your problems. In other words, congratulations.

19

STRATEGY

PILOTS VERSUS STAFFING

If you can't depend on an agent or manager for your first script assignment—and you can't—how do you get one? Strategy and tactics will vary depending on the circumstances. New writers fall roughly into two categories: working folks and recent grads. Working folks have made a living before Hollywood, perhaps writing professionally in another field but just as likely working in law, business, government, the military, medicine, teaching, whatever. What they have in common is life experience outside of an academic environment. Consequently, they're less inclined to want to start as writers' assistants or in some other nonwriting capacity. They want to be hired as writers. By contrast, most recent grads would be thrilled to become writers' assistants, the common route for students fresh out of school. Whichever group you belong to, there are two paths to getting your first writing job: the pilot route and the staff writer route, each with advantages and disadvantages.

The Pilot Route

This path certainly sounds more exciting. You sell a pilot and are suddenly thrust into the forefront of the business. It can happen. Not only is it unlikely, however, but it also contains a hidden hazard: by leapfrogging over a course of apprenticeship, you may forfeit practical knowledge that can sustain a long career.

Here's a best-case scenario: somehow, you manage to get your spec pilot to a studio, which loves it, sells it to a platform, and pairs you with an experienced showrunner. (Under virtually no circumstance will a studio let you attempt to run your first show by yourself.) The show succeeds; the showrunner mentors you to the point that after two or three seasons you're allowed to take the reins. When the series eventually runs its course (as all must do), not only are you sought after for your next pilot, but you have the savvy to run it by yourself, should the show be produced. This is winning the lottery. You get all the benefits of apprenticeship while building your reputation as writer-producer and series creator.

Now for a dose of reality. Most pilot scripts that get bought are not produced; most that are produced are not picked up to series; most new series fail; and, should your series succeed, finding a collaborative showrunner is far from assured. Some showrunners seek to wrest control from newcomers. Less alarming, but equally unhelpful, your showrunner may lack the experience to be much of a mentor, no matter how well intentioned. Their priority is going to be their own survival, not the progression of your learning curve.

Your only protection against such forced marriages is to have a significant say in choosing your partner. The studio may not grant it, particularly if they have a writer on a showverall deal they're trying to amortize, but assuming you have input, the most important quality you're looking for is belief in your material. Does the showrunner get what you're after? Beyond that, is this someone you feel comfortable with, someone you trust? Experience matters, too, of course, but I'd rather take my chances on an inexperienced showrunner I connect with than a veteran who leaves me feeling uneasy. Do your due diligence—ask around, make plenty of phone calls about candidates—and make your decision accordingly. In the event your spec pilot becomes a series, be aware that your initial job title may not be at the writer-producer level; even if it is, your effective role may amount to little more than staff writer. It all comes down to your showrunner partner.

Because most pilots don't become hit series, perhaps the most pernicious pitfall for newcomers I've seen is the trap of the perpetual pilot writer, what I dub the "Hail Mary syndrome." Here's how that works: You write a pilot that gets sold. This puts money in your pocket—around $75,000 is the norm for an unknown writer in broadcast—and gets you an agent or manager or both, if you don't have reps already. So far, so good. You do some rewrites for the studio and the network, but the pilot doesn't get produced. Bad luck, but hardly the end of the world. Your reps encourage you to write another pilot. You take the next six months to do so, but it doesn't sell. It happens. Write another, they say. You do. It sells—it may even get produced—but doesn't get picked up to series. Back to the drawing board. Your next pilot doesn't sell.

You get the picture. You're twenty yards from the goal line but can't reach pay dirt. Meanwhile, what seemed like a head start increasingly appears to be a burden. You're getting older, your income is sporadic, and you're not getting the apprenticeship that friends working on staff are receiving. You tell your reps you want to get staffed, but they dismiss that, insisting that your breakthrough is only a script away. The truth is, they don't want a first down; they want a touchdown—a Hail Mary pass: all or nothing. That's easier for them than trying to place you on staff. And with a bench full of other pilot writers just like you, they need only one of you to score to have a good year.

Consequently, after four or five years of writing pilots, you find you have to pursue staff work on your own, trying to convince showrunners that despite your apparent success as a pilot writer, you're willing to start at the bottom. Compared to peers who've been writing steadily on other shows, however, you're behind. And compared to fresh-faced prospects just out of school, you may appear a bit stale—and expensive. I've seen it happen to good writers. Finding they can't get staffed, they reluctantly conclude that their only way out of the pilot trap is to double down—keep writing pilots, hoping for that Hail Mary pass to connect. But here's the good news: Your odds of selling a spec pilot are so remote that you probably won't have to worry about the perils of overnight success.

The Staff Writer Route

If you want a long career in television, particularly as a showrunner, you need to know all that goes into the production of a series, and the best way to learn that is by serving some form of apprenticeship on one or more series. This can happen on your own show, as described above, but the more likely path is working on others' shows, beginning as a staff writer, the lowest rung on the ladder, and working your way up to story editor, then executive story editor, and then into the writer-producer ranks.

Staff work allows you to get on-the-job training as a writer, producer, and collaborator while being paid a handsome wage—a one-hour script for broadcast currently pays around $43,000; that's in addition to your weekly salary, which starts around $4,000. You'll meet colleagues with similar ambitions and come to value many of them as friends. Throughout, you'll be compiling a mental checklist of what to do and what to avoid when you run your own show—assuming you even want to run a show. Not everyone does, which is fine. It's perfectly possible to enjoy a satisfying career as a television writer without ever becoming a showrunner. You'll likely live longer, too.

Is there a downside to staff work? Sure. Because most series don't last long, you might find yourself looking for your second job before you've had the chance to learn much of anything in your first. Compounding matters, shorter seasons and "mini-rooms" (writers rooms that disband before production begins)—both staples of streamers and subscription cable—are denying writers opportunities to obtain hands-on experience in production and postproduction. As a result, you may be promoted from one job title to the next without knowing much more about producing than you did before. Another problem with shorter seasons is that roughly the same cohort of mini-room writers may move from show to show, freezing out opportunities for newcomers.

Finally, not every show is a greenhouse of personal growth. Showrunners are paid to produce episodes, not prodigies. If they can keep the trains running on time by being exemplars of enlightenment, fine; but if they can do it by destroying young souls, also fine (from a corporate perspective), provided their behavior doesn't lead to litigation or bad press. So although a genuine apprenticeship is invaluable, it's hardly guaranteed. Nevertheless, I still consider staff work the bedrock of a productive career.

Young writers today have told me they view writers' assistant as the first rung of staff work, an important apprenticeship in itself, and I see their point. A successful comedy writer I know gushes about her experience: "I personally think everyone should have to work as a writers' assistant before becoming a writer. It helps you learn how to read the room and observe the flow of things without feeling the pressure to participate. It's the perfect on-the-job apprenticeship!"

Obviously, this writer and I came up at very different times in the business and through very different routes, which leads me to reemphasize: consider the source of all advice, use your judgment, and chart your course accordingly.

20

TACTICS

MAKING IT HAPPEN

How do you get your first writing job? The short answer: any way you can. Chances are your first sale as a professional writer will be for an episode of an existing series rather than for a spec pilot, so we'll concentrate on that. While it's possible you could sell a pilot, it happens so rarely that each success story becomes its own exception to the rule. Even so, much of this chapter will apply to those circumstances as well.

For recent grads, the route to a first assignment typically begins with being an assistant of some kind, which leads to a freelance script, which can, in turn, lead to a staff writer position. Of the variety of assistant positions on a series, the two most coveted are the showrunner's personal assistant and the writers' assistant whose job is to make notes in the writers room, but any job that puts your nose up to the glass will provide an opportunity to observe, absorb, and eventually lobby for a script. While waiting for their break, some assistants progress to script coordinator (the position responsible for inputting and distributing outlines, drafts, and revisions). Because script coordinators work with showrunners at all hours and under all degrees of hysteria, they have unique access to the inner workings of a series.

Regardless of whatever office job you land, the goal is to turn it into a script assignment. This doesn't mean ignoring your assigned duties; to the contrary, you should do those exceptionally well, above and beyond the call, demonstrating your initiative and commitment. While doing so, however, seek out a champion on staff, a sympathetic writer willing to critique your writing and eventually pitch you to the showrunner. It may take several seasons—perhaps several series—but this approach has paid off for many assistants who had the persistence to keep at it.

Working folks have a different challenge than recent grads. Having established themselves in another field, not only are veterans of the work world less inclined to start out as assistants, but the business is also less likely to see them that way. Assistant positions are considered entry-level jobs; most showrunners in their thirties or forties would feel uncomfortable having assistants the same age or older, as would the rest of the staff. So the challenge for someone entering television from another field is to get your material in front of a showrunner who will consider you as a writer from the start. Regardless of the quality of their spec material, most newcomers coming at the business from this angle don't get put on staff without executing a freelance episode first as an audition piece. Unfortunately, not many freelance scripts are handed out each year—and they often go to writers' assistants or other people already working on a series. So the bar for entry is high. Your ability to clear it will depend on your resourcefulness, resilience, and resolve.

Showrunners are the ultimate target for your spec material, obviously, but any writer or employee on a show is a potential avenue to the showrunner. Studio and network executives can also be valuable contacts, particularly current executives (those execs assigned to ongoing series) whose responsibilities include recommending writers for both new and existing shows. If you've managed to land an agent and/or manager, use them, of course, but expect your first sale to come through your own efforts, which means exploiting every personal contact you have. If your aunt went to school with someone whose college roommate now works for a studio, track that person down.

When you do land a meeting with any of these people, minimally make it into what's known as an "advice-referral" interview. By making it clear you're looking for guidance rather than a job (necessarily), you put the other person at ease. The more specific you can be in your questions and goals, the better. You'd be surprised how many people are willing to help, but you have to let them know how. Where appropriate, ask how they got where they are and what they would do in your position. Can they suggest other people to contact, other avenues to explore? What would you have to do to come back in a year and get hired?

Should you get your spec material to a showrunner, ask as many people as you can to recommend you in an email or phone call. Every showrunner has a perpetual slush pile of scripts to read, but the more a showrunner encounters your name, the more likely they are to look at yours—and if your submission connects, you'll get a meeting.

Before that meeting, do your homework: Learn all you can about the show, studio, platform, and showrunner. Your goal is to sell yourself, emphasizing not only your writing ability but also your background, resourcefulness, and work ethic, all of which will help generate stories and contribute to others' stories in the writers room. Make it a conversation, not a performance. Be a good listener; let the showrunner set the tone, but be prepared to jump in if things lag or you feel you haven't been able to put your best foot forward. By WGA rules, a showrunner can't ask you to pitch story ideas without paying you, but feel free to comment on what you like about the show and suggest possible directions it might take, should the opportunity gracefully arise.

Do *not* tell a showrunner what they're doing wrong or how to make their series better. You'd be surprised how many newcomers do that out of a combination of nervousness, arrogance, and ignorance. Err on the side of enthusiasm—genuine enthusiasm. Showrunners know bullshit when they hear it, so keep things real, but do find a way to tell them how much you'd like to write for their show and how hard you'd work for them.

One thing to avoid: Do not ask the person to let you know if they hear of anything. If you make a good impression, you'll stick in a showrunner's mind, but none will actively scout job opportunities for you, so it's both presumptuous and naive to end an interview on that note.

Should an offer for a freelance episode and/or staff position ultimately result and you don't have representation, you'll have no trouble finding agents willing to take 10 percent of the money you've just earned by yourself. The showrunner might even suggest their own agent or manager.

That's a straightforward, stripped-down version of how things can work under ideal conditions. Most writers have to lobby hard to get that first showrunner meeting. Looking for extra leverage, some turn to fellowship programs, script competitions, or forms of script reading, so a quick word on each is in order.

Fellowship Programs

As of this writing, the major broadcast networks plus Warner Bros. Studios and HBO offer fellowship programs that provide not only training but also potential placement on one of their series for a season, with a goal of promoting fresh voices in the industry. Such programs are open to all unproduced writers and typically require a spec pilot and a spec episode to be considered. The competition is fierce, and the status of these programs in constant flux, so get the latest information from the WGA's Inclusion and Equity Department (contact details are available online at the WGA West website at https://www.wga.org).

Though these programs provide great opportunities, they can also provide unique challenges. Despite having earned their break, fellowship writers may find themselves stigmatized once they get placed on a show. The reason? Their salaries are paid for by the fellowship programs, not the studios—that is, they come free, leading some showrunners to view fellowship writers as perhaps less qualified than the rest of the staff. It's an unfair bias, but where it exists, showrunners tend to give fellowship writers minimal attention during the season and, unsurprisingly, tend not to pick up their options for a second season when their salaries would come out of the show's budget. As one fellowship alum told me, "You have to make yourself invaluable, so they have to invite you back." That's true for all first-time staffers, of course, but it can be particularly true for fellowship writers. Nevertheless, the programs have launched an impressive number of careers, so if you're lucky enough to get the opportunity, grab it.

Script Competitions

An award from a script competition can generate interest in you, but not all contests are created equal. A veteran Hollywood career coach I know advises: "Only apply to the top-tier competitions and only list them if you're the winner or runner-up. That's what agents and managers are looking for. Don't waste money on contests no one's ever heard of." If you've written a screenplay that won a prestigious award, let people know, but your emphasis should be on television competitions that turn heads.

Script-reading Services

The Black List is the best known of several companies that, for a fee, will assess and rank your work—which performs a valuable service for agents, managers, and executives looking for new material. Presumably. My career coach friend calls this industry sector "predatory bullshit," adding, "Maybe if you're living in the middle of nowhere and want some allegedly professional feedback on your work, one of these services might make sense, but you never know who's reading your material or how qualified they are to make comments." You can research these firms online and make your own decisions.

Targets of Opportunity

Many first-time writers want to start out on a prestigious streaming or cable series. Not only are such opportunities highly sought-after, however, they're also inherently limited by the paucity of episodes. And while it's possible to get an assistant job on a high-profile show, it's less likely you're going to get your first script there. Furthermore, the more exclusive the series, the greater the pressure and smaller the margin for error for newcomers.

As I said in chapter 3, there are two types of television shows: teaching hospitals and private hospitals. In a teaching hospital, the showrunner acts as chief resident, taking you on rounds, exposing you to a wide variety of patients, letting you treat some without killing any. In a private hospital, the showrunner is the chief surgeon, leading an elite team of specialists expected to operate with a minimum of supervision. Make a mistake and you not only lose the patient, you lose your job. You can find both types of shows on all platforms, but it's more common to find teaching hospitals where orders are longer and the critical spotlight dimmer. For those reasons, I encourage new writers to consider broadcast as a starting point.

Broadcast

In broadcast, you'll be given the opportunity to do more, learn more, and earn more than at most other platforms. Broadcast has been the training ground for generations of top TV writers, and the opportunities continue today. In recent decades, broadcast series have featured twenty-two episodes per season, providing virtually year-round employment for writers. Although that may change as broadcast pivots to shorter orders to compete with cable and streaming, the number of prime-time hours remains fixed and must be filled with content of some sort. It can't all be reality programming, which means demand for scripted drama will remain high. And broadcast pays the highest WGA minimums. Sweetening the pot, on a select number of broadcast shows, residuals from reruns and international sales continue to be a significant source of additional income.

Creatively, broadcast may not be the table in the cafeteria where the cool kids hang out, but it still has the capacity to deliver well-crafted series that satisfy mainstream appetites. And don't kid yourself: writing for any broadcast show will be a demanding job that calls on everything you have to offer. Most important, because broadcast series typically retain their writing staffs throughout production, you'll experience all phases of making a show: prep, shooting, and post. Such opportunities are increasingly rare on streaming and other platforms employing so-called mini-rooms that disband before filming. Long-running broadcast hits are in constant need of fresh blood to keep churning out scripts. If I were running one of those successful franchises, I'd rather hire an enthusiastic rookie than a cynical veteran who looks down on the work.

Despite these selling points, if you have no aptitude for broadcast, forget it. Only pursue opportunities where you can do honest work. But if you're drawn to any of the genres that broadcast does well, you might find not just a start there, but a home.

Basic Cable

Right up there with broadcast is basic cable, which shares many of broadcast's advantages and enjoys a few of its own. Because basic cable isn't exclusively dependent on advertising (it receives additional subscription money as part of consumer packages), it can succeed with fewer viewers, allowing for bolder, "niche" series. Creatively, basic cable has demonstrated it can punch well above its weight (*Better Call Saul, Breaking Bad, Mad Men, The Walking Dead, The Shield*). And there are plenty of teaching hospitals in basic cable. There have to be, because so many experienced writers migrate to premium cable and streaming once they've earned their stripes. As a result, showrunners in both basic cable and broadcast are prone to hiring less experienced writers looking for a break.

On the downside, the pay in basic cable is generally lower and the seasons shorter than in broadcast, meaning less money and greater instability. And despite broader artistic license, episodes still must conform to strict running times and include act breaks. I believe such discipline can lead to heightened creativity, particularly for writers learning the ropes, but some writers find it an impediment. Overall, basic cable operates with the corporate discipline of broadcast while striving to compete artistically with the high end of subscription services. It can be a winning combination.

Subscription Cable

The obvious appeal of subscription cable is the creative excellence of its finest work. Unrestrained by advertisers' concerns and other curbs on content, premium cable set the bar for quality years ago and continues to compete at the highest level. In the most luxurious cases, subscription series are produced on a scale closer to feature films than broadcast television. But the medium's success makes it a buyer's market not necessarily friendly to new talent. Though well-known names flourish in premium cable, lesser-known writers can find wages low and gestation periods long for new series—with no guarantee of production. Even in success, subscription series employ short seasons, resulting in proportionately downsized annual income. And residuals and profit participation remain a relative mystery compared to the more transparent financial models of broadcast and basic cable, where creators have equity in their own projects, and residuals are based on clearly trackable data regarding reruns and secondary markets. So although subscription cable remains a great destination for high-quality content, it can be a tough neighborhood for newcomers to enter. Private hospitals only; interns need not apply.

Streamers

The streaming world is a bit of the Wild West; anything goes. Many streaming execs appear to be making things up on the fly, which can be both exhilarating and terrifying. Although the landscape is shifting, Netflix dominated this industry sector in its first decade (beginning with *House of Cards* in 2013) and thus provides the logical model for discussion. With a staggering number of shows being produced each year, Netflix has created tremendous opportunity for writers, but just how generous the platform has been with them isn't clear. For all its visible success, Netflix remains an enigma to most writers, including showrunners. The company is notoriously opaque with viewer data, which gives execs the upper hand in negotiations. Netflix owns and produces most of its content, which can range from high-end series with exorbitant budgets to foreign ventures made on a shoestring. Writers' experiences can yo-yo just as wildly. I know colleagues who have had a fine time running Netflix shows, but I also have a friend who ran a Netflix show in Mexico where he was the only writer being paid WGA wages and constantly found himself fighting for working conditions equivalent to those on American productions.

Netflix's power has allowed it to subvert some long-standing writers' traditions, most significantly through introduction of the mini-room, a misleading term that covers a host of different situations—from a handful of writers who meet for a few days to flesh out a series premise to a fully staffed room meeting for twenty weeks to break stories for a thirteen-episode season. By generally accepted definition, all mini-rooms dissolve before production, curtailing the opportunity for writers to participate in prep, shooting, and post. Consequently, should you find yourself working in a mini-room, it will be up to you to seek out as much knowledge in these areas as you can on your own. Some showrunners will be sympathetic, but all will be hamstrung by their production schedules and budgets.

Because Netflix owns virtually all its content, as of this writing, the company can show a series in perpetuity without revealing how many times it's been viewed, avoiding the pro rata residual payments mandated for reruns in broadcast and basic cable. In most cases, Netflix buys out showrunners and writers up front, keeping them forever in the dark about how their show actually performed. It's been said that the most creative writing in Hollywood has always been done by the accountants, and the practice continues today.

Every three years, the WGA negotiates with the Association of Motion Picture and Television Producers to maximize compensation and protections for writers, but streaming is such a fast-moving target that it's hard for the WGA to keep up with just how writers are being squeezed. As this market segment matures, I expect things will settle down to the point where the WGA can identify the most exploitative streaming practices and propose measures to address them, but eternal vigilance will always be required.

Streaming is understandably alluring for the new writer, but entry is difficult and the terrain can be tricky. Streaming has been a buyer's market in its first decade and appears likely to remain so, at least in the short term. For writers, that's been a decidedly mixed bag. On the one hand, there's the promise of virtually unlimited creative opportunity backed by feature-quality production values. On the other, there are suppressed wages, reduced authority, opaque financial protocols, and compromised working conditions for writers. It's a volatile environment already showing signs of internal upheaval. If you find yourself on a streaming show, congrats, buckle up, and expect a wild ride.

* * * * * * * *

As you pursue your tactics, there are a few things you should keep in mind.

The Fastest Gun Syndrome

No matter how quickly you make it in Hollywood, there will always be someone younger, more successful, and seemingly happier than you are. So if your self-worth is based on being the fastest gun in town, forget it; there's always going to be someone faster getting off the stagecoach. One secret to my longevity is I don't read the trades. Not only are they full of lies and half-truths, their major purpose is to make you feel that whatever you're doing is not enough. My advice: concentrate on the work, be thankful for what you've got, and let *Deadline Hollywood* deal with the rest.

The Rocket Man Syndrome

Some writers' careers take off in a blaze of glory. But what goes up like a rocket can come down like a rocket. I knew a talented but raw writer on *Remington Steele* who fast-talked his way into a lucrative deal with the hottest producer in one-hour drama; it was all over the trades. (Okay, occasionally I peek.) But his ambition took him well beyond his capabilities. Shortly after his heralded ascendance, he was fired and never worked in the business again. Literally. He just disappeared. There's a moral in there for those willing to find it.

Sail Your Boat

I've found that navigating a television career is more like sailing than riding a rocket—or even piloting a motorboat. A motorboat muscles its way through the water, but a sailboat relies on the wind, which requires skill, humility, and patience. Sometimes the wind is at your back, but just as often it's in your face, and because you can't sail directly into the wind, you have to tack many times to reach your destination. Another factor: a sailboat needs a keel for stability. Without it, you sideslip all over the place. In Hollywood, the wind is a product of several factors: the studios, the networks, prevailing market conditions, and dumb luck. You can't control it; you can only try to harness it. As for the keel, that's your center, your sense of self. Protect that with everything you've got because you'll need it to stay on course as you tack and tack again with your eyes on the horizon.

21

DECISIONS, DECISIONS

A CASE STUDY

I recently came across an email exchange from 2016 with my former assistant at *Army Wives*, a promising writer and graduate of USC School of Cinematic Arts. After working on *Army Wives*, she was hired as an executive assistant at a major TV studio. Our correspondence ties together much of what I've been saying about routes to writing. I offer it as an example of real-world job hunting.

She wrote:

> I need some advice. I interviewed to be the writers assistant on the new Netflix show about hip-hop in late 1970s New York that was created by Baz Luhrmann and will be run by Shawn Ryan. Baz had someone he wanted from his camp to be the writers assistant, but they offered me the script coordinator job. I really liked Shawn and his assistant and it sounds like a cool, well-done project, but, from a career standpoint, I wonder if it's the right call, since almost everything I've written has been comedy. I guess I just consider myself a comedy writer. And I'm not sure what the track is for a script coordinator—I don't want to get stuck!
>
> I'd love to know what your thoughts are—I feel a little nervous that I'll take this, and then an opportunity will come up with a comedy or something like that. And, even though what I'm doing now isn't the most thrilling job in the world, I really

like the people I work with, and they've been very good to me and very helpful when it comes to my writing and career stuff. On the other hand, this seems like an interesting show and potentially a better stepping stone than a studio job.

I replied:

As with every job opportunity, there are at least two important aspects to consider, the superficial and the substantive. The sizzle and the steak.

Put another way: What's this going to do for my profile/visibility/viability? What's this going to do to improve and perhaps even platform my work?

On the face of it, working on what appears to be a hot new project that will generate buzz with star players on the platform of the moment gives you considerably more bragging rights than working for a studio. It tells the industry you're traveling with the right crowd, which suggests you bring something to the table, if only the ability to charm the right people, which is not something to be laughed at—I'm certainly not suggesting that's the case, but it's actually an important component of success out here. The question then becomes, what do you do with such cachet? Will it help get you closer to what it is you want substantively?

So that brings us to the second area, what you'd be doing. From a versatility standpoint, being a script coordinator is a good thing, a transportable skill that is critically important to any show. It is a demanding job, however, often requiring long and unusual hours. The script coordinator can't go home until the script under fire is done. On the plus side of that, however, a reliable script coordinator often becomes more than a functionary; she can evolve into something of a confidante to the showrunner(s) involved because the position inevitably involves late-night and weekend calls under stressful conditions. There are also those quiet moments when it's just the showrunner and the script coordinator either waiting for notes or catching a collective breath. I've frequently collapsed in the script coordinator's extra chair as a long night wore on.

So, a good script coordinator becomes a valued member of the whole writing/production process. Does it help you become a better writer? Well, you become intimately familiar with every change that happens on every script. Literally. Because you're responsible for those. Does it get you into the writers room? Depends on the show, on conditions, on whatever arrangements you make individually. Generally, especially once production begins, I would say no. Your job is to keep the scripts in order and coordinate the various related documents the script coordinator is responsible for. Doesn't mean you can't get into the room or benefit from all the creative talks that go on. It's just to say your job is to be at your battle station when needed.

Now as to the material itself, comedy versus drama. In an ideal world, yes, you'd want to work on a comedy if given the choice. But this is the choice in front of you right now. And it appears a pretty alluring one. Certainly, it would seem to be closer to the engine room of writing than your current position. Now that might not be true, especially if you're reading a lot of scripts right now at the studio and learning a lot about how and what to write. You have to decide that. But, leaning toward the new offer, in today's world of increasingly sophisticated single-camera comedy, it seems to me that there's plenty of "cross-learning" that can happen on a drama with a comedic component (and I certainly hope that a hip-hop drama involving Baz Luhrmann has some lighter touches to it).

Finally, allow me to point out that you are not yet a produced writer of either comedy or drama, so concerns about being typed or getting stuck, while understandable, should be minimal. The fact is Hollywood doesn't type you until you've been responsible for produced work by which you can be typed. And being typed is less likely in today's fluid world of television than it was in previous decades. The lines are increasingly blurred not only between film and TV, but comedy and drama. Migration is highly possible between the various spheres. It seems to me that working on the hip-hop show would only type you as hip (no pun intended), which I think would be helpful to you as a comedy writer.

When the time comes for you to get your first produced credit as a writer, then I think you'll have more reason to consider what statement you're making with your work, how you're being perceived, but even then, I'd caution against being overly cautious. The important thing is getting produced. Someone actually paid you for your words. That's the first hurdle. That tells the business you are a viable writer. I'd worry about being typed after your fourth or fifth or tenth or twelfth script. . . .

So, you have to add it up: What do you get from the new job? What do you give up? What doors does it open? What doors does it close? Another critical factor is quality of life. Are these good people to hang around with or will your mental/emotional health be threatened? Very important to consider. As a corollary, I know you like the folks you work with now—which is great—but comfort alone is no reason to stay in a job that is not getting you closer to your career goals or has already gotten you as far as it's going to get you. I just throw that into the mix to make your decision more difficult.

Oh, and then there's money. But that should likely be the least of your concerns. The right decision on all the other factors should ultimately lead to the most profitable course in all respects.

My two shekels. Hope they're of some use.

Coda: she took the job as script coordinator on the Netflix show, which turned out to be something of a disaster—canceled after one season, a rarity for Netflix at the time—but she came through it just fine. She and her writing partner quickly became staff writers on several popular half-hours, rising through the ranks to the writer-producer level, and they recently got their first shot as showrunners.

22

PAY DIRT

STAFF WRITER TO EXECUTIVE STORY EDITOR

You're now a staff writer. Congratulations. Typical backstory: You were a writers' assistant, had supporters on staff, and got the job when last season's staff writers were bumped up to story editors. Or, entering from another field, you managed to get your spec material in front of a showrunner who hired you. However you got here, well done. You're in the army now, although a rather strange army in which rank is relatively meaningless. Technically, the hierarchy on a writing staff in ascending order is: staff writer, story editor, executive story editor, coproducer, producer, supervising producer, co-executive producer, executive producer.

All showrunners are executive producers, but not all executive producers are showrunners. In fact, "showrunner" itself is an unofficial term; you won't find it in any WGA contract because showrunning involves producing responsibilities beyond the WGA's sole jurisdiction over writing services. Consequently, on series with multiple executive producers, from the outside you need additional knowledge to identify the showrunner.

From the inside, it's far easier. If the organizational chart for most conventional businesses resembles a pyramid, on most television shows it's more like the sun hovering over the horizon. There's the showrunner on top and everyone else on a straight line underneath, all doing essentially the same job: pitching stories and writing scripts. There are notable exceptions, certainly, but to understand what anyone actually does on a particular series, you have to observe them in action—or inaction.

In all cases, the fundamental job of every writer on staff is to serve the showrunner. Figuring out what that means will constitute a large part of your success. For staff writers, it usually translates into contributing ideas in the writers room and writing a script—if you're fortunate enough to get an assignment. On broadcast shows with twenty-two episodes, you can hope to get at least one script. On short-order shows, like so much else in this business, it depends on the showrunner.

On some series, the showrunner's instructions will be clear, on-the-job training plentiful, and personal progress steady. On other series, directions will be murky, training nonexistent, and the atmosphere chaotic.

When you show up for your first staff job, it will feel like the first day of high school. Unfortunately, when you show up for your second staff job, it will also feel like the first day of high school. There's a bit of *Groundhog Day* involved in episodic television: every series begins at square one, with staffers nervously checking each other out, afraid of being unmasked as frauds. You may be given an office or a desk, but much of your time will be spent in the writers room (typically, a conference room or converted office space filled with whiteboards and bulletin boards, dominated by a long table littered with dry-erase markers, index cards, and bowls of candy and other unhealthy snacks). This is the engine room of most series, where stories are created. A few showrunners don't use a room, relying instead on a one-on-one approach to break episodes; some showrunners attempt to write all episodes themselves, but both cases are exceptions.

(The COVID-19 pandemic forced television series to resort to virtual writers rooms using Zoom or other communication platforms. As with much of corporate America emerging from that crisis, most shows today feature a hybrid approach to the writers room, splitting time between virtual and in-person rooms. The principles in this chapter pertain equally well to all rooms regardless of configuration.)

In most rooms, all writers are expected to contribute to story discussions, supervised by the showrunner or a designated number two. Individual writers subsequently peel off to write their own outlines and scripts as assigned by the showrunner, so the room is in constant flux. Mini-rooms are exceptions; often, because all stories are expected to be broken before the room disbands, you're required to stay in the room throughout, doing any individual work outside of office hours.

As for lead time, on a well-run broadcast show, the period involved from initial idea to shooting script can range from seven to nine weeks. When pressed, it can be done in a week or less, but if you do that too often, the machinery breaks, leading to production shutdowns, the bane of every showrunner's existence. And even if a show manages to keep shooting under hysterical conditions, episodes written in such a rush usually show the strain.

Some writers rooms are meritocracies, others hierarchies. Some are friendly, others snake pits. I heard a writer once liken the writers room to "a delicate fish tank," in which pH, temperature, and different species all must harmonize for the room to thrive. It can take time to get it right—and some rooms never do. So prepare for the worst and hope for the best. The goal is to do well enough to have your option picked up for another season, or, if your show goes down, to develop a sufficiently good reputation to be hired on another show.

Here are some tips for survival.

Show Up

It's been said that 90 percent of life is just showing up. In television, that means arriving early and staying late. Anticipate. Be prepared for the next day's work. Put in extra effort where appropriate without being obsequious.

Shut Up

Although you've been hired to contribute, it's better initially to err on the side of brevity than verbosity. There'll be plenty of time to show you've got game. First, establish you're a team player through a balance of humility, restraint, and respect. Look, listen, and learn.

Be Positive

Your job is to pitch solutions, not problems. Don't criticize an idea without having a suggestion to replace it. There are a variety of ways to do this without inviting hostility: "I love that; I was wondering if it also makes sense to consider . . . ." Pay attention to how veteran writers express criticism effectively and adopt best practices.

Don't Keep Score

You may feel pressure to put points on the board, but be patient. Ease yourself into the game. In a well-managed room, no one's keeping score. Offer an idea when you have one, but don't force it. As a new writer, being quiet and thoughtful is unlikely to bother anyone. Constant chatter, on the other hand, can become annoying.

Be Open to Criticism

There's a cruel calculus to TV writing in that it's harder for a novice to take criticism than a pro. You'd think it would be the opposite, that the veteran would resent notes and the rookie welcome them, but it's not so. Old pros have been through the process enough times to know that it costs them nothing to listen. If a note can improve their material, they'll take it, regardless of the source. By contrast, rookies tend to see notes as an attack on their competence, so they instinctively go on the defensive. And when a rookie does take a note, it's often with the intention of doing "least harm" to what's already there, which isn't helpful to the script, the showrunner, or your progress as a writer. I once heard a midlevel writer-producer tell a roomful of rookie staffers, "The biggest problem we have as young writers is that we fall in love with our stuff. You have to learn to let it go. The best script will evolve. Be open to change because writing is rewriting. Don't take things personally if you can help it. It's not about you; it's about the show." Spot on—to which I'd add, don't be so pliable you won't defend anything, but once you've been heard by the showrunner, accept the verdict and move on.

Expect to Be Rewritten

When you're assigned a script, at some point on most shows it's going to be taken away from you. The showrunner is either going to rewrite it themself or hand it to someone else to rewrite it. How early this happens and how much rewriting is involved are clues to how well the showrunner thinks you've done. When the final shooting script appears, it may be a mere polish or it may be a page-one (i.e., total) rewrite. Most showrunners are happy if a first draft by a veteran writer comes in 60 percent there—and will be satisfied at 50. So don't judge yourself too harshly if your first efforts undergo heavy revision. Some showrunners will explain why certain changes were made; others won't. In most cases, the best feedback will be the changes themselves. On a good show, the shooting script will be better than the one you turned in, so do all you can to learn from that. If you feel the shooting script is only a lateral or inferior variation on your own, at least you have a better sense of what the showrunner's looking for.

Avoid Factions

Hollywood has been called high school with money. On television staffs, cliques can form, usually based on complaints about the showrunner, fellow writers, or the direction of the show. Stay out of it. Keep your head down and do your work.

Don't Diss the Showrunner

Some showrunners are saints, others sinners; most fall somewhere in between. All showrunners, however, are working their asses off to do a job you can't possibly understand if you haven't done it yourself. It may be tempting to take potshots at the showrunner with fellow writers or friends. Don't. Word gets around, and though it's unlikely to hurt the showrunner, it will almost certainly hurt you, painting you as someone who can't be trusted. When confronted with less-than-stellar leadership, the military has an expression: "Salute the rank, not the individual." (I'm talking about routine work issues, of course. If you encounter unacceptable personal conduct, that's a different matter. In such cases, discuss how to proceed with your fellow writers and your reps.)

Take Walks

The air can get hot in the writers room, literally and figuratively. It's important to remind yourself there's a world outside of the third-act break of the current script. Take a stroll, clear your mind, breathe the smog, dodge the traffic.

Learn What's Expected on Set

As a staff writer, you may be asked to "be on set," particularly on a broadcast or basic cable episode you've written. On-set responsibilities can vary, but usually entail acting as the showrunner's surrogate, ensuring that things go as the showrunner intended—from actors' performances to shot selection, coverage, and crew safety. By strict definition, these functions fall under the director's jurisdiction, but many showrunners want an extra measure of creative reinforcement from a staffer. Being on set is a balancing act. On the one hand, you want to get along with directors; on the other, you don't want to be second-guessed by showrunners for "mistakes" they think you should have prevented during shooting. As a staff writer once told me, "You don't want to be known as someone who can't handle the set." To me, that's a big burden to place on inexperienced shoulders: sometimes an unrealistic—even unnecessary—one. Nevertheless, you need to be prepared.

Ideally, the showrunner will give you a clear protocol to follow on set and will share this with the director (see chapter 32), but most series don't exist in an ideal world. Some showrunners themselves don't have a firm grasp on what to do on set but will assume that you do. If you find yourself in this confounding situation, seek advice—from fellow writers on staff, the line producer, the director-producer, anyone whose opinion you respect. Get the information you need to succeed.

* * * * * * * * *

All the above has been directed at staff writers. Turning to story editors and executive story editors . . . it's the same thing. Despite title bumps, you likely won't be doing much more than you did as a staff writer. You'll know more and might enjoy more seniority, but on most one-hour series, there's little distinction among staff writers, story editors, and executive story editors except weekly pay, which is established by WGA minimums. The big divide on writing staffs is between the non-producer ranks and writer-producer ranks, though even here the contrast often has more to do with status and money than capability or function. Nevertheless, while recognizing that titles are arbitrary and capricious, the next big step on your journey is the day you cross the line from being a mere writer to something more—a hyphenate.

23

BOTTLENECK

WRITER-PRODUCERS

It's exciting to tell family and friends you're no longer just a writer but a writer-producer—no need to go into detail; they won't understand, anyway. Accept their congratulations and feel good about yourself, but don't be fooled. As mentioned earlier, the organizational chart of a typical writing staff more often resembles a horizontal line rather than a pyramid. Essentially, you and your colleagues will all be doing the same thing: breaking stories, structuring outlines, and writing scripts. Although you may be given some actual production responsibilities, your principal value will be as a writer, not as a producer; on series that employ mini-rooms, you likely won't be doing any producing at all.

As a result, you and your fellow hyphenates will find yourselves engaged in a race to the middle, where a bottleneck develops. The only definitive step up on most shows is the number-two position—the writer designated to run the room in the showrunner's absence. But not every show has a clear number two, and even on those that do, the opportunity to take over the reins from the showrunner is increasingly rare in today's market, dominated as it is by short-order series with limited lifespans. Not only are most showrunners reluctant to step away under prevailing circumstances, but most shows don't last long enough for a peaceful transition of power to occur.

Consequently, climbing the ladder as a writer-producer requires patience.

That said, it's perfectly possible to be happy for years without doing much more than writing. I should know; I did it. And you may decide after witnessing enough showrunning that you don't want to get to the top. A proven writer-producer is an asset on any staff—with the added benefit that you don't go home with a showrunner's ulcers.

If your ambition is to run a show, however, your short-term goals as a writer-producer should include learning all you can about all phases of showrunning and mentoring junior staff members. Not only is paying it forward part of your obligation as a successful writer, but it's also gratifying, a reminder that you've actually learned things along the way that are valuable to others. And you may develop relationships with younger writers that bear fruit when you're in a position to hire—or they're in a position to hire you.

If the showrunner assigns you production responsibilities, seize them. If you're expected to stay rooted in the writers room, make the best of it and learn what you can about production on your own. You'll find that most folks in production, from heads of department on down, are happy to share their expertise with someone who's genuinely interested.

A word about personal finances: As a hyphenate, you'll likely be making more money than you thought possible. Do not run out and buy a Tesla. Things can change in a heartbeat. Saving money gives you the leeway to choose projects; debt forces you to take the next job that comes along. Some writers thrive under such pressure, but unless you're one of them, be prudent with your good fortune. Get sound financial advice before making serious investments. Consider incorporating. By creating what's known as a loan-out corporation, you'll gain legal benefits and tax advantages. If you don't have a lawyer who handles incorporation, ask colleagues to recommend someone.

A bit more about timeline: when I broke in during the last hurrah of broadcast television, once you were staffed on a series and proved your worth, people would know who you were. It was a much smaller club, and with a bit of luck you could expect to keep working for a long time, hopscotching from show to show like choosing stepping-stones across a stream. That's not true for most writers anymore. To begin with, getting that first script assignment is more difficult, for a host of reasons: increased competition, shorter orders with fewer staff positions and freelance episodes, mini-room cohorts moving in virtual herds from show to show, and the decline of development deals, resulting in more veteran talent on the market. And once your current job goes away—as every job does eventually in this business—there's no assurance the next one will come any time soon. There is no reliable calendar for series development anymore; shows come and go in a ceaseless blur. And the industry has become so vast, with so many platforms and players, it's hard for anyone to know who's doing anything, much less to be aware of a promising young writer who's just had an episode produced on a short-order series somewhere on the edge of the known universe.

Consequently, you have to scramble from job to job, often with the same job title—or even taking a hit—to stay employed. This is the way things are now, and part of your necessary skill set is the ability to see things clearly and navigate accordingly.

But do try to have some fun along the way. Once you become a showrunner, the responsibilities make it more difficult. Heavy is the head, and all that. Nevertheless, that's where we're going next.

24

MEANS OF ASCENT

ROUTES TO THE TOP

For most writer-producers, the drive to the top isn't simply about fame and fortune, but creative control: you want to write and produce a series your way. How to reach the summit? Here are five common routes.

Create Your Own Show

This is the most traditional path and the one most under your control. You write it, you run it. This applies only to experienced writer-producers, however. If you're new to the business, the studio will insist on pairing you with a veteran showrunner. You can object, but you're unlikely to succeed—and shouldn't want to; running a show by yourself as a newcomer is tantamount to career suicide. As noted in chapter 23, being assigned a showrunner can be a blessing or a curse, so be wary.

Even if you find the ideal partner, it's critically important to have "the conversation" before formalizing any collaboration. The conversation is a nuts-and-bolts talk about division of labor—how the show is actually going to run. Unless you're part of a preexisting writing team, there's no such thing as "co-showrunning." Someone has to be in charge, and if you're a first-timer, it's not going to be you. This doesn't mean you can't be a significant part of the process, but you need to talk about it, ask the awkward questions: how's the room going to work? What do you see me doing from day to day?

Many promising collaborations at all levels of the business have been torpedoed because the parties involved didn't have the conversation. Consequently, they made unfounded assumptions about each other. One top showrunner I know had it happen to him when he agreed to executive-produce a pilot written by a writer on his staff. When production began, it turned out the writer expected to be treated as a full equal, which led to arguments before the veteran finally threw in the towel. Subsequently, the pilot failed, and the old pro walked away having relearned a valuable lesson: have the conversation.

Be Promoted from Within

This used to be a common path, particularly in broadcast when there were a healthy number of long-running shows generating spinoffs, each spinoff needing twenty-two episodes a season. Successful creators would hand off an established series to a proven deputy and proceed to create more shows themselves. Today, with fewer reliable broadcast hits, showrunners tend to stay in the saddle longer than they used to. Basic cable is much the same. And creators of short-order subscription series tend to oversee the entire run. Nevertheless, being promoted from within remains a viable route. Your ascent may begin with elevation to the number-two position: the writer who runs the room when the showrunner's not there. It's a great way to get a taste of the full-on experience of showrunning.

Being promoted from within has distinct benefits: you don't have to assemble a writing staff or production team from scratch; the creative content, corporate culture, and production protocols are familiar. The principal challenge is earning the respect of your colleagues. Yesterday, you were a peer; today, you're the boss. Writers might be jealous and actors might get naughty, testing what they can get away with now that "Mom" or "Dad" is gone. There's no playbook on how to handle the transition other than to deal with such issues as honestly and adroitly as you can.

Take Over Someone Else's Show from the Outside

There are two types of takeovers: "friendly takeovers," in which a departing showrunner invites you to take over a series, and "hostile takeovers," in which the preceding showrunner has been fired—sometimes for bad behavior, more often for unacceptable or late scripts, sometimes both.

A friendly takeover is like being promoted from within except you have to familiarize yourself with the established personnel and culture. A hostile takeover is more reminiscent of Leo Tolstoy's observation about families: every unhappy show is unhappy in its own way. The only common factor with hostile takeovers is hysteria. The studio's hemorrhaging money, the production schedule is in shambles, and everyone's running scared. I wouldn't recommend it as your first showrunning gig. Though execs can't blame you for the catastrophe you inherit, they *will* hold you responsible should the show get canceled on your watch. They're certainly not going to blame themselves.

Be Assigned to an Inexperienced Creator

A number of series each year are created by inexperienced television writers who need veteran help. In the three previous examples, the showrunner is the sovereign who holds the scepter. In this instance, however, I encourage showrunners to think of themselves more as prime ministers, with the responsibility to advise and persuade rather than the authority to make unilateral decisions. Even though you technically outrank the creator and could likely arrogate full control if you tried, you will promote more harmony and better results by taking this approach.

The creator's biggest fear with arranged marriages is that you're going to take their show away, so your first priority is to assure them that's not the case. You're there because you like the show and want it to succeed—assuming you mean it. (If you don't, then what are you doing there?) One showrunner I know who works with inexperienced creators puts it this way: "Your vision, my guidance."

Unfortunately, there are situations where a studio marginalizes the creator as soon as they've acquired a pilot, hiring an experienced showrunner to rewrite the script and subsequently run the show with virtually no regard for the creator—not a good or honorable arrangement for anyone. It happened to me on a newly launched basic cable network. I liked the script and the writers, but the studio execs smugly confided they had serious doubts about both, which made me wonder why they had bought the project in the first place. I walked away, telling the writers to watch their backs. The series never got made. In fact, soon after my experience, the network itself went out of business. Karma can be a bitch.

Be Asked to Join a Project

This final path is relatively new and applies most commonly to premium cable and streaming platforms, whose deep pockets and clout give them the ability to assemble projects piece by piece—intellectual property, actors, director, showrunner—in whatever order they choose. Under the traditional pilot model, a project begins with a writer either pitching an idea or submitting a script. In this paradigm, however, a writer might be the last element to be brought on board. It's a form of in-house packaging.

If you're invited to join such a project as showrunner, be aware that you inherently surrender some autonomy because the show didn't originate with you. At the far end of this spectrum is Marvel Studios, which has resorted to using the term "head writer" in place of showrunner on many of its series. Marvel reserves the key leadership role for the studio itself, granting the head writer and director roughly equal footing on a subordinate tier, routinely installing a pair—or more—of nonwriting execs in the writers rooms, a fact of life that writers must accommodate as cheerfully as possible. Marvel is an isolated example involving a wildly successful studio controlling a vast inventory of intellectual property governed by a labyrinthine mythology. But Marvel isn't the only shop where showrunner authority has been eroded of late. It's been a trend at the high end of the streaming and subscription cable spectrum. Should you find yourself in such circumstances, heightened flexibility and resourcefulness will be required. The goal is to maximize influence where you can't exercise strict control. Keep a cool head, be genuinely collaborative, and you may change minds about the value of having a showrunner in charge.

25

FASTBALLS AND PASSED BALLS

THE ART OF PITCHING

There are essentially two ways to get your own show on the air: write a spec pilot or pitch your series, which in success leads to a pilot script and eventual series order. The spec route is easy to understand: you write it, they buy it. Pitching is more arcane. Although the concept is simple—sell your idea through a personal presentation—the execution is not. Pitching requires a combination of substance and showmanship that doesn't come easily to many writers. A spec pilot is writing. A pitch involves performance.

For writers, the obvious appeal of a spec pilot is that no one else is involved. But that's the downside, too; even the best writers can benefit from good notes. Furthermore, not all spec pilots get read in a timely fashion, if at all, and many execs won't look at a script once they think it's past its freshness date. For execs, the benefit of a spec script is they have something in their hands to judge. But that blessing also contains a curse: a spec pilot limits execs' ability to shape a series, particularly because spec pilot writers tend to be more resistant to notes than those who go through the pitch process. Execs prefer projects where they feel more like valued collaborators than passive observers.

The fundamental advantages of a pitch for writers are pragmatic. To begin with, you don't have to worry about whether execs are going to read your script. You're in the room with them, so you know you have their attention. Furthermore, with a pitch you don't commit to writing a script unless someone's willing to pay for it. For execs, it's easier to listen to a pitch than read a script. And, as mentioned, a pitch allows them to get creatively invested from the start.

Any discussion of pitching, like so much else in this business, should begin with William Goldman's first rule of Hollywood: nobody knows anything. There's as much hot air expended in this town about what makes a good pitch as there is about what makes a good script.

Here's my take: a good pitch is one that sells. Some writers claim you have to mount a slick, visually sophisticated multimedia presentation to get this done. Others say a simple verbal explanation is all that's needed. Both methods— and everything in between—have worked. I know a writer with no detectable social skills who sold a series while reading from notes, never once making eye contact with the execs in the room. I also know writers who've gone into meetings with awesome pitch decks and come away empty-handed.

What's most important is the quality of your idea, of course, but that's only half the battle. You can pitch, but executives must catch; knowing how to communicate with execs is the difference between throwing a fastball and a passed ball. Consequently, there are two critical aspects to any pitch: what you say and how you say it—the content and the delivery.

Content

You need to know as much about your series as you can to say as little as possible in your pitch. That may sound counterintuitive, but concision implies mastery; you have to know a subject well to summarize it succinctly. Well-prepared writers, while equipped to go into as much detail as execs might ask for, will highlight only the most enticing elements in the formal portion of their pitches. A common mistake is to immediately plunge into a rambling description of the pilot episode, effectively sucking all the air out of the room. I know. I've done it. With that in mind, here are some tips for developing your pitch.

Pilot Story

What kind of episode do you plan to open with? A premise pilot that throws your lead characters together for the first time? A "typical episode" that thrusts the viewer into the middle of an established situation? A "first chapter" that begins a densely plotted serial? Although you'll include only the most tantalizing details in your pitch, you need to know the structure of your initial episode.

Logline

This is your series in one sentence. When someone asks what your show is about, this is the answer. It should be an intriguing description of the premise and the promise. The logline may end up directly in your pitch or you may use it to set up a pitch. Regardless, the discipline of constructing a logline forces you to drill down to the essence of your concept. No matter how complex your series may be, if you can't describe it in a single line, odds are you need to think about it some more.

Tagline

This is the hook you'd see on the poster for your series. It differs from a logline in that it doesn't need to describe the series, only promote it in a catchy way: "Once upon a time, in a galaxy far away. . . ." The farther from P. T. Barnum you are as a personality, the more you may find this exercise pointless, even distasteful, but it's simply another way to focus your thinking, to hold a different facet of your project up to the light.

Theme

What's the emotional spine of the show? Beyond its importance to you as the writer, a strong theme assures execs there's a deep emotional well to draw upon for the life of the series, not merely a gimmick or clever setup that could quickly run dry.

The World

Where does your show take place, and in what time period? What special rules might apply? The more specific you can be in visualizing your world, the better.

Tone

What's the feel? Is it funny, intense, clever, moving? Of course, a good script—and series—will feature a range of different tones, but what's the predominant mood of your show? In conveying tone, comparisons to movies and TV shows are inevitable. Used sloppily, this can be a crutch for lazy thinking, but applied properly, the "recombinant" approach is a vivid form of shorthand: "It's *24* meets *Star Wars*." That's terrible, but you get the idea: a thriller about stopping a terrorist threat in space.

Main Characters

Be prepared to discuss your main characters in detail, but how much detail will vary from pitcher to pitcher and catcher to catcher. Some writers routinely write extensive bios of their characters before starting a script. Others begin with character sketches and fill things in as they go. Similarly, some execs are happy with brief character descriptions in a pitch; others might insist on more complete backstories, throughlines, and emotional arcs. Personally, I favor the "less is more" approach, siding with Oscar-winning writer Paddy Chayefsky, who observed:

> It is a common illusion that dramatists sit down and preconceive a detailed biography and character study of each character in a script. To a professional writer, this would be a palpable waste of time. . . . It is inevitable that the preconception of the character will change a thousand times during the course of construction in order to satisfy the demands of the storyline. . . . Generally, the characterizations are devolved from the incidents of the main story and not preconceived. It is, of course, not as simple as that. . . . Obviously, the characters are not deduced merely from the incidents—because the

> incidents are derived from the characters. Writing is such a confused business of backing and filling, of suddenly plunging into the third act while you are still pondering the first act.

Episodic Structure

Is there anything unique or unusual about the structure of your series, a distinctive template each episode will follow? Are episodes self-contained or serialized? How many storylines run through a typical episode? Is there a teaser? Are there time jumps?

Bible

It has become increasingly common for execs to want to hear some form of "bible" during your pitch: story ideas that shepherd the series though the first season—and perhaps beyond. Bibles can be brief or they can be, well, biblical in length. David Simon's bible for the first season of *The Wire* ran seventy-nine single-spaced pages, but there are unique aspects to that, notably Simon's background as a crime journalist, his stature in the business, and his professional history with HBO. You can find Simon's bible and other examples online, although be wary of provenances: some bibles appear to be written by studio execs after a series was sold.

The value of writing a bible has as much to do with your own preparation as it does with potentially giving execs a blow-by-blow account of how your series unfolds. As with crafting detailed descriptions of your main characters, there's an element of transparent fiction in writing a bible because storylines and characters will inevitably change once actual writing begins. Nevertheless, you need a good sense of your story arcs to sell your concept, delineating mile markers for various plotlines and character developments.

Opinions vary about giving execs a physical copy of your bible or similar documents at pitch sessions. The WGA strongly opposes such "leave-behinds," believing writers should be paid for all written work. I agree. Once a studio has bought your pitch, you can deluge them with all the paperwork they want.

Conviction

Last, but far from least, if you don't believe in what you're trying to sell, no amount of slickness will be able to disguise the emptiness at its core. Your pitch should likely begin with your personal attachment to the project, what drew you in. Good execs recognize genuine passion—and its absence. Conviction alone won't sell a series, but lack of it will be fatal.

Delivery

A good pitch balances the sizzle and the steak. You've got maybe fifteen minutes to sell yourself and your concept. Fifteen minutes might seem short—the pitch session itself can go considerably longer with questions and conversation, but I suggest fifteen minutes as a form of self-imposed discipline—and demonstration of mercy for your audience. (I'm not joking entirely; most execs will form a positive or negative impression of your project before those opening minutes are up.) Think of your planned presentation as the "elevator pitch," the one you'd give a stranger who enters the elevator with you on the twentieth floor going down. By the time you hit the lobby, that person should be dying to see your show. A successful pitch doesn't try to cover everything; it teases so that the listener wants to hear more—and will pay to get it.

There are several factors to consider when crafting a pitch.

Your Audience

Your pitch will adjust to match your listeners. You might begin with a conversational pitch to your reps, which then becomes a more formal pitch to a POD (a development company with a "production overall deal"), if one is involved. The POD execs might help turn your pitch into a multimedia presentation ready to throw at a studio. And a studio will give further refinements before you pitch to a platform.

You

How you see yourself—and how you choose to project yourself (not always the same thing)—greatly affect your approach—or should. Kimberly D. Elsbach, a professor of management, did firsthand research on the television pitch process for a 2003 article in the *Harvard Business Review* and discerned three archetypes of effective pitchers: showrunners, artists, and neophytes. Her conclusion: "By successfully projecting yourself as one of the three creative types and getting your catcher to view himself or herself as a creative collaborator, you can improve your chances of selling an idea." Her categories and advice remain as relevant today as they were twenty years ago.

Showrunner

If you identify as a showrunner, you've likely had experience with pitches before—perhaps even with the execs you're pitching to, which suggests a more relaxed approach, essentially treating the execs as creative peers, which is both flattering and effective. The subtext: "We all know how these things work; I don't have to sell my expertise to you, so let's talk about how to make a great show together."

Artist

I know a former playwright who has the aspect of a disheveled college professor. He mumbles, speaks barely above a whisper, yet always hooks execs with his intellect, sincerity, and passion, a prime example of "the artist." Artists score points with their clearly unique, spontaneous sensibilities, which run counter to the more polished approach of "the showrunner." Elsbach notes that this persona is hardest to fake because artists "don't play to type; they are the type." If you have to think about whether you belong in this category, you probably don't. Sorry.

Neophyte

The opposite of showrunners, neophytes don't try to hide their inexperience but make a virtue of it, presenting themselves in Elsbach's words as "eager learners." She writes: "They consciously exploit the power differential between pitcher and catcher by asking directly and boldly for help—not in a desperate way, but with the confidence of a brilliant favorite, a talented student seeking sage advice from a beloved mentor."

If you're not a showrunner and you're too well-balanced to honestly present yourself as an artist, then it's likely your pitch should take on aspects of the neophyte.

Rehearse, but Don't Memorize

The distinction between rehearsing and memorizing is like the difference between having a conversation and delivering an oration. The first is fluid and interactive; the second, fixed and one-sided. Though a pitch involves performance, it's closer to stand-up comedy than traditional theater. Good stand-ups appear to be inventing their act on the spot for your personal enjoyment, when in fact it's the result of hours of rehearsal. Such preparation allows the performer to read the room and adjust on the fly for each show. There will be key phrases and descriptions you'll want to include in every pitch, but don't be enslaved to an extensive script. Concentrate on the structure of your pitch. Familiarity, not formality, is the goal.

Visual Aids

Some folks insist you can't sell anything these days without a look book or pitch deck; I know of one studio that enters every network pitch with a mock-up of the poster for the series. Other successful writers downplay the importance of such props, but it's hard to ignore them entirely if a studio or network will mark you down for failing to provide at least some eye candy. It pays to get the latest advice in this area, calibrated to whomever you're pitching to.

Because the COVID-19 pandemic forced writers to pitch virtually via Zoom and other platforms—and such pitches have continued at some studios— it's important to note how remote pitches affect the nature of the session. During an in-person presentation, the visuals support the writer. In a virtual presentation, the writer supports the visuals, turning the writer into more of a narrator than a pitchman and the execs more into viewers rather than listeners. Consequently, you want to be sure your visuals are compelling and move briskly to maintain interest. And you want to get out of the visuals as quickly as possible to resume "face-to-face" contact with your audience.

At best, visual aids not only help execs envision your series but also demonstrate the depth of your thinking. At worst, they're a superficial means to mask a poorly thought-out concept, the so-called lipstick on a pig. No matter what pyrotechnics you plan to use in the room, remember that visual aids can't substitute for the intrinsic value of your concept; they can only enhance it.

Pitch Killers

To counterbalance the three positive archetypes in her *Harvard Business Review* article, Elsbach identifies four negative stereotypes of pitchers: the pushover, the robot, the used-car salesman, and the charity case. I've seen them all, and you don't want to be any of them.

The Pushover

This is the writer who will immediately abandon an idea or embrace a new one at the slightest suggestion during a pitch. Such mutability suggests the writer either doesn't know or doesn't care enough about the project to defend it.

The Robot

This writer has failed to heed advice about rehearsing, not memorizing. The results are monotonous and unconvincing, the opposite of being able to think on one's feet—an essential quality for a showrunner.

The Used-Car Salesman

Like a dog with a bone, this writer keeps trying to sell the same thing repeatedly, even when it's clear the buyers want something different. Such intransigence can quickly become obnoxious.

The Charity Case

More than anything, writers in this category make it clear they need a job. Desperation lies just below the surface everywhere in Hollywood, an uncomfortable reality that execs don't want to be reminded of—and they certainly aren't going to reward it. Charity cases may evoke pity, but they're not going to make a sale.

* * * * * * * *

Ultimately, as in baseball, pitching is an art, not a science. Once the game begins, it's just you on the mound, using all the skill and cunning at your command to get the ball over the plate and into the catcher's mitt.

III

RUNNING THE SHOW

26

THE IMPOSSIBLE JOB

SHOWRUNNING DEFINED

Nothing can prepare you for your first showrunning job. Each year as I survey the incoming class of the WGA Showrunner Training Program, I'm reminded of the moment in *Lord of the Rings* when Frodo meets Strider at the Inn of the Prancing Pony. "Are you frightened?" Strider asks. When Frodo says, "Yes," Strider responds, "Not nearly frightened enough. I know what hunts you." Writer-producer Liz Friedman, an SRTP alum, says, "Showrunning is like being beaten to death with your own dreams."

If that seems an unusually sober introduction to showrunning, it's meant to be. Yesterday, you were just another writer. Today, you're the CEO of a multimillion-dollar corporation with more than 150 employees. You're responsible for all creative decisions that go into the production of a series. You hire writers and fire writers. You approve the hiring of all key personnel and oversee their work. You supervise outlines and scripts, handle notes from executives, manage actors, collaborate with directors, and coordinate with the line producer to stay on time and on budget. You hire editors and have final cut on all episodes. These responsibilities might be modified by platform and circumstance, but this is showrunning at its fullest. To get a graphic picture, here's an organizational chart of a traditional broadcast or basic cable show.

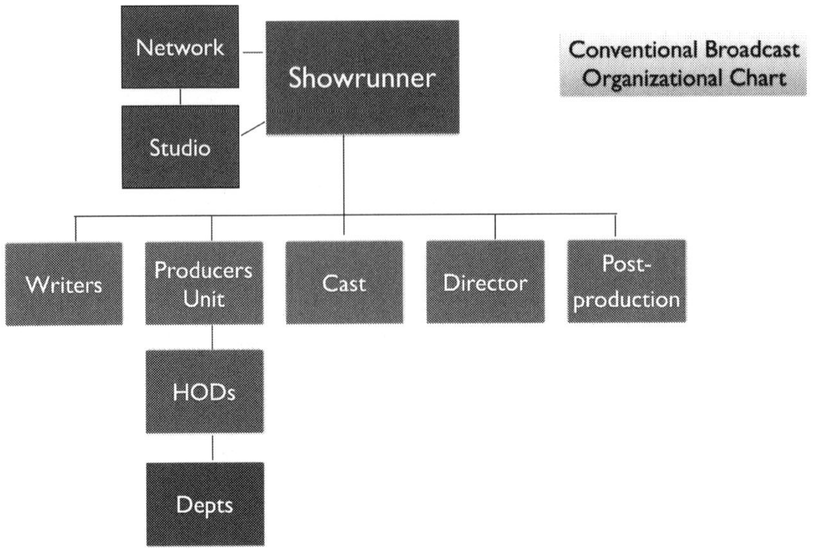

Credit: Author

This is highly simplified. For example, the producers unit—the line producer, director-producer, and any others with actual production authority—will have considerable interaction with the director in making an episode. And the director, in addition to leading the cast and crew on set, will also interact with department heads and editors. Nevertheless, as a thirty-thousand-foot view, it lays out the showrunner's preeminence. What's significant to note is that on creative issues, essentially everyone reports through you, which is why I put the showrunner on the same level as the network and studio. Execs may control the money, but you command the troops. Premium cable and streaming may alter the architecture by elevating the studio, network, and/or director in various combinations, but this chart serves as a basic introduction.

Traditionally, the showrunner supervises all three phases of production: preproduction, shooting, and postproduction. Under the broadcast and basic cable model, these areas will overlap as scripts continue to be written while other episodes are being shot, prepped, and edited; subscription cable and streaming tend to separate writing and production, which alleviates the need for extensive multitasking but creates its own peculiar showrunner headaches down the road. (These will be discussed later.)

As showrunner Glen Mazzara points out to members of the SRTP, "showrunner" is the only job title in Hollywood (informal though it may be) that incorporates the word "show," and it's no coincidence. Your job is to keep the show running, as in, "The show must go on." If it doesn't, if you're forced to take a shutdown for any length of time for virtually any reason, you've failed—not fatally, perhaps, but you're in trouble. To avoid such crises, showrunners must be masters of multitasking.

To illustrate the plate-spinning required under a traditional broadcast setup, here's "a day in the life" of a showrunner in the middle of the second year of a series.

A Day in the Life

6 a.m.: Episode 10 begins shooting day 2 on location.

6:15-7:30: Wake up; read writer's draft of Episode 13. Needs work.

8-9: At office, continue yesterday's rewrite of Episode 12. Crisis call from set. Lead actor having trouble with line. Cancel lunch.

9-10: Concept meeting with director on Episode 11.

10-11: Give notes to writer of Episode 13. Look at casting tape for uncast part on Episode 10.

11-11:30: Studio notes on Episode 14 outline; they don't like it.

11:30-12:30 p.m.: Sit in with editor for final notes on producer's cut of Episode 8. Crisis call from set. Lost afternoon location.

12:30 - 2: Music and F/X spotting on Episode 6.

2-2:30: Network notes on Episode 12 (which you're already rewriting). They have problems. Cancel shrink appointment.

2:30-4: Writers room; work on Episode 15 outline. Approve prop design for Episode 10 scene. Review Episode 14 notes with writer.

4-4:30: Studio notes on cut of Episode 7. Cancel dinner plans.

4:30-5: Discuss studio notes on cut of Episode 7 with editor.

5-8: Ask studio for breakage for guest star role in Episode 11. Continue rewrite of Episode 12. Go home to watch dailies.

Credit: Author

If you add it up, this showrunner is working on nine different episodes in the same day. Episodes 6, 7, 8, and 9 are in post; episode 9 isn't included because the director is working on the director's cut. Episode 10 is being shot. Episode 11 is in preproduction. Episodes 12 through 15 are in some form of being written. This schedule is hyperbolic, but only slightly; it certainly conveys the way it *feels* to oversee a broadcast show at full flood. And keep in mind that in this example there are still seven episodes to be conceived before reaching the season total of twenty-two. It makes my heart race just thinking about it.

How is it possible for any one individual to manage it all? It's not, really; not all the time, anyway. And this will be true for showrunners on any show on any platform. You have to know these things and then tuck them away somewhere in a corner of your subconscious where they don't interfere with your ability to think—or breathe. Good execs know that television is a crapshoot; most shows are not hits. Consequently, how you conduct yourself is as important as how your show performs. You can be in charge of a moderate success but alienate the studio and platform, short-circuiting your career. Conversely, you can preside over a flop but emerge as a leader whom execs are eager to work with again. It's all a matter of performance: how well did you run the show?

27

WHAT IT TAKES

DIMENSIONS OF LEADERSHIP

One of the astounding aspects of showrunning is how a writer can be catapulted from hanging out at Starbucks one day to leading a multimillion-dollar enterprise the next. What qualifies a writer for that rocket ride? Very little, in most cases. By nature, writers are extraordinarily ill-equipped for the job. To illustrate, in the WGA Showrunner Training Program (SRTP), I present a slide that asks, "What Is a Writer?" and lists the following pairs of characteristics:

Gregarious	Loner
Brooding	Congenial
Secure	Insecure
Selfish	Generous
Trusting	Paranoid
Diplomatic	Impulsive
Decisive	Indecisive

I ask the class to choose one quality from each pair. They invariably respond:

Loner
Brooding
Insecure

Selfish
Paranoid
Impulsive
Indecisive

I then present a second slide listing the same qualities under a new title, "What Is a Leader?" This time, the answers come back:

Gregarious
Congenial
Secure
Generous
Trusting
Diplomatic
Decisive

You get the picture. I end with a third slide: "The Challenge: How to Get There from Here?"

Loner	→	Gregarious
Brooding	→	Congenial
Insecure	→	Secure
Selfish	→	Generous
Paranoid	→	Trusting
Impulsive	→	Diplomatic
Indecisive	→	Decisive

Up to now, all you've had to worry about was yourself. But as showrunner, you hold the fate of a small army and tens of millions of dollars in your hands. From a corporate perspective, you've been handed an enormous loan for which the studio expects significant return on investment. They rely on you to manage things, which presents the fundamental challenge facing first-time showrunners: going from writer to manager. And when I say "manager," I mean it in the most inspiring terms: a confident leader in charge of a complex organization.

It's not an easy transition, and no one gets there overnight, but it begins with awareness. For the SRTP, I cheekily present

"Management Theory in Five Minutes or Less," focusing on two pioneers in the field: Abraham Maslow and Douglas McGregor. I explain how McGregor, expanding upon Maslow's psychological analysis of human motivation, postulated two opposing theories of management: Theory X and Theory Y. Theory X, based on traditional views of labor dating to the Industrial Age, basically assumes that people are no good. More specifically, it asserts that the average person:

- has an inherent dislike of work and will avoid it whenever possible;
- has no ambition, wants no responsibility, and would rather follow than lead;
- is self-centered and unconcerned about organizational goals; and
- is therefore motivated only by money and security, suggesting a "carrot and stick" managerial approach of rewards and punishments.

This theory supports what is known as "authoritarian management."

Theory Y, reflecting Maslow's influence, particularly his well-known hierarchy of needs, holds a sunnier view of the human condition, suggesting:

- Work can be as natural as play or rest.
- If a job is satisfying, addressing higher fulfillment needs, people will be committed to the organization.
- If people are committed to the organization, they will be self-directed.
- Under these conditions, people will seek responsibility, not avoid it.
- Imagination, creativity, and ingenuity can be used by a large number of employees to solve work problems.
- High results can be obtained by aligning organizational and individual goals, seeking to utilize each person's quest for fulfillment as a motivator.

This approach leads to the "participative style" of management. To me, it also suggests optimal conditions on a television show. The sad truth, however, is that many shows fall far short of these aspirations. Why?

The answer is hinted at in a list of characteristics that McGregor compiled to describe the Theory X manager:

- Results-driven, deadline-driven to exclusion of all other factors
- Issues deadlines, ultimatums, instructions, and edicts
- Demands, never asks
- Shouts
- Threatens
- Does not thank or praise
- Does not invite or welcome suggestions
- Does not practice team building
- Holds on to responsibility, but shifts accountability to subordinates
- Poor at proper delegating, but believes delegates well; thinks giving orders is delegating
- Seeks culprits for failures or shortfalls
- Seeks to fix blame rather than learn from experience
- Takes criticism badly and is likely to retaliate; vengeful, recriminatory
- One-way communicator; poor listener
- Unconcerned about staff welfare or morale
- Short-tempered; intolerant
- Distant and detached
- Aloof and arrogant
- Proud, often to the point of self-destruction
- Antisocial
- Fundamentally insecure, possible neurotic
- Unhappy

After running through this sorry catalog, I ask the class how many of them have worked for this person. All hands go up. It's a grim comment on the business. No showrunner sets out to be such a regrettable human being, so why do so many end up affecting their writers this way? The answer is, because showrunning is a heat-seeking missile that will find every chink in your psychological armor and blow it to pieces, unleashing all your worst tendencies, transforming you into the boss from hell.

To provide a positive model, I share Maslow's "self-actualizing characteristics," which I find an apt description of the Theory Y manager:

- Sees problems as challenges, situations requiring solutions
- Not susceptible to social pressures; nonconformist
- Democratic, fair, nondiscriminating
- Socially compassionate, possessing humanity
- Comfortable with oneself
- Spontaneous and natural, true to oneself
- Accepts others as they are
- Sense of humor directed at oneself or the human condition, rather than at the expense of others

This is the goal. Though some of the above might seem obvious, if you've never thought about such things before—particularly in relation to your own work and responsibilities—the truth can dawn like an epiphany. Ultimately, it boils down to this: be the boss you'd like to work for.

The Twelve P's

As showrunner, you'll be called upon to be different things to different people at different times. Over the years, I've compiled a list of what I call the Twelve P's.

Producer

Up to this point, although you may have held a writer-producer title, you've likely done little actual producing. Now, you're expected to know what you're doing. If you falter, your show will be produced around you, so you need to fill in whatever gaps exist in your knowledge. You don't have to be equally good at everything, but you do need to know your strengths and weaknesses well enough to delegate effectively. Small example: I'm not great with wardrobe (as my wife often reminds me), so I always deputize a qualified writer to review important wardrobe decisions with me.

Even if you're confident in many areas, you still must delegate or you'll never get through your day. As a wise showrunner once told me, "You can do anything, but you can't do everything." First-time showrunners are often reluctant to delegate, fearing it reveals weakness rather than strength. It's understandable; plus, you don't know who you can rely on when starting out. Experienced showrunners know, however, that delegation doesn't diminish authority; it extends it, while making others feel like valued members of the team. If athletic skill can be defined as getting maximum results from minimal expenditure of energy, effective management can be described in much the same way. Delegate or die.

As a corollary, if you let a bottleneck develop at your door, keeping work from proceeding until you personally have addressed whatever problem has just come knocking, then you've effectively reduced the collective workload of your entire team to one person: you. It's a prescription for early burnout and ultimate failure.

Problem Solver

To keep a bottleneck from forming, you have to determine just what is and what is not a problem. Not everything that flies into your field of vision demands a personal response, so consult a mental checklist to evaluate situations as they occur:

- Is this really a problem? If not, forget it.
- If so, is this a problem rising to my level of attention? If not, have a subordinate take care of it.
- If it requires my attention, how urgent is it? Do I need to handle it now, or can I put it off while concentrating on other things? (Veteran showrunner John Wells literally does not look at his cell phone during the day, knowing

that if he's hired the right people, virtually all routine problems will get solved without his involvement. I'm not that hands-off, but then, I'm not running multiple series, either.)
- What are my options? Every problem has more than one possible solution.
- Make a decision and act on it.

As all leaders know, decisiveness is the essence of command. People are looking to you for answers. Better to make a poor decision than no decision, which erodes confidence in your leadership. You learn from your mistakes and move on.

Potentate

This is a fancy word for power holder. As showrunner, you will quickly discover you have more friends than you ever knew because you now have the power to provide jobs and benefits—real-world stuff. While it's thrilling to assemble your own team, having power often means disappointing as many people as you gratify. This can be especially tough with writers you know. If you think a friend can write your show, great, but, if not, they won't be your friend for long when you find yourself doing a page-one rewrite of their latest script on a Sunday night under deadline pressure. As Peter Parker discovered, with great power comes great responsibility. And when it comes to hiring, your first obligation is to make decisions that help you make the best show. If you don't succeed, your show doesn't succeed, and your career takes a hit. Hard truths. Of course, your power extends far beyond hiring and firing. As captain of the ship, you determine how it operates and where it's going. Everything that happens, for better or worse, happens on your watch. If you're not willing to assume the mantle of authority, you can't lead.

Professor

You'll think it's obvious how you want your show to be written; your writers won't. They'll need to be shown—through discussion, margin notes, and your own rewriting of their stuff. You might feel presumptuous instructing anyone how to write, to which I offer this from a successful showrunner: "I tell my writers, 'I'm not here to tell you what great writing is. All I can tell you is what I like and what I don't like. And it's my show, so as long as I'm in charge, your job is to write what I like.'" This deceptively simple summation was the result of years of therapy and lays out a fundamental truth: it's your show. No one on your staff, not even the most devoted writer, is going to care about it as much as you do. And no one has as much to gain or lose as you do. Like it or not, you're in charge, so give yourself permission to lead. Don't assume; teach.

Psychologist

This is a sneaky "P," but an important one. A key facet of showrunning is motivating and managing diverse personalities. You need to figure out what makes people tick. Some need to be cajoled, others nurtured, others given a swift kick in the pants. This applies not only to writers but to everyone you deal with, including execs. It forces you to be a chess player, looking several moves ahead: if I do this, what's likely to result?

Politician

Despite what has been playing out on our national scene of late, politics is the art of compromise. You will exhaust the patience of executives and others around you if you make every disagreement a fight to the death. You must seek middle ground and let the other side win at least some of the time to preserve your influence and reputation. As is said of the US House of Representatives: before you save the world, you have to save your seat." In the SRTP, we hand out a slim book titled *Difficult Conversations: How to Discuss What Matters Most*, by Douglas Stone, Bruce Patton, and Sheila Heen of the Harvard Negotiation Project. It's an excellent guide to framing and resolving conflicts, both personal and professional. I highly recommend it.

Paradigm

Consciously or not, as a showrunner, you model behavior for your writing staff and others who work with you. If you're a screamer, for example, if you treat people badly, then members of your team will feel it's okay for them to do the same. If you demonstrate grace under pressure, then that becomes the standard. Similarly, if you share credit, spreading praise among others rather than arrogating it to yourself, you will create a more harmonious workplace while developing a reputation as an inspiring leader.

Professional

In an industry with no formal training or peer review, the concept of professionalism might appear problematic, but there are professional standards to uphold. To begin, familiarize yourself with both the WGA guidelines on treatment of writers (laid out in the Minimum Basic Agreement) and relevant sections of the Directors Guild of America's *Creative Rights Handbook*. Both are available free online. Beyond explicit dictates, there are implicit standards for showrunners to uphold. Credit-grabbing is a good example. As showrunner, you're expected to do a healthy amount of rewriting, but that doesn't entitle you to add your credit to another writer's episode or to remove another writer's credit entirely. Doing so not only affects that writer's professional standing but also takes potential residual money out of their pocket. The WGA has an arbitration process to determine final credits, but few writers will openly challenge a showrunner, fearing reprisal. Ethical practices are hard to police, so it's up to you to do the right thing.

Parent

Like it or not, every show is a family. If you create a show, you're literally the parent. If you take over a show, you're a stepparent, with all the distinctions that implies. In either case, actors, writers, and others will be looking to you for approval, encouragement, boundaries, discipline, consistency, fairness—all the qualities of a real parent. Now, you may refuse to assume parental responsibilities, but that doesn't mean you're not a parent; it means you're a dysfunctional parent—and all the behavior that subsequently results on your show will resemble that of a dysfunctional family. Some people will act out, others withdraw, and a few will try to exploit the power vacuum left by your abdication of authority. If you're a parent in real life, all of this will be familiar. If not, you'll learn quickly: expect to be tested, demand to be respected, hope to be rewarded.

Protector

Of your many responsibilities, chief among them is the need to create a safe environment in the writers room and beyond. This means setting a tone that promotes free expression without fear of being talked over, bullied, or diminished in any way. On set, it means providing physical safety for cast and crew. Although this specific responsibility falls most directly to the line producer and director's unit, your emphasis on safety will reinforce its importance. Regarding actors, the cast needs to know they can come to you with questions and concerns. The message you want to transmit to everyone is that you're there to make the best possible show and will protect and defend the team to make it happen.

Showrunner Mike Schur says that writers in a writers room can be in creative mode or survival mode, but not both. If they're in survival mode—worried about their job status or anything else that threatens their sense of well-being, they can't be in creative mode. Your job is to monitor the room to be sure your staffers are in creative mode, and if not, to take steps to get them there.

Priest

As showrunner, you may hear things from colleagues that you never expected to hear—deeply personal things. The business can be hard on everyone, and some coworkers will turn to you for guidance. Though you have neither time nor bandwidth to be everyone's confessor, there will be moments when your role is to listen, counsel, or console. Displaying compassion and understanding on such occasions is your privilege—and obligation.

Person

Ultimately, you're just one person trying to do an impossible job, so you need to reserve some compassion for yourself. You may be tired, you may be angry, you may want to take the next helicopter off the mountain, but look down. You've come a long way. Take pride in that. You're doing okay.

28

WHERE AM I?

CONTEXT

One size does not fit all in showrunning. Not even close. You may be the sole creator of a series with complete freedom to fill out your production team, you may be taking over an existing series with little opportunity to make new hires, you may be assigned to a series as part of a package assembled by a studio—there are countless variations, each with its own parameters of responsibility governed by the culture and protocols of a particular studio and platform. How do you know where you are? Here's a guide.

Business Model

The economic factors that drive your studio and platform will dictate your budget, schedule, creative format, and corporate culture.

Broadcast

- Still favors twenty-two episodes per season, but may be scaling back
- Weekly episodes utilizing act breaks
- Advertiser-driven
- Showrunner has considerable control

Basic Cable

- Generally, eight to thirteen episodes per season
- Weekly episodes utilizing act breaks
- Driven by combination of advertising and consumer fees
- Showrunner has considerable control

Subscription Cable

- Generally, eight to thirteen episodes per season
- Episodes are seamless; no act breaks
- Generally, weekly episodes
- May use mini-rooms, letting writers go before production
- Subscription-driven
- Showrunner may have less control than in broadcast and basic cable

Streaming

- Generally, eight to thirteen episodes per season
- Episodes are seamless; no act breaks
- All episodes drop at once; binge-watching is goal
- Uses mini-rooms, letting writers go before production
- Subscription-driven
- Showrunner may have least control because of studio/network/director influence

Production Setup

How and where your series is produced affects your line of command and patterns of communication.

Los Angeles

- Keeps you close to cast and crew

Remote Location—HQ in Los Angeles

- Challenges your ability to stay close to cast and crew
- Increases importance of line producer, director-producer, and other heads of department on location
- If location is in different time zone, complicates communications between LA and set

Other

- Variations include housing writers and editors on location; in the case of international productions, all creative personnel may be overseas, but the majority of notes could come from execs in the States.

Production Partners

Who are the execs you deal with on a regular basis? How do they rank in authority and capacity to affect your work? As buyer, the platform usually holds the upper hand, but there are situations where studios and other players exert considerable influence.

Studio

The company that finances and delivers the show, responsible for the budget, which gives them a prominent voice in all major creative decisions.

POD

A company with a "production overall deal" (or "production only deal") that helped assemble the series and owns a piece of it. Not all series involve a POD. On those that do, however, the execs can be a source of support or annoyance.

Platform

The company that distributes the show. In broadcast, the network licenses a series from a studio for a set period. In streaming, the network typically owns the content—and the studio making it. There are many variations between these two poles.

Other

The global nature of the business has created opportunities for international partners to participate in American productions. Similarly, any company that brings money to the table may become part of the landscape you have to navigate.

Daily Team

The list below is hardly exhaustive but suggests how different circumstances can alter the composition and conduct of your working team.

Line Producer

Indispensable under any setup, responsible for physical production of the series, including staying on schedule and on budget.

Director-Producer

Particularly critical on remote-location shows. The showrunner's surrogate to deal with cast, crew, and guest directors. If you're not budgeted for it, you might have to do without.

Director

During broadcast's heyday, an episodic director (as distinguished from a pilot director) was considered more an efficient craftsman than a creative influence. Although that culture still exists on certain platforms, the trend toward more sophisticated series has elevated the director's prominence in many cases, particularly on streaming and premium cable series.

Nonwriting Producer

Not a part of every show but common enough to mention; considered a member of your creative team, but not expected to do any writing. An effective nonwriting producer can relieve pressure on you—helping manage certain executive relationships and handling post, for example, allowing you to concentrate on other priorities. An ineffective nonwriting producer is someone you're stuck with—a POD exec, for example, or your lead actor's manager, anyone with sufficient clout to get the title and potentially complicate your day.

Nonexistent Producer

A variation on the nonwriting producer; someone you don't have to deal with but who drains money from your budget. Financially a pain, but operationally less of a problem than an intrusive nonwriting producer.

* * * * * * * *

Every show presents unique challenges. You'll figure out where your series fits by bumping into walls as you navigate the maze. Some things will be within your control; others, beyond it. Knowing the difference will help you conserve energy, increase effectiveness, and preserve sanity.

29

ALLIES

ASSEMBLING YOUR TEAM

The day you become a showrunner, your phone doesn't stop ringing until the day you stop being a showrunner. You need a team to get through it all. To begin, you need an assistant to maintain your schedule, screen calls, and represent you to the outside world. Prior experience as a writers' assistant or production assistant—anything that reflects working knowledge of the showrunner's world—is valuable but needn't be a strict prerequisite. The showrunner's assistant is a gateway job that can launch a career; virtually all writers' assistants want to be writers, so you may want to read a writing sample to see if this is someone you'd enjoy mentoring. In any case, choose wisely, with special consideration for those who can benefit most from the opportunity.

In assembling the rest of your team, you need hire only the key players, who can subsequently recommend or hire subordinates themselves. Who are the key players? I've listed six that I believe are essential for all showrunners to hire: line producer, director-producer, production designer, director of photography, casting director, and coproducer (postproduction).

Line Producer

The line producer is your right hand, responsible for maintaining the budget and running physical production. The "line" in the title refers to the line items that make up a budget. All heads of department (HODs) report to the line producer, who reports to you. This arrangement allows you to concentrate on creative matters while the line producer sees to the nuts and bolts of actually making things happen. Some say there's an inherent conflict for line producers in terms of their obligation to you and their obligation to the studio, but I see it more as a tightrope to be walked. A line producer once described the job to me this way: "You tell the showrunner, 'Don't worry, we're gonna make the show you want; leave the studio to me.' You then walk down the hall and tell the studio's head of production, 'Don't worry, we're gonna stay on budget; leave the showrunner to me.'"

A good line producer knows how to navigate that high wire, faithfully serving both masters. Some showrunners, however—especially first-timers—distrust this balancing act, wanting to be sure the line producer is on "their side," which isn't necessarily a healthy attitude. The fact is, you want your line producer to have a good relationship with the studio so that they can fight for things that matter to you when conflicts arise. Conversely, you want the line producer to tell you what's possible and what's not, offering options on how to keep your show on schedule and on budget. It ultimately comes down to trust, which begins with your hiring process.

As with any position, talk to at least three candidates and do your due diligence beforehand. During the interview, does the person show genuine passion for your project or is this just another job to them? Be frank about your production experience or lack of it and see how they respond. Is this someone you can learn from, someone you'd like to work with? Be honest, because you're going to be in touch with the line producer every day—and many nights.

Director-Producer

If the line producer is your right hand, the director-producer is your left, responsible for handling creative matters on set, directing some episodes, breaking in guest directors, maintaining good rapport with cast and crew, generally keeping an eye on all creative elements of production. Not every one-hour series has a director-producer. It's an expensive position that some studios deem unnecessary. On a remote-location show, however, I think it's essential. Be advised, however: the director-producer is your surrogate on set and thus commands considerable authority, which can be abused, especially on a remote-location show when you're far away. In such situations, it's easy for cast and crew to feel neglected, creating an "us versus them" mentality. Left unchecked, this can generate smoldering resentment that leads to open rebellion. A responsible director-producer will douse such embers before they ignite; an underhanded one will blow on them. So be wary, but also know that a trustworthy director-producer can be a critical component of your success—and a real friend in need.

Director of Photography

An effective DP in television is not only a skilled artist but a master of time management and team building. A good DP helps directors make their day, motivates the crew, and elevates cast morale. So, in addition to assessing résumés and highlight reels, check out these qualities when doing your due diligence. Of the six key hires, the DP is likely the position you'll have least contact with once the look of the show is established, but the importance of finding the right one should not be underestimated.

Production Designer

The production designer is responsible for the overall look of your show, supervising the art director and coordinating the work of others who create sets, costumes, and other visual elements. An effective production designer is one-third visionary, one-third craftsman, and one-third realist. Vision is necessary to imagine what will make the show come alive on-screen. Craft is required to express those concepts in ways that others can execute. Realism is demanded to deal with budget constraints, shifting conditions, and creative temperaments. Production designers have long enjoyed special prominence in movies, where they often work with directors well in advance of shooting. Historically, television hasn't afforded such close collaboration, but this is changing, particularly on some premium platforms.

If you've never talked to a production designer before, don't fret. Mentioning movies and series you think are relevant to your show and putting together a "look book" (a compilation of relevant images that appeal to you) are effective ways to initiate conversation. Candidates will come with their own ideas, of course, which may inspire you. The goal is to get on the same page.

Casting Director

Casting directors are unsung heroes in the industry, scouring the globe for talent and fighting for actors they believe in, even though casting directors usually don't get a vote in the final selection process. The casting director's role is critical in pilots but remains vitally important throughout the life of a series; finding the right guest actor can elevate any episode and might result in a recurring role. A casting director will come to an interview armed with ideas that could persuade you to consider roles differently than you had before. As with all members of your team, you want someone with genuine passion for your project who's willing to go the extra mile to make it succeed.

Coproducer (Postproduction)

The coproducer in post—sometimes referred to as an associate producer—is your partner in the final rewrite, there to ensure that the finished episode gets done to your satisfaction. The job begins before production with hiring editors. Because the best editors don't stay on the market long, an effective coproducer will know who's available and arrange interviews before another show can grab them. The coproducer will sit in on editor interviews to ask pertinent questions and provide valuable insights afterward. The coproducer also helps hire the music supervisor, visual effects coordinator, and other positions critical to the finished look and sound of your show. Though not as flashy a position, perhaps, as line producer or director-producer, the coproducer is your copilot when bringing in an episode for landing.

* * * * * * * *

Beyond these six hires, every show has specific needs requiring special attention. Costumes might be a critical component of your show, or makeup and hair. If your show features romance, sex, or physical encounters of any kind, an intimacy coordinator should likely be a part of your team. If it's an action series, the stunt coordinator is key; if a high school musical, the choreographer and music director move to the head of the class. Visual effects are no longer the exclusive province of sci-fi; most shows today utilize some form of VFX for a range of "invisible assets" like set extensions and establishing shots. If VFX figures prominently in your series, a VFX coordinator will be an important hire.

And so forth. Your line producer and/or director-producer can help winnow lists for these and other positions, in which case you need only to meet the leading contenders before signing off.

A final note: As showrunner, you have a professional and moral obligation to make inclusion, equity, and diversity priorities to remedy historical barriers to underrepresented constituencies. Not only is this the right thing to do, but experience has shown that a diverse workplace results in a greater range of creative output than a homogeneous setting. If you haven't spoken to any BIPOC (Black, Indigenous, and People of Color) candidates or members of other historically marginalized groups, try harder. If your circle of contacts is limited, broaden your reach by enlisting the studio, the Writers Guild's Inclusion and Equity Department, and others to help. If you're a BIPOC writer or member of any underrepresented group, then I'm preaching to the choir.

When it comes to production positions, Craig Siebels—writer-director, producer, and instructor in the WGA Showrunner Training Program—discovered that when he delegated diversity hiring to heads of department, inevitably they'd report back that they couldn't find anyone. Typically, they'd wait until they had only one slot left and couldn't find a diverse candidate to fill it. And it might have been true at that late point in the game. So moving forward, Craig came up with a rule: he didn't tell HODs which position they had to fill but insisted that the first hire in each department be a candidate from an underrepresented group. That solved the problem.

30

THE MANTRA

FOUR WORDS TO LIVE BY

It takes an army to produce a television series. As showrunner, you're directing troops on multiple fronts every day, so it's easy to get distracted and ignore your highest priority, which is the writing. Everything else can be delegated; the work will get done—not to your total satisfaction, perhaps, but it will get done. Not so with writing: As is said, "If it ain't on the page, it ain't on the stage." Consequently, the essence of showrunning can be reduced to four words:

QUALITY SCRIPTS ON TIME

This is what you've been hired for. Succeed and you'll be a hero to your writers, cast, crew, and executives. Fail and you'll be chased by the hounds of hell until you or your show collapse. Likely both. Breaking it down:

Quality Scripts

If your scripts aren't good, then what are you in this for?

On Time

No matter how good your writing may be, if scripts are late, you compromise the ability of everyone working with you to do their best work. Be late too often and you'll exhaust your cast, crew, budget, and, quite possibly, your time in office. Late scripts lead to production shutdowns, which in turn lead to new showrunners.

* * * * * * * *

If you can deliver quality scripts on time, your show won't necessarily succeed, but if you don't, it certainly will fail. The next six chapters are devoted to putting this mantra into action, from hiring writers to firing writers and everything in between.

31

MONEYBALL

HIRING WRITERS

First-time showrunners often approach hiring a writing staff as if filling positions in a military platoon: you need a lieutenant as your number two, followed by sergeants, corporals, privates, and so forth, each performing their assigned, well-understood tasks. It's a logical model that would make sense—if it worked. As explained earlier, titles are relatively meaningless on writing staffs, where hierarchical responsibilities might not exist at all. So I've come to think of hiring writers more like choosing a pickup team for baseball: you show up at the park, see who's available, make your picks, and manage according to the skills of your players. A winning team does not necessarily mean the most experienced or even the most naturally gifted players. An eager rookie might prove more valuable than a cynical veteran.

In his autobiography, Bruce Springsteen talks about how he assembles a band: "You're not looking for the best players. You're looking for the *right* players who click into something unique. . . . The primary math of the real world is one and one equals two. . . . But artists, musicians, con men, poets, mystics, and such are paid to turn that math on its head, to rub two sticks together and bring forth fire."

Take it from the Boss: you're looking for a group that can create fire—on a budget. You have to spend your money wisely.

Here's how that works typically: the studio gives you a writing budget, which you're free to allocate as you see fit. This allowance will vary widely from show to show. Let's say your writers' budget is $60,000 per episode. A potential number two might cost $30,000 per episode. (The amount will fluctuate depending on inflation, a writer's experience, and their agent's aggressiveness.) Hiring a pricey veteran may be the best decision you could possibly make—or the worst. If you spend $30,000 on a purported number two, you now have $30,000 left to spend. You could pick two midlevel writers at around $15,000 each or one midlevel at $12,000, plus a story editor and staff writer. If you don't choose an expensive number two, you can buy more players. It's Monopoly with real money. Depending on the studio, you might also be able to add a writer from a fellowship program (see chapter 24), which can expand your room without diminishing your budget.

Rather than assuming what slots I'm going to fill beforehand, I read a ton of scripts to get a sense of who's available, line up potential hires, interview candidates, and negotiate from there. I don't let résumés take precedence over my own sensibility and judgment. With a tip of the hat to author Michael Lewis, it's "Moneyball"—maximum bang for the buck, often achieved by choosing overlooked writers or diamonds in the rough.

How to find writers? It takes time and persistence. Mostly, it takes reading, lots of reading. The moment your series is announced, you'll be flooded with recommendations from executives, agents, managers, colleagues, friends, and distant cousins. You don't have to read all these candidates, certainly, but there's no harm in accepting submissions. I've learned to respect names that come from development execs, whose job is to find writers to help you succeed. As a plus, writers recommended by development execs come "preapproved" by the studio, which isn't a huge deal but can't hurt. Be wary of agents and managers who will try to fob off as many of their clients on you as they can; make them be selective, suggesting writers best suited for your show.

As recommendations pour in, I collate and compare lists. If a name appears more than once, I move that person's script up the pile. Same goes for suggestions from people whose opinions

I value. If someone's worked on a show I admire, that's another reason to bump a script up. Remember, you're not making hiring decisions, merely ranking submissions to be read. At some point, you have to stop reading and start interviewing, so where a script sits in your pile is critically important. The next Shonda Rhimes or Aaron Sorkin may be lurking in the sixty-seventh script, but if you stop reading at the sixty-sixth script, you'll never know.

You might know colleagues you want to hire, which can cut down the number of slots to fill, but be wary of hiring on familiarity alone. You're looking for the best writers for your show, not just a pal to make you feel more comfortable in the room—although that could become part of the mix. Be resourceful in seeking out writers. Recruitment efforts can begin long before your project is greenlit. Whenever you see a TV episode you particularly like, make a note of the writer and possibly invite them to lunch or drop them an email. What writer doesn't like hearing that someone admires their work? In addition to a pleasant conversation, you'll be adding to your network of potential collaborators.

When your show becomes real, put out the word to as many sources as you can about the qualities you're looking for. Contact organizations and individuals who can recommend suitable candidates, particularly writers from backgrounds different than your own. Only when I've collected a critical mass of scripts from a diverse pool of candidates, anywhere from fifty to eighty scripts, do I begin to throttle back. The selection process then becomes a bit like house hunting. Sometimes the first house you see is the one to bid on; other times you'll look at dozens before making an offer. And, like house hunting, because you don't always get the property you want, you need to make a prioritized list of prospects.

You're under no obligation to read an entire script. I try to give the writer the benefit of the doubt, but time is precious. If after a few pages I've read nothing to hold my interest, I begin flipping through, and if I don't promptly land on anything that makes me sit up, I put it down. Among your submissions, you may get a produced episode of an ongoing series. If so, check the provenance. Most of the time, it will either be the writer's own draft or one slightly revised by the showrunner. In some cases, however, it might be a total rewrite that doesn't reflect the writer's work at all, in which case you likely should move on.

Once you've found at least twice as many writers as you can afford to hire, it's time to schedule interviews. Interviewing involves not just intellectual judgment but chemistry and instinct. You've already determined that the person sitting across from you can write; now it's a question of whether they can write for you and your show. Is this someone you'd enjoy seeing every day? Not every candidate has to be a charming extrovert—in fact, many good writers are not social butterflies but can still be valuable members of your team.

One thing you can't afford is a toxic writer, so you need to apply what's politely referred to as the "no-asshole rule." Due diligence is essential. Find out how a writer performed on other shows. Michael Schur divides writers into two categories: firefighters and arsonists. You want firefighters, writers who look to solve problems, not inflame them. Showrunner Matt Nix characterizes writers as patriots or mercenaries. You want patriots who believe in your show and will give it their all.

Most writers are nervous at the start of an interview, so I do what I can to put them at ease by complimenting them on their own work. That usually takes them by surprise and helps jump-start a conversation. When the talk turns to your project, assess whether the writer has done their homework. Can they discuss the series with depth and understanding? Do they have intelligent questions and comments? WGA regulations prohibit you from soliciting story pitches during a job interview, but you can certainly ask for a writer's take on your concept. A strong candidate will come prepared to discuss characters and possible creative avenues.

You may find writing teams you want to interview. The obvious advantage of a team is economical, two writers for the price of one, which can be a great help in filling your room with different voices. But hiring a team doesn't give you twice the literary output of an individual writer. When it comes to scripts and production responsibilities, the WGA makes it clear that a team should be thought of as a single entity, not to be divided, which is only fair, although you hear stories all the time about teams being exploited by frantic showrunners. Don't be one of them.

When you've completed your interviews, you'll have three groups of candidates: those you're dying to hire, those you're willing to hire, and those you don't want to hire. Rank the writers in that first group—most expensive first because signing them will affect whom else you can afford—and submit the list to the studio. Under most circumstances, you'll get quick approval; you might have to do some persuading with lesser-known writers, but you can push for your choices.

Once the studio's creative execs have signed off, business affairs steps in to handle negotiations. Do not talk money or contracts with writers during this period. That's why writers have reps and studios have business affairs execs: so you can keep your hands clean. As negotiations play out, you might have a marginal role to play. For example, if the studio balks at a writer's demands, you can let them know just how badly you want that writer. Occasionally, a writer may call you, usually to complain about being lowballed by the studio. The simplest thing to do is politely decline to discuss it, saying you're not authorized to do so, which is true. Failing that, you can listen sympathetically, but don't make any assurances; you're an employee of the studio and can't be perceived as advocating against them. Ultimately, contracts are the studio's call.

As individual deals get done, you'll have the pleasure of calling writers to let them know they got the job. It's one of the joys of being a showrunner. But I believe you also have a reciprocal obligation to call the candidates who didn't get the job. Those conversations aren't as much fun but are equally important. Most of the time, writers who don't get hired are left hanging, waiting for a call that never comes; the bad news usually comes from their agent. As one who has been in that position, I think writers are owed the courtesy of being told promptly they weren't hired—by you. It gives you the chance to say how much you enjoyed meeting them, reiterate that you're a fan of their work, and explain that hiring a staff involves many factors, including salary, experience, and personal backgrounds. No writer is going to like you for delivering bad news, but they will respect you. Once all your calls have been made, you can get down to business—putting your staff to work.

32

THE TALK

SETTING THE TONE

When you assemble your staff for the first time, your goal is to make them feel welcome and secure. But you also want to use the opportunity to establish expectations that set the tone for the entire season. And you do that with "the talk."

The talk can be set up any number of ways. Veteran showrunner Yvette Lee Bowser, my half-hour counterpart in the WGA Showrunner Training Program, uses what she calls "the benevolent lie" technique: "Some of you have asked how I feel about cell phones in the writers room." Nobody asked, of course, but the pretext allows Yvette to get down to business without sounding bossy. Another colleague favors a more formal approach, arranging a meeting with the entire office staff, including writers' assistants, that can run two hours or more. And there are countless variations. Showrunner Melinda Hsu Taylor begins setting the tone before the room assembles by sending her staff an email laying out her views, including ideas on "how to foster a writer-and-family-friendly environment that also results in better work and a more fulfilling daily existence."

Whatever your style, the talk shouldn't be a random collection of thoughts, but a well-considered presentation. I begin by congratulating the group, letting them know how excited I am to be working with them. I then have everyone introduce themselves, which breaks the ice. Beyond that, the order and manner in which you address things are up to you, but here are topics to consider.

Schedule and Process

- Share your overview of the season, beginning with how many days you've set aside for general discussion before plunging into breaking story.
- Distribute the writers' schedule (discussed in the next chapter).
- Explain how you assign scripts. I've found that writers like to know their assignments as early as possible; it relieves stress and allows them to begin tracking story developments affecting their own episodes. One tip for broadcast and basic cable shows: don't make assignments in descending order based strictly on seniority or you'll soon be left with a depleted room containing only less experienced writers as others depart to write outlines and episodes. "Hopscotch" to maintain a balance. It might be you don't want to make assignments until you've gotten the chance to work with writers in the room for a while, which is fine. Do what makes the most sense for you.
- Discuss your outline format. How long and how detailed do you want outlines to be? Over the years, I've settled on ten-page outlines following a set format (discussed in chapter 36). You'll have your own preferences.
- Explain your approach to giving notes and rewriting. I explain that I give writers as much opportunity to incorporate notes as possible, but all scripts eventually go through my computer for at least a polish. If the reasons for my revisions aren't clear, the writer is welcome to talk to me about them.
- Identify the writer designated as your number two, who will run the room in your absence. I explain that if that writer is unavailable, I'll name someone else to take over

as needed. You may not know who your number two is when the season begins, so you might skip this, waiting to see who emerges as a natural lieutenant.

Room Rules

- *Hours of operation.* Assuming you have a room, when do you want it to start and end? By laying out reasonable hours, you promote goodwill, especially among writers with families.
- *Punctuality.* If your room starts at 10 a.m., is it a "soft" ten or a "hard" ten? If you expect writers to begin serious work on the hour, make that clear so they can arrive earlier if they want to schmooze. In any case, late arrivals are a source of irritation that can lead to further problems, so let them know punctuality matters.
- *Cell phones.* My policy is no phone calls during room hours, except for family calls. Family takes precedence over work.
- *Laptops.* Laptops should be used only to take notes—no texting or shopping on Amazon. Nothing is more disrespectful than a writer playing internet hooky.

Office Staff and Crew

- Everyone on the show, from office staff to dolly grip, is to be treated with respect. No exceptions.
- Share your view of writers' assistants. Review their responsibilities. How do you see assistants involved in the writing process, if at all?
- Review other housekeeping items that are part of the daily rhythm of the office.

The Room

- Lay out how your story process works.
- I emphasize that the room is a safe environment with zero tolerance for rudeness or personal abuse. Mutual respect and common courtesy prevail; don't talk over people, don't bully. You expect passionate disagreements during story discussions, but debate should focus on the work not on individuals.
- Observe the no-sniper rule: don't criticize an idea without a suggestion to improve it.
- Don't hoard ideas for your own episode. Share everything. Your stroke of genius might show up in someone else's script, and theirs might show up in yours. We're a team. When one episode shines, we all shine.
- My office is the court of appeal. If a writer has been heard and overruled in the room, you expect them to let it go in the moment, but they're welcome to talk to me privately afterward to press the argument one more time.
- If a writer feels they've been mistreated in any way, they should talk to me. I provide appropriate contacts at the studio and WGA so that writers have someplace to go if they think I'm the problem and don't feel comfortable talking to me.

Additional Responsibilities

The following pertain only to shows that retain writers through production:

- The major role of every writer is to write. Assuming that's going well, every writer helps produce their own episodes, from prep through post. Part of my goal is to help everyone on staff get to where they want to go as writer-producer (and the showrunners I admire feel the same).

I deputize staffers over the course of a season to help cover certain areas, like casting, wardrobe, and social media. The practice varies from showrunner to showrunner.

On my shows, writers are expected to watch dailies on their own to stay current. When a writer's episode is being produced, that writer is responsible for providing a concise dailies report, emailed to me and the entire staff, summarizing what was shot and remarking on anything of note. If there's a problem, they need to let me know immediately. But I also want to hear about anything that's particularly good so that I can call the individuals responsible and let them know.

Regarding being on-set, I typically send writers to set for the last days of prep to cover final production meetings, the read-through (if the show uses one), and the first days of shooting. I can't spare them for the entire length of production, nor do I think it's necessary. You may have a different take. The accepted wisdom on some shows is that a writer must be on set at all times, to which I ask, why? If scripts are on time and directors well-prepped, why should a writer have to be at the director's elbow—or over their shoulder—during shooting? The usual answer—to ensure everything gets done as the showrunner intended—implies a lack of faith in both the director and the show's creative process, at least it does to me. I believe strongly in writers gaining on-set experience, but it's chiefly for their education and benefit, not for the benefit of an individual episode itself. But I find myself in the minority on this. Regardless of your position, your obligation is to properly prepare writers for their behavior on-set. Here are my chief instructions:

- The set belongs to the director. A writer's notes should be discussed with and delivered through the director.

  Writers should tread carefully when giving notes on set. Rookies tend to jump in prematurely, commenting on performances while the director and actors are still work-

> ing things out or citing missed coverage before the director has finished their shot list.
>
> The writer is my surrogate on set but shouldn't make decisions above the authority granted them. If writers have questions on how to proceed, they should call me.
>
> Writers should resist the temptation to get too chummy with cast members on set. Actors—some innocently, others not so much—will take advantage of starstruck writers to lobby for script changes or similar favors.

Showrunner Shawn Ryan distributes a detailed document to his writers titled *Prep/Shoot/Post Etiquette,* which lays out how he expects his staff to perform in each of these areas. He opens with a friendly, but firm message: "Congratulations! You've written an episode of television and now it's time to make sure that it's prepped, filmed, and edited as best as it can be. So how do you do this? Well, at least on this show, here's how I'd like you to do it." Shawn concludes six pages later in a similarly confident, encouraging manner: "Everything listed in this document should be considered in the following context: you are the defender of this episode. You will need to compromise at times and you will end up disappointed occasionally, but FIGHT for the best episode you can get. Every decision you make, every action you have with a cast or crew member should raise the question, 'What is best for the show and for this episode?' Also. Have fun in prep and production. It's contagious." Who wouldn't want to work for a showrunner like that?

Social Media

Let your staff know your take on using social media. The studio and network might have established policies, so check first. Generally, you don't want staffers disclosing storylines or behind-the-scenes activity unless it's part of a calibrated marketing campaign. Similarly, unless instructed otherwise, writers shouldn't engage in public dialogue with viewers, which rarely ends well. A few showrunners appear to delight in stirring up controversy through social media, but do so at risk to their shows and reputations.

Personal tweets and similar messages also warrant a word of caution. Staffers shouldn't tweet negatively about other staffers or anyone else associated with the show. This may seem obvious, but it happens more often than you'd expect. A brief mention—without sounding like a school principal—may save you a headache down the line.

Any Questions?

- It's a good thing to ask for questions at regular intervals during the talk—and throughout the season. A variation of this is, "Does that make sense?"
- When the talk is done, your staff should feel they're in good hands, led by a thoughtful, well-organized leader. By giving them a solid framework of working conditions, you've freed them to concentrate on the creativity ahead.

* * * * * * * *

Any questions?

33

THE ART OF DISCOVERY

MANAGING THE ROOM

Most showrunners use a writers room to break stories. A few prefer one-on-one conversations; these are usually veterans who don't feel the need for a room to shape episodes. Some creators of short-order series don't use a staff at all, choosing to write everything themselves. These exceptions prove the rule, however. What follows are suggestions on how to get the most out of a room.

Get Organized

UCLA basketball coach John Wooden put it best: "Failing to prepare is preparing to fail." Running a show is a race against time. Use time well and you buy room to maneuver. Spend it poorly and you're at the mercy of the clock, forced to make deadline decisions under pressure. As showrunner John Wells is fond of saying, when you're on time, you pay wholesale; when you're behind, you pay retail. To which I'd add, when you're really behind, you pay whatever's necessary, but it may not be enough to save the situation, the show, or yourself.

Being organized—knowing what needs to done and in what order—is the key to effective time management. And being organized begins with a writing schedule, the timetable that dictates when outlines and drafts are due so that scripts can hit their prep dates and your cast and crew can do their jobs.

Typically in broadcast and basic cable, the studio will give you a production schedule, showing when episodes are to be prepped and shot. You construct a writing schedule by working backward from that, calculating where the major steps in your writing process must fall to keep the cameras turning. For most shows, those steps are: story discussion, outline, drafts, shooting script. When making your writing schedule, you must factor in time for notes from the studio, the network, and potentially other parties as well.

Under this model, the goal is to start writing far enough in advance to build a reservoir of at least four or five scripts before production begins, then keep writing on schedule to maintain that buffer. Under production models utilizing a mini-room that disbands before production, you need to map out sufficient time to get what you need from your writers before they're released.

Below is a writers' schedule from *The West Wing*, a quintessential broadcast drama, drawn up by John Wells, who took over the reins from Aaron Sorkin in season 5.

This illustration takes you through the second half of the season. Each writer is assigned by initials. Episode 11 is only shown partially, so our analysis begins with episode 12. The first date, "Story," on September 29, represents the initial outline delivered to studio and network, which means the story itself was actually broken in the room and vetted by John before then, so we have to back up about two weeks to get an accurate sense of when the script's journey truly began. The "Revised Story," due a week later on October 6, incorporated whatever notes John and the writer had agreed upon with the studio and network. Then the writer had two weeks to turn in the "Writers Draft" on October 20. During the ensuing week, John and the staff provided internal notes on the script, followed by studio and network notes, ultimately resulting in a "First Draft" on October 27, which was sent to production to begin prep the next day, October 28. Further revisions during prep accommodated production concerns, director's notes, and other factors, ultimately resulting in the shooting draft. Under this system, the "First Draft" is a bit of a

"West Wing" 2005-06 Writers Schedule
October 14th 2005

Episode 11 – BW

First Draft	Thurs, Oct 13
Preps	Tues, Oct 18
Shoots	Thurs, Oct 27

Episode 12 – EA

Story	Thurs, Sept 29
Rev. Story	Thurs, Oct 6
Writers Draft	Thurs, Oct 20
First Draft	Thurs, Oct 27
Preps	Fri, Oct 28
Shoots	Tues, Nov 8

Episode 13 – DC

Story	Sun, Oct 9
Rev. Story	Sun, Oct 16
Writers Draft	Sun, Oct 30
First Draft	Sun, Nov 6
Preps	Wed, Nov 9
Shoots	Fri, Nov 18

Episode 14 LO'D

Story	Wed, Oct 19
Rev. Story	Wed, Oct 26
Writers Draft	Wed, Nov 9
First Draft	Wed, Nov 16
Preps	Fri, Nov 18
Shoots	Thurs, Dec 1

Episode 15 JS

Story	Thurs, Oct 27
Rev. Story	Thurs, Nov 3
Writers Draft	Thurs, Nov 17
First Draft	Thurs, Dec 1
Preps	Fri, Dec 2
Shoots	Tues, Dec 13

Episode 16 LS

Story	Thurs, Nov 3
Rev. Story	Thurs, Nov 10
Writers Draft	Thurs, Dec 1
First Draft	Thurs, Dec 8
Preps	Thurs, Dec 15
Shoots	Mon, Jan 9

Episode 17 JW

Story	Sun, Nov 13
Rev. Story	Sun, Nov 27
Writers Draft	Sun, Dec 11
First Draft	Sun, Jan 1
Preps	Tues, Jan 10
Shoots	Thurs, Jan 19

Episode 18 PN

Story	Sun, Dec 4
Rev. Story	Sun, Dec 11
Writers Draft	Sun, Jan 8
First Draft	Sun, Jan 15
Preps	Fri, Jan 20
Shoots	Tues, Jan 31

Episode 19 LO'D

Story	Thurs, Dec 15
Rev. Story	Thurs, Jan 5
Writers Draft	Thurs, Jan 19
First Draft	Thurs, Jan 26
Preps	Wed, Feb 1
Shoots	Fri, Feb 10

Episode 20 EA

Story	Sun, Jan 15
Rev. Story	Sun, Jan 22
Writers Draft	Sun, Feb 5
First Draft	Sun, Feb 12
Preps	Mon, Feb 13
Shoots	Thurs, Feb 23

Episode 21 DC

Story	Thurs, Jan 19
Rev. Story	Thurs, Jan 26
Writers Draft	Thurs, Feb 9
First Draft	Thurs, Feb 16
Preps	Fri, Feb 24
Shoots	Tues, Mar 7

Episode 22 JW

Story	Thurs, Feb 2
Rev. Story	Thurs, Feb 9
Writers Draft	Thurs, Feb 23
First Draft	Thurs, Mar 2
Preps	Wed, Mar 8
Shoots	Fri, Mar 17

Credit: Courtesy John Wells

misnomer, as it represents the culmination of several prior drafts and is essentially a finished script. Seven working days after prep started, the episode began shooting on November 8. Adding it up, including two weeks of story generation, that's seven weeks from idea to prep, eight and a half weeks from idea to shoot date. So roughly two months per script.

But, like tectonic plates moving beneath the earth's surface, the process overlaps. Look at episode 15, for example, whose Story is due on October 27. Episode 11 begins shooting on the same date; the First Draft of episode 12 is also due. The day before, the Revised Story of episode 14 was turned in; on October 30, the Writers Draft of episode 13 is expected. It's a five-ring circus—and, on top of that, there are always three episodes in various phases of postproduction. This is the pace of an extremely well-organized broadcast show producing twenty-two episodes a season. Imagine what it's like on a show that's not well organized!

This system works well for John, who formally convenes a writers room only three days a week to accommodate his personal schedule. (He's always running multiple shows). John maintains that this scheme provides sufficient time to generate the DNA of good episodes—and I see his point. His system doesn't prevent writers from continuing to work together when he's not around; in fact, he encourages it, but this schedule allows him a comfortable balance between showrunner control and writer initiative.

One successful showrunner I know shook his head when I shared John's method with him. "I wish I could do things like that," he said. "Just never works out that neatly. Some scripts take longer, some don't." Even if you can't always abide by a schedule, it's vital to have one to know where you are and what you may need to do to catch up. As former president and five-star general Dwight D. Eisenhower said, "In preparing for battle, I have always found that plans are useless, but planning is indispensable." John represents the far end of the spectrum when it comes to organizational discipline. There are many variations on schedules and how to make them work. Your challenge is to find a model that you can make work for you.

Honeymoon

In the traditional broadcast model, the interval between the beginning of the writers room and the beginning of production is what I call the "honeymoon period," a seemingly luxurious stretch in which you and your staff can ponder ideas without the pressure of looming deadlines. Like all honeymoons, however, it's fleeting—and not quite real. Production will soon be devouring scripts. In the streaming world, production itself isn't the guillotine waiting to fall; rather, it's the imminent dissolution of the mini-room—a softer blow, perhaps, but one with equally ominous implications. As showrunner, you have to fight the temptation to kick back during the honeymoon period. This is the time to get ahead. Delay will come back to kill you.

Big Picture

To steal another line from Coach Wooden: "Be quick, but don't hurry." Despite the need to get a jump on the season, don't rush. Begin by talking about the big picture, the season as a whole, before attempting to break individual episodes. What's the background of the show, your influences and hopes for it? Run down the characters, set down possible mile markers for pivotal events: at episode 6, this happens; by episode 9, this happens, and so forth. Such landmarks are destinations to work toward. Some will adjust or even disappear as discussions play out, but they provide a framework to work with.

Although you invite full participation in these discussions, you'll likely do much of the initial talking yourself. Your writers will be looking for direction. The more pipe you lay, the better. By contrast, it's discouraging—even dismaying—for writers to have a showrunner enter the room and ask, "Okay, so what do we think this show is about?" Only the greenest writer would find this approach inspiring. Veterans would recognize it for what it is: a prelude to disaster. A proverb I often quote in the writers room: "If you don't know where you're going, every road will take you there." Provide a path that writers can follow.

The Problem with Brainstorming

Many showrunners begin their rooms by inviting writers to "brainstorm," which typically involves throwing out a torrent of ideas over several days of open-ended discussion. It's fun and promotes collegiality among staffers, but I've found it rarely results in scripts. What typically happens is a writer says, "The rodeo." To which everyone responds, "Love it!" "Awesome, dude." "Genius." So "rodeo" goes down on a list of possible stories, as do all subsequent ideas, received with equal enthusiasm. At the end of a few days, the lengthy compilation is taped to the wall—where it remains largely ignored for the rest of the season.

It's not that these entries are without merit, but they're not story ideas; they're notions, themes, the equivalent of a screenwriter saying he has a great premise for a movie: "World War II." Days or weeks after the brainstorming is over, when your staff returns to the list expecting to find inspiration, what they often find instead is disappointment. "What was that idea about the rodeo again?" "Our heroes go to the rodeo." "Yeah, but why?" "I dunno. I just thought it was fun." And that's the end of that "story"—or merely the beginning of the laborious pick-and-shovel work that goes into creating any episode from scratch.

In *Group Genius: The Creative Power of Collaboration*, author Keith Sawyer uses empirical evidence to argue that individuals and groups who are given clear instructions—a problem to be solved and a grading system based on uniqueness and value—produce fewer overall ideas than traditional brainstorming groups but come up with more useful ideas. He concludes: "Competition, mixed with loosely specified goals, can be just the right recipe for group genius."

Influenced by Sawyer, I came up with my own approach to brainstorming for a scriptwriting course I taught at Harvard in the winter of 2008 when the WGA was on strike. To kick-start students' stories, I gave them four phrases to complete before proceeding to outline:

1. What would happen if . . . ?
2. I like this story because . . . .

3. I see it going this way . . . .
4. At the end, I want the audience to feel . . . .

The responses provided raw material I could work with. The first question provides a premise—ideally a conflict, the backbone of any story: somebody wants something; something's in the way. The second yields a personal connection—why the writer wants to write this, which is critically important; without a personal connection, why are we discussing this? The third requires a sense of direction—not a detailed structure, but some inkling of movement and scope. The final question speaks to theme, what viewers might take away from the story. Add 'em up and you get more than a one-line idea; you get the biography of an idea.

When both the course and the WGA strike were over, I took this system back to *Army Wives*, where it ultimately sparked more episodes than we'd managed to come up with in previous seasons using the classic brainstorming approach—and morale didn't suffer. Generating usable material more than compensated for whatever initial disgruntlement writers might have felt about being assigned homework that was going to be "graded."

Listen to All Voices in the Room

It's not enough to have diverse representation in the room; as showrunner, you have to listen to what others have to say. During a virtual WGA seminar I conducted, a participant typed in this question: "What's the best way for white showrunners to create a work environment where people of color are a major part of the creative process, not merely diversity hires at the lower level?" I answered to the best of my ability.

Afterward I received several thoughtful suggestions from BIPOC writers, including this email that I believe has value for all showrunners:

> White showrunners need to realize that BIPOC writers in a Hollywood writers room have spent their whole lives hiding

parts of who we are in order to occupy historically white spaces. There are beliefs we hold, histories we know, and stories we tell that are constantly being held back. That's because full truth can be dangerous. Being totally honest when it isn't welcome can cost your job, your freedom, your life. While no one's life is on the line in a writers room, there are still social, political, and economic costs for BIPOC writers to be fully honest in this primarily white space. If your room is a place that doesn't value the totality of every writer, it will be a difficult space to occupy, let alone be creative in. If you want your room to be a place that allows full creativity to flow, there are many ways to encourage that on a daily, case-by-case basis.

If you think a topic is too political, but a BIPOC person is telling you it's just part of daily life, listen. There's very likely a golden pitch in there. If a BIPOC writer tells you something they have experienced in the room or in their lives is about race, take their word for it. Don't spend time trying to convince them there's an explanation for what they've been through other than race. Arguing that point will only aggravate them, waste time, move you no closer to solving the problem at hand, and prevent them from speaking up in the future.

When you don't understand something, ask. If you feel your question might be silly, ask it in private. Ask the small questions, but research the big cultural and historical things. Don't push off the job of educating the room on the few BIPOC writers in the room. Consultants from nonprofit agencies abound, dying to educate writers. Let them do their jobs.

Sit in discomfort. If you're moving off a topic because it doesn't work story-wise, fine. But if you're shutting it down because it makes you feel guilty or sad, sit in that. Process it. Your show will get better. Your characters will feel richer. It will unlock a new level of creative flow and authentic storytelling that will make your work stand out in the crowded marketplace. If you find trying on these new practices difficult, remind yourself that these efforts are nothing compared to the constant politicking and self-censoring that BIPOC writers have to deal with every day.

Process

All showrunners lead rooms in their own way, but most follow a pattern: general discussion leads to specific episodes, which in turn move from an overall premise to scenes, ultimately fusing into an overall structure, at which point the assigned writer disappears to write an outline, reappears to receive notes, then disappears again to write the script, aided and abetted by further notes. With mini-rooms, writers likely will be expected to stay in the room throughout the entire story-breaking process, writing their own material outside of office hours, even after the room has disbanded.

Ensemble dramas typically use multiple storylines, referred to as "A," "B," and "C" stories (and sometimes "D" and even "E") in order of importance. Even straight-ahead police procedurals tend to thread in one or two personal storylines to fill out the hour. For those shows that don't use interwoven stories, the process is less complicated, but that doesn't make it any easier. You're still staring at whiteboards for hours trying to be brilliant.

In my process on an ensemble drama, we break individual storylines on separate boards to be sure each has its own natural rhythm—a beginning, middle, and end. This is particularly critical on series that employ act breaks, because you can't predicate five or six act breaks on the "A" story alone without torturing the drama; you need moments from the "B" and "C" storylines to create requisite suspense and emotion to get through the hour.

Once the stories are broken, the beats are written out on colored note cards, using a different color for each story. A beat is often synonymous with a scene, the distinction being that a beat denotes a development within an individual storyline not necessarily a wholly independent scene. Several beats from different stories can occur sequentially within the same location under one continuous scene heading, like a bar, hospital corridor, or squad room. In *Northern Exposure*, for example, one scene in the bar might include conversations among three different sets of characters, each conversation representing a different story beat.

The average pace of television storytelling has accelerated dramatically over the decades. On *Northern Exposure*, we figured there were roughly twenty-four beats to an episode: twelve for the "A" story and six each for the "B" and "C" stories, on average. A typical scene might run two to three pages. Today, it's not uncommon for a one-hour episode to contain forty to sixty beats, with few scenes running more than a page. Which got shorter first, the scenes or the audience's attention span? It's hard to know. Technology has certainly played a part; the latest cameras make it possible to shoot more quickly and under a broader range of conditions than ever before, encouraging writers to write more scenes and directors to shoot more shots within those scenes. As a result, twenty-four beats in a one-hour episode would seem slow by contemporary standards, although there are exceptions, usually found at the high end of premium cable and streaming, where there's sufficient confidence in the material to let scenes play out to their own natural rhythm. Broadcast, by contrast, appears committed to keeping the pedal to the metal at all times.

Once the requisite number of beats are created in the room, we begin "the weave," as I call it, assembling the episode act by act, putting cards in place on a bulletin board under act headings. Here's where you discover problems that weren't immediately apparent while forming individual stories. For example, your "A" story takes place over three days, but the "B" story takes only one day and the "C" story takes two. Or you have no obvious act 2 break. Or your lead character disappears for three consecutive acts. Consequently, there's a lot of push-pull during the weave, tweaking to make everything fit into a coherent series of escalating events.

When the weave is complete, I often let it sit overnight before sending the assigned writer to outline. The temptation, particularly in the middle of a long season, is to kick an episode out the door before it's ready. Taking the extra time up front can save enormous time later, because fixing a story in outline is far easier than fixing it in script, when you have to reverse engineer everything back to the outline to determine just where things went off the rails. A final review of the outline in the room, led by the writer, allows one more crack at refining things while giving me the opportunity to ensure the writer owns the material before departing to write it up.

The Art of Discovery

The major challenge in running a room is managing the art of discovery. As Robert Frost said: "No tears in the writer, no tears in the reader. No surprise in the writer, no surprise in the reader." Without discovery, writing is dead on arrival. Without a road to follow, however, writers on staff can get lost. Consequently, your job as showrunner is to provide a clear vision of what you're after while allowing writers enough latitude to make their own discoveries without fear of being shut down. It's not easy.

Some observations about managing the story process:

- Every story breaks differently. Some break front to back, some back to front; others follow the "golden spike" model—you lay track from both coasts, hoping to meet in the middle.
- Be suspicious if a story breaks easily. Most good stories break hard.
- Breaking stories week after week is largely a matter of creating problems, then solving them.
- Strive for tough creative challenges. The harder the problem, the more satisfying the solution—and the story.
- If a story seems to proceed at a slow pace on the board, it's often because you're killing time to get to the climactic scene. A possible solution is to pull up the climax. Writers will howl if you do because that's all they've got. Which is the problem—the story is undernourished. By pulling the climax forward, not only do you hold the viewer's interest, you force the writers to find more story.
- Observe the partygoer rule: Arrive late and leave early. Applied to scenes, it makes for vivid storytelling.
- Take it from Raymond Chandler: "When in doubt, have a man come through a door with a gun in his hand." Sometimes that's a literal solution; sometimes it's figurative. In either case, it thrusts surprise into the story—and wakes up your writers.

- Only play the cards you need to win the trick. If you have a rich storyline going, get out of scenes as "cheaply" as you can, maintaining audience interest while hoarding your trump cards to be played later to maximum effect.
- Be judicious with "icebox questions." The term is attributed to Alfred Hitchcock, who reasoned this way: If a viewer enjoys a movie, comes home, goes to the fridge for a slice of angel food and a glass of milk, and then suddenly thinks, "Hey, wait a minute, how did . . . ?"—that's an icebox question and is totally acceptable. If, on the other hand, the question occurs while the viewer is actively watching the movie, taking them out of the moment, that's not acceptable. Hence, especially on mystery shows, when a plot hole is discovered during the writing process, writers will often ask, "Is that an icebox question or do we have to do something about it?"
- Use self-deprecation to promote creativity. "This isn't it, but . . . ," "This will never work, but . . . ," "This is terrible, but . . . ," "This is the worst idea ever, but. . . . " Such professions of inadequacy are common in the writers room and serve a valuable purpose: they allow the speaker to get an idea into the world without having to fully defend it. The subtext is, "Look, I think there may be something to this, but don't kill me if there isn't." Very often, such "terrible" ideas lead to good ones. And sometimes, "the worst idea ever" turns out to be a winner, with others saying, "What's wrong with that? It works."
- Use "house numbers" to keep story development moving. A relative of "This isn't it, but . . . ," a house number is a facile solution to a story problem that you plan to improve on later. I'm not sure how the term came about, but here's how it's used: "Okay, the house number is Sam gets a text from the office with the killer's real name." You can do better, but right now you have more pressing matters to solve. If you can't come up with a house number, another useful phrase is, "Let's put a pin in it," which means we'll come back to it later. The point is to not get bogged down by relatively unimportant details when constructing a story.

- Embrace euphemisms to steer conversation. "Is there any value in considering . . . ?" and its many variations are useful phrases to employ when wishing to get a writer to drop whatever bone they've been gnawing on and get them to hunt in a new direction: "I love that Julie walks out on Jim, but is there any value in considering it might be the other way around?" This stratagem has the virtue of making subsequent discussion a conversation rather than a matter of attack and defend. Of course, there are times, especially with a writing staff you've come to enjoy, when you can be blunt. One showrunner I know sings out with a smile, "Hate it!" and the room moves on. Writers love her.
- Invoke Picasso when dealing with real-word issues: "Art is the lie that tells the truth." I frequently paraphrase this when working with real-world situations that require compression of characters and events. (I say, "Art is the little lie that tells the bigger truth.") If such manipulation serves the higher truth you're striving for, then I think it's justified in most cases.
- Be clear with instructions when tasking another writer to lead the room in your absence. I tell my deputy to contact me if the room reaches an impasse or wants to reverse course on something I've already agreed to. Few things are more disheartening for a showrunner than reentering the writers room to find that all the pretty writing that had been on the whiteboards only a few hours before has been replaced by acres of empty space. Better for the room to stand down if you're unavailable than to dismantle the beginnings of something you liked.
- Keep reasonable hours. Ideas rarely get better as the night gets longer; you only convince yourself they do, a delusion that disappears the next morning. You want writers to come to work each day refreshed and excited.
- Maintain esprit de corps. "We're all in this leaky boat together," my first boss, Michael Gleason, would say to us all the time on *Remington Steele*. If nobody panics, we'll get to shore eventually—or at least go down laughing.

- Avoid time vampires. On broadcast and basic cable series where writing continues into production, you need to conserve as much of your time and energy as possible for the writers room and writer-related problems. Therefore, during the normal course of a season, I keep set visits to a minimum, avoid rewriting during room hours (that's what early mornings, late nights, and weekends are for), stay out of the editing room until it's absolutely necessary for me to be there (the edit bay is where showrunners go to hide), delegate casting responsibilities as much as possible, and look at dailies outside of office hours. That's my list of time vampires. Whatever's on your list, don't let them suck your blood.

Moguls

Should success smile on you as a showrunner, you may have the opportunity to run more than one show at a time. Typically, while one series is enjoying a healthy run, you're asked to create another—or perhaps supervise a writer to create another. Being such a mogul is a remarkable achievement, but it comes with a price. The more projects you supervise, the less time you have to spend on any one of them. To be effective, you must be extremely well organized, delegate more, and, in my opinion, inherently care less about individual episodes and the writers behind them. You simply can't afford to be as emotionally invested as when running a single show. I've never aspired to run more than one show at a time—nor has anyone ever asked me to, which is just as well; I think I'd have trouble letting go. It's a choice.

34

MAKING THE MAP

OUTLINES

Outlines and scripts have long been the standard documents used in television. Recently, however, there's been a trend toward additional pre-outline paperwork under various names: "pitch-outs," "story areas," "story arenas," "story documents." Such material provides executives with earlier input on a story, which often translates into more opportunities to say "no" before ideas can be fully developed. A showrunner I know had an episode idea rejected by a Netflix exec because he was told it didn't fit the series' "taste cluster," whatever that means. I suspect the chief impulse behind such pre-outline scrutiny is fear: executives are afraid to commit money without being backed up by algorithms and/or superiors. The rationale, as with much of traditional television bureaucracy, often has less to do with promoting success than justifying failure: "Hey, don't blame me; we went through all the steps." For most showrunners I know, pre-outline documents amount to little more than irritations that waste time while doing little to actually move ideas along. In my experience, outlining is where the real work begins to turn stories into episodes, so that's what I'll concentrate on here.

For me, outlines serve at least four valuable functions:

1. They give the writer a road map to follow.
2. They give the showrunner a sense of creative control. Knowing that the bones are solid, you can still salvage a good episode if a first draft is a disaster.
3. They give production a jump on prep, allowing the line producer to troubleshoot challenges that might otherwise prove insurmountable or excessively costly.
4. They give the studio and the network their rightful bite of the apple. A good executive will be a thoughtful first reader of your material, providing constructive feedback.

Outlines can run from three to thirty pages or more. It's largely up to the showrunner. The longer the outline, the less room for improvisation for the writer, which puts heightened emphasis on discovery at the outline stage. Most outlines function as charts for a dance band: the notes are there; all that remains is for the writer to play them with appropriate expression. At the other end of the spectrum, exceptionally short outlines are like charts for a jazz band: the melody is stated, followed by twenty-four bars of improvised solo. Take it.

Showrunners who favor extended outlines seek to protect themselves against unwelcome surprises from both writers and executives. Surprises in television are like throwing a pass in football: three things can happen, two of which are bad. A long outline lays everything out for all to comment on in detail in advance of the script. (Of course, this assumes execs will stand by the outline when the script appears, which isn't always the case, but minimally, a long outline provides a comprehensive baseline that showrunners can refer to should they encounter executive resistance at the script level.) Outlines from series like *Lost* and *The Closer* could run twenty-five to thirty-five single-spaced pages. Here are two pages from a twenty-six-page outline for *Lost*.

Essentially, all that remains to turn this outline into a script is to put it through Final Draft. There may be some tweaking, of course, but basically, what you see is what you get. Both the script and resulting episode hewed closely to this outline.

LOST
Episode 218 Outline
"Dave"
Edward Kitsis & Adam Horowitz
2/9/06

A Hurley-centric recap resetting Hurley's pre-lottery life. We see Hurley on the island confessing to Jack that he was once in a mental institution. We see Hurley later visiting Leonard at that institution and hearing the numbers. We see Hurley confessing to Charlie his crush on Libby. From Hurley, we move to the Henry situation and the disturbing discovery that he is indeed an Other...

TEASER

INT. HATCH - MORNING

OPEN CLOSE on WIGGLING TOES. RACK FOCUS to see they're LOCKE's toes. He's testing them in a shot reminiscent of "Walkabout." WIDEN to JACK, making his post-lockdown diagnosis of Locke's hobbled condition as KATE watches.

Jack lays it out as best he can. There's good news and bad. The good? His left leg is only bruised. The bad? Well, the right leg... it's fractured. How bad, Jack can't tell without an x-ray. It may just be a hairline. Either way, Locke's gonna have to be off it for some time.

During this, Kate's curiosity is percolating about something else. The fucking PALLET of FOOD that just showed up. Could it be related to the "lockdown"? Jack doesn't know. Right now he's focussing on Locke's condition. To Kate: "Back at camp, there's a wheelchair I recovered from --" Locke SNAPS SHARPLY. "No. I don't need a wheelchair."

Jack eyes Locke. That wasn't exactly a measured response. "We have some crutches, John. Will that do?" Locke nods. Crutches will be fine. Jack sends Kate off to get them.

As Locke watches her go, SAYID enters. Heads for the armory. A man with a dark purpose. Wordlessly, he enters the armory. And in case we forgot just what was IN there, we've got Locke. And he sure as hell hasn't forgotten --

"What are they doing to Henry?"

Right. There's a guy in there. A guy who they just learned is a FUCKING OTHER.

Jack says that they now need to be more careful with Henry. Sayid and Ana Lucia are retrofitting the armory to serve as a more... appropriate holding area.

Credit: Courtesy ABC Signature

This concerns Locke. "Don't hurt him. I gave him my word I would not let him be harmed." Jack is thrown. "Why would you do that?" Because, Locke explains, during the lockdown Henry had the opportunity to escape but didn't. "He came back for me, Jack. Why would he do that?"

Jack is skeptical that Locke's loyalty has been adequately earned. Posits his own theory. "He came back because he thought his story was going to check out." OFF LOCKE, point taken --

INT. HATCH - ARMORY - A LITTLE LATER

HENRY is being tied up. ANA LUCIA questions him --

"What's your name? Your real name? What are you <u>doing</u> here?" Henry is quiet. He stares vacantly into the distance. Ignores Ana Lucia.

Now it's Sayid's turn. "You're not going to speak to us now?" Henry remains tight lipped. Sayid nods. He sits down across from Henry. Stares at him for a long loaded moment.

Sayid then proceeds to deconstruct (and at the same time recap) Henry's story. How he knew the specs of the balloon, had anecdotes about owning a mining company, how he concocted a story about a dead wife.

Sayid: "All very convincing. You're obviously smart. And that concerns me. But what should concern <u>you</u> is that it's only a matter of time until everyone else in our camp finds out that you're down here." Through all this Henry remains STOIC. Sayid: "And if you think I'm alone in my feelings of what needs to be done to you, you are sadly mistaken."

A beat. Sayid lets that just fucking hang there. Then: "Isn't that right, Ana Lucia?" Ana Lucia pulls the CHAIN TIGHTLY around Henry's limbs in answer.

And suddenly Henry's expression transforms... He's no longer stoic. No, what we now see is unmistakable. <u>We see FEAR</u>.

EXT. BEACH - DAY

Sandy beaches. Waves crashing. Bright sun... and the sound of HUFFING and PUFFING. WIDEN to FIND HURLEY and LIBBY bursting into frame, SPEEDWALKING. Libby leads. A sweating Hurley tries to keep pace. That's right, folks, she's got him EXERCISING.

Libby: "Isn't this nice?" Hurley forces a smile. Says it's almost as nice as... breathing. Libby offers encouragement. "Trust me, you're gonna feel so much better.

Credit: Courtesy ABC Signature

By contrast, showrunners who employ extremely short outlines cede a significant amount of control to the writer, putting faith in the writer's ability to translate ideas into scenes. On *Northern Exposure,* we used three- or four-page outlines, which were submitted exclusively to showrunner Josh Brand, who refused to take studio and network notes (and had the clout to pull that off). To generate a short outline—what I called the "transparent outline" because you could easily see the bones—I would first write a much longer version for my own purposes in stream-of-consciousness style, including smatterings of dialogue. I would then compress it for Josh. Below is page 3 of my four-page outline for the episode "Kaddish for Uncle Manny." The "A" story involved Dr. Joel Fleischman needing to assemble a minyan (ten Jews) in the middle of remote Alaska to say Kaddish, the Jewish prayer for the dead, for his late uncle. Maurice, the town's leading citizen, has put out a cash reward for Jews to come participate. The "B" story involved deejay Chris, his brother Bernard, and a blood feud with a West Virginia family. The "C" story involved bartender Holling, his wife Shelly, Dr. Fleischman's assistant Marilyn, and a Cajun dance contest.

As you can see, this approach to outlining is a world apart from *Lost.* It's essentially shorthand between the writer and showrunner, barely more than notes, implying an inherent fluidity between outline and script. In fact, none of these scenes appeared in the shooting script in the same order as they appear here, and much of the content was changed. For example, the moment when Joel thanks Maurice was transferred to an earlier scene, and the sentimental exchange between Joel and his uncle in the dream sequence was dropped altogether. That said, I couldn't have written the script without this outline. It was a sketchier map than those used on most shows, but it still laid out the territory to be explored.

When I became a showrunner, I developed an outline process that falls somewhere between the poles of *Northern Exposure* and *Lost.* As implied above, I believe an outline is a map, not the journey; discovery should continue through the script process, as it did on *Northern Exposure.* But as showrunner I also want sufficient control to "guarantee" a script, as in the *Lost* paradigm.

INT. BRICK – DAY Marilyn tells Holling she's dumping him as her dance partner. He's too tall. Holling's surprised, hurt; was it something he did or said? Marilyn shrugs. It isn't personal. It's business.

Maurice introduces Joel to two more Jews. We can see Joel's bothered. Something doesn't feel right, tries to articulate his feelings to Ed. Wants to do right thing for his Uncle, but also for himself. Unburden his grief. So odd, this dilemma. Should be happy with what's happening, but isn't.

EXT. WOODS – DAY Maggie, on a walk, comes upon Bernard sitting on a stump, listens as Bernard talks about his imminent annihilation tomorrow and his inability to stop it.

JOEL'S DAYDREAM A Sergio Leone western; Joel deputizes a row of Jewish lawmen in long coats (the deputy stars are Jewish stars); Uncle Manny's there, wonders what's going on; Joel explains, though doesn't feel right to him; he doesn't know these guys, feels awkward making them help out; Manny says it's okay, it's thought that counts. Joel and Manny admit their deep affection for each other. Joel turns to dismiss deputies. When he turns back, Manny's gone. Joel wakes up in his office chair, thinks.

INT. MAURICE'S CABIN – DAY Joel goes to Maurice, wants him to call off the hunt. Saying kaddish for uncle is intimate, not the kind of thing he feels comfortable sharing with strangers. But he appreciates what Maurice did, one of nicest things anyone ever did for him. Shakes Maurice's hand, impulsively hugs him, to Maurice's great discomfort. Get a grip, Fleischman.

INT. DANCE HALL – NIGHT The Cajun dance contest. Holling's not happy. Shelly sees it. With everyone except Joel present, Marilyn and Livingston dance; they win.

EXT. CICELY – DAY High noon. The participants show up. Bernard makes a final argument. What happens if the Miller boys win – which seems likely? Where do they go from here? Chris and Bernard are last of the line. The feud is over. But the feud is the defining element in their lives. The boys – and Chris – appreciate the need for the feud, they need to hate each other and anticipate the future havoc they'll wreak on each other. So the fight is avoided and the boys depart, happy to be as angry as they were when they arrived.

Credit: Author

I've come to settle on a ten-page outline, which not only makes writers drill down on the essence of each scene but also provides a brisk reading experience for executives. The outline provides all the information needed by the writer, showrunner, line producer, and execs. Scenes are identified by sluglines—the same headings that will appear in the script. Production days and nights are included to help production get a jump. All the DNA for an individual scene is incorporated in a paragraph, conveying intent, arc, and tone. Below is a sample from *Army Wives.*

ARMY WIVES

Episode 710
Studio/Network Outline – 02/26/13

"Reckoning"
By T.J. Brady & Rasheed Newson

Previously On:

- Roland tells Joan if she goes to Army War College, their marriage is over. (Ep. 709)
- Gloria gets a letter from Patrick, breaking off their relationship. (Ep. 709)
- Penny dies after a car accident; Denise helps deliver her healthy child. (Ep. 709)
- Maggie grounds Caroline for drinking and lying about it. (Ep. 709)

Episode 710 begins a week after 709.

ACT ONE

Day 1
1. INT. MONTCLAIR HOUSE – DINING AREA – DAY

As LATASHA feeds TUCKER, the dog, she calls for the kids to get ready for school. DEUCE appears, reminds his mother that he's supposed to start trumpet lessons today. She's enthusiastic until he hands her a slip of paper - $250 for a trumpet. She says they'll rent one for now; that's still a $100 deposit. If he sticks with it (unlike karate), they can talk about buying later. Latasha looks at her check register, the balance at $140. She sighs, begins writing a check…

2. INT. HALL HOUSE – DINING AREA – DAY

As CAROLINE gets up from the breakfast table, MAGGIE reminds her to come home right after school. Caroline, snippy: "You don't have to tell me a thousand times." TANNER smirks. Caroline: "Shut up!" As Caroline goes, OFF Maggie, doing her best…

3. INT. TRUMAN APARTMENT – KITCHEN – DAY

GLORIA listlessly cleans up after breakfast as HOLLY enters, tries to lift Gloria's spirits, reminds her that Penny's baby is safely in Charlie's arms. Gloria acknowledges, but says she can't stop thinking about how Penny died alone. Gloria: "That poor girl's parents wouldn't even come up to claim the body. She just got shipped down to Florida like some package. Who knows if anyone even showed up for the funeral?" Holly encourages her to focus on the positive. Gloria: "What's positive? Life's not fair. Good people die. Others let you down…" Holly knows enough not to push it. OFF Gloria, sad…

4. EXT. AFGHANISTAN – FB RENO – DAY

CLOSE ON a photo of a baby. REVEAL HECTOR, holding the photo, surprised by the feelings the picture has stirred in him. TIM (O.S): "Hey, is that your kid?"

Credit: Courtesy ABC Signature

A few things to point out: because *Army Wives* was a serial, I asked the writers to list the scenes for the "Previously On" teaser that began each episode. This was not only helpful for execs who might need reminding, but also took the burden off the editors. To help production, we also indicated when the episode started in relation to the previous episode—is it ten seconds or two weeks later? Characters are put in FULL CAPS when they make their first appearance, just as in scripts, which makes it easier to track the cast.

Some showrunners don't tolerate much deviation, if any, from outlines. "What happened to that line?" is a common query. Other showrunners are looser. Josh Brand was an extreme example. On *Northern Exposure*, he didn't care if you followed the outline or not. All he cared about was whether the script worked. If it did, great. If it didn't, pointing out that you'd adhered to the outline wouldn't save you. "Your job is to write," Josh would say. It was a very different way of running a show.

Again, I take the middle ground. I believe outlines should firmly establish the episode's structure but leave room for inventiveness within individual scenes. If a writer finds the structure a problem, they know to come to me before making changes. Because the outline has already gone through a layered vetting process with the studio and network, however, structural problems usually don't arise.

If you find yourself getting behind on your writing schedule and must choose whether to give an extra day to an outline or to the initial writing of the script, give it to the outline. Scripts can be rewritten throughout prep if necessary, but if the story doesn't work, not only do you have to reverse engineer everything back to the outline level, but there will also be hell to pay if you make changes that affect production elements already being prepped. Get it right the first time—if you can.

35

DRAFTS AND DISAPPOINTMENT

SCRIPTS

Perhaps the biggest surprise awaiting new showrunners is disappointment. You handpick a staff, invest tremendous energy into arcing the season, breaking stories, and writing outlines, then first drafts come in and . . . let's just say, they don't live up to expectations. Instead of being elated, you're shocked, even angry, to find yourself behind where you thought you'd be.

It's a common problem with a simple explanation—and it's not the writers; it's you. You expected too much. Veteran showrunners are happy if a first draft from a young writer comes in 40 percent there. Sixty percent is outstanding. Anything higher brings tears of joy. Vets know that most scripts require significant notes and at least some time in their computer. Why? Because writers can't read your mind. All they can read are the pages you've written to date, which on a new series usually amount to a pilot and perhaps a bible and assorted pitch documents. To expect your staff to extrude perfect scripts from such limited material is to set yourself up for frustration.

A successful showrunner I know said of her first-ever staff, "For the first year and a half, I hated them all and wanted them to go away. I rewrote everything, got no sleep. When I heard writers in the room talk about what they'd done on the weekend, I wanted to shout, 'I don't have weekends because of you!' Then I thought, maybe it would be better if I spent more time showing them what I want, because this isn't working. I need to let them more inside my head." Exactly. You must show them the way even as you're finding it yourself.

A secondary explanation for disappointing drafts can be chemistry; some writers simply won't get your show. This doesn't mean you hired a bad writer, only that you hired someone who couldn't write what you want. Showrunner John Wells tells participants in the WGA Showrunner Training Program (SRTP) that if two writers out of five succeed in the first year of your series, you've done well. You aim higher, of course, but the point is clear: not everyone is going to work out.

In any case, no first draft is going to be the script you would have written. How could it be? The crucial question is: does it work anyway? If so, hallelujah. If not, you give notes in the hope that successive drafts improve. Of course, that will largely depend on the quality of your notes.

Giving Notes

Giving notes is an art, not a science, and every showrunner handles it differently. When I began, margin notes on printed scripts were the standard. Here are a few pages from the first produced script I ever wrote, emphatically annotated by Michael Gleason, showrunner of *Remington Steele.*

The notes were a direct line from Michael's brain to the writer through the point of a red felt-tip pen—very old school but highly effective. There was no question what he liked and didn't like, what he wanted you to do in the next pass, and what he never wanted to see you do again, ever. He didn't rewrite on the page. Instead, he pointed out problems for you to solve. If your next pass didn't come up, he'd do some rewriting himself, but the idea was to do it yourself.

Margin notes remain a prevalent form of commentary, although most showrunners today embed them digitally in a Final Draft file or equivalent. Not only can you make more detailed observations with such software, but you can also revise comments before sharing them. And unlike my handwriting, the general note: I wouldn't mind a little more Mildred in the first act.

up to page 22: what is Laura + Remington personal story?

July 18, 1983

There is, at the moment, no personal story of any kind for Laura and Remington.

Story needs more drive, urgency, umph!

REMINGTON STEELE

"NIGHTMARE IN STEELE"

Given the story, this may not be the most appropriate title we can come up with.

By

Jeff Melvoin

Do we want to continue running line Mildred/Laura/Remington? & Have Remi's confession?

PROD. # 3702

MAJOR QUESTION —
SHOULD WE KEEP MR X?
If yes build him as a character.
See him in act I before funeral.

Credit: Author

46

CONTINUED

LAURA
We'll explain on the way back.

DANNON
Can I stretch my legs first?

LAURA
Sure.

Dannon and Fred get out of the limo. Instantly A SHOT RINGS OUT from somewhere and strikes the ground near Dannon.

LAURA
Get down!

Everybody does, using the limo as cover.

DANNON
Shoot back, Mr. Steele!

REMINGTON
Actually, Frank, I've always preferred thinking my way out of tight spots to the use of violence.

DANNON
You don't have a gun, huh?

REMINGTON
Precisely.

Fred tries to get in the car, but ANOTHER SHOT sends him diving back into the dirt.

LAURA
(to Remington)
You said this case was like "Mirage." When the detective in that movie got in trouble, what did he do?

REMINGTON
Actually, Laura, he was killed.

LAURA
Oh, great.

CONTINUED

Credit: Author

62

THE BELL

still ringing.

LIGHTNING

flashes through a window of the room.

DANNON

feels the world revolving around him.

DANNON
(a whisper)
No.

THE BELL

from the clock DISSOLVES INTO:

THE BELL

from the nightmare.

CUT TO:

EXT. LAURA'S CAR - NIGHT

moving quickly through rain-drenched streets.

INT. LAURA'S CAR - NIGHT

Laura drives.

REMINGTON
But how can you be sure it's her?

NO, I WON'T "CALL IT A HUNCH"!

LAURA
Call it a hunch, but I think that box of plant food is going to unmask the killer.

REMINGTON
If you're right, we don't have much time.

STANDARD DETECTIVE SHOW LINE.

ABOUT WHAT?

CONTINUED

Credit: Author

66

CONTINUED

MR. X

bandaged up, walking with a cane toward them. In obvious pain.

MR. X ~~(CONT'D)~~
Very clever woman. Been following her for a while now.

LAURA
You're supposed to be in the hospital.

MR. X
Had to get here. Stop her.

REMINGTON
From what?

MR. X
Murder. Seems she's been married eight times in the last five years.

Laura, Remington, and Dannon exchange looks of disbelief.

MR. X ~~(CONT'D)~~
Lost all her husbands quite mysteriously, string of accidents, bodies never recovered for one reason or another. The company was bothered by the "coincidences," especially because of the insurance involved.

DANNON
(comprehending)
She wanted me for my money.

REMINGTON
She thought you were a wealthy banker.

DANNON
I can't believe it.

LAURA
(not unkindly)
The cat became the canary.

CONTINUED

WE MUST ALSO EXPLAIN WHY FRANK HAD THIS AMNESIA, i.e. THE WOMAN THAT HE TRULY LOVED OUT OF ALL THOSE HE MARRIED TRIED to kill him; EMOTIONALLY HE COULDN'T FACE THAT.

WOULDN'T THIS be great if we learned this earlier, perhaps in Hospital Scene, AND OUR people HAD to figure out which one OF FRANK'S wives SHE IS. (NOW THAT'S A GOOD MYSTERY) USING THE clues they (LAURA, REM AND AUDIENCE HAVE been supplied wit

great premise FOR A SHOW BUT TOO late to mean ANYTHING when it comes this LATE IN STORY. This should Be part of the mystery.

This is all great, But earlier so they HAVE A killer to UNMASK!

Credit: Author

notes are legible. Typically, I'll email the first draft back to the writer with my notes, then invite them in to discuss.

With all notes and script sessions, I try to observe three rules:

1. Begin and end with praise. Honest praise. No matter how troubled a draft might be, you can always find something positive to begin with, even if it's "I can really see the makings of a terrific episode here." All writers are nervous after turning in a draft. The first thing they want to know is: did you love it or hate it? There's no in-between. And here's the deal: as a showrunner, you can be given a script that needs a 70 percent rewrite and spend an hour with the writer reviewing copious notes, but if you begin and end with praise, that writer will emerge feeling energized, even inspired. Some showrunners call this "the shit sandwich" approach—criticism layered between two slices of compliments—but no matter how you characterize it, delivered sincerely, it works. Because it sends a clear and essential message: "I'm on your side. You're okay. We're going to get through this together." As a writer, you need that lifeline to keep going. On the other hand, if you're handed a script that needs only a 30 percent rewrite but begin by emphasizing your disappointment, it will take twice as long for that writer to turn in a second draft that's not half as good as it could—and should—be.
2. Make your notes about the writing, not the writer. At the outset of a heavy notes session, I make a point of reminding the writer that this isn't a referendum on whether they're a good writer or not—they are, or they wouldn't be here. It's not about them, it's about this thing, this draft lying on the desk between us.
3. Honor the power of the question mark. This humble grammatical device has the magical ability to transform any judgment into a conversation. Consider the difference between the margin note "trite" and "trite?" The first is a condemnation, the second an invitation to discussion. Of course, you've already determined the moment is trite, but the question mark allows the writer to come to that

conclusion without losing face: "Yeah, I see your point. I can change that."

There are plenty of other approaches to giving notes. One successful showrunner I know invites the writer into his office to make script changes with him on a large screen. I don't know how much the writer actually contributes to such sessions, but I appreciate the logic: if you're going to rewrite the script, anyway, there's nothing to lose and potentially much to gain by having the writer at your elbow to see how your mind works. It's all a matter of individual style, comfort level, and time management.

Inevitably, I've found there comes a point when you have to take over a script. It could be late in the game, when all that's needed is a polish, or it could be early, when, in your judgment, heavy revisions are required that exceed the writer's ability to execute them. In some cases, you might let the writer continue to work on an act or storyline while simultaneously assigning another writer to do the rest. Sometimes under deadline pressure, group writing may be required, resulting in a "Frankenstein" script—a creature of disparate appendages that you must animate with a bolt of your own lightning.

In most cases, the writer handling the final rewrite will be you. In my experience, the reliable number two you can count on to handle major rewrites is largely a myth. Such writers do exist, certainly, but in small numbers and for relatively short periods because they're quickly hired away to develop their own series or run other shows. Consequently, you're better off planning to do the heavy lifting yourself. If you happen to find a number two who can lighten the load, be pleasantly surprised and hold on to that writer with every means at your disposal.

Having a script taken away can be a demoralizing experience for writers, so sensitivity is required. Often the best you can do is thank the writer for their effort and explain you'll be happy to talk about subsequent changes once your draft is done. It can be tough, but ultimately, it's your reputation on the line, not the writer's. Before I distribute a rewrite, I compare it to the writer's last draft to be sure I haven't merely made changes to make my presence known. If that's the case, I'll restore the writer's words as best I can. Such things matter to writers, particularly young writers, who comb a script for every line of theirs that remains. I know I did.

Read-throughs

Some showrunners use read-throughs, also known as table reads, to refine scripts. Others don't. A lot has to do with logistics. Read-throughs rely on having scripts available on time with a cast that can be assembled, at least virtually, before every episode, usually at lunch hour—and it's voluntary for actors (although few will refuse). I have no idea how many one-hour shows use read-throughs, but I suspect fewer than half because of the logistical challenges and, sadly, the inability to consistently deliver suitable scripts on time.

As the name implies, a read-through isn't a rehearsal per se, but rather a chance for the cast to literally read through the script with the director presiding and writing staff listening, if only through a phone connection. Some actors try to give a performance at read-throughs, others throw the lines away; most fall somewhere in between. Regardless, read-throughs provide a baseline for discussion at the tone meeting (the final discussion of creative matters between showrunner and director, discussed in chapter 40). They also allow you to tweak scenes and catch actors' mispronunciations and misinterpretations.

Read-throughs can be morale boosters for actors, particularly at the beginning of a series, because the entire cast often doesn't get the chance to gather during a typical episode. On one-hour dramas (unlike half-hour comedies, in which read-throughs are critical fixtures), cast enthusiasm for read-throughs will likely fade over time, but it's fun while it lasts. On a long-running show, some actors might fall into the habit of reading the script for the first time at a read-through, which can be exasperating, but at least you know they've read it before shooting begins.

One inevitable ramification of a read-through is actors' notes. I encourage the cast to contact me with questions as soon as they receive a shooting script, which, presumably, is days before the read-through. Regardless, many will wait until after the read-through, so schedule your time accordingly. It's unlikely your series will suffer without read-throughs—I didn't encounter my first read-through in television until *Army Wives*, more than twenty years into my career, but found there are definite benefits if you can pull them off.

Script Length

It often takes several produced episodes on a new show to determine an average script length that keeps you on time and on budget. In broadcast and basic cable, which must conform to strict running times, a shooting script that's too long can result in entire scenes being dropped in the edit bay, which might hurt creatively but will always hurt economically. Minimally, the time and money spent on the excised sequences could have been put to better use enhancing scenes that remain in the episode. On the other hand, if a script generates a director's cut that's too short, you're forced to vamp in postproduction, dragging out scenes in the edit that should have been trimmed. Theoretically, it's possible to shoot additional material after principal photography has been completed, but most studios in broadcast and basic cable approve such expenditures grudgingly, if at all.

So on balance, it's better to be too long than too short. The fact is that most episodes won't suffer fatally if you have to drop a scene or two. The goal, of course, is to find that sweet spot in length that delivers sufficient footage to play with, but not so much that you have to drop scenes. In broadcast, I've found the ideal broadcast script produces a director's cut that's four to five minutes over airtime (as of this writing, forty-two minutes and thirty seconds). It's an imprecise science, of course. On platforms without rigid parameters, a comfortable length will relate more to satisfying the shooting schedule and budget than screen time.

Batting Average

You strive to make every script great, but by definition, it's impossible for every episode to be "the best." John Wells shares this rule of thumb with members of the SRTP: in a twenty-two-episode broadcast season, 20 percent of the scripts will be outstanding, 40 percent will be good to very good, 20 percent will be okay, and 20 percent will be lousy. If you accept that, he argues, it's a lot easier to get through the season. I don't disagree—I just never stop to think of the numbers; it can be too depressing. I keep my head down, hoping for the best each time out.

That said, one of the beauties of television is that it can surprise you. There will be a point in your education as a showrunner when you have to let what you consider a mediocre script go to production because you've run out of time. A month later, however, when you look at the director's cut, you're surprised—and delighted—to find it's better than you thought. It could be that the actors or director brought it up; it could be you misjudged the script. In any case, you've dodged a bullet.

Conversely, you'll have the less pleasant experience of seeing a script you thought was great turn out to be only okay. As in the first example, you won't always know why. The value of such experiences is to recognize that the creative process will always contain an element of mystery, so you do the best you can and keep moving.

John tells members of the SRTP a pertinent story about William Stafford, the poet laureate of Oregon from 1975 to 1990. Stafford was notably prolific, turning out one or two books of poetry a year. He rose early each morning, began a poem, taught class, then finished the poem that night. When someone asked what he did if the poem he was working on wasn't very good, he said, "I lower my standards." Experienced showrunners will smile at that.

36

THE SACK

FIRING WRITERS

Hiring writers is fun; firing writers is not. But there are steps you can take to make the process manageable and reasonably humane. "Generally, showrunners are confrontation-averse babies," showrunner Mike Schur told members of the WGA Showrunner Training Program. "We don't think of ourselves as managers; we think of ourselves as goof-offs. In your mind, you may think you're not qualified to make decisions, but that's not modesty, that's shirking responsibility. There comes a moment when you realize you're the one everyone's looking at, the responsibility falls on your shoulders, you have to make a decision. Don't run away from those moments. Those moments are what makes a showrunner."

And few moments are more important than firing a writer. Retaining dead weight puts strain on you and your staff. Allowing a toxic writer to operate freely poisons a room. Both situations erode respect for your leadership; either can lead to the cancellation of your show. So while the hope is to be thrilled with every writer you hire, you need to know how to proceed when things don't go according to plan.

Firing the Underperforming Writer

Most jettisoned writers are not fired in the classic sense but simply let go when their options expire. An option is a contractual provision that allows the employer to either renew or terminate employment at a fixed point in time. Not only is this the most painless way to part company, it's also the most practical, because releasing a writer before their contract lapses rarely allows you to replace them; the writer still must be paid, and the studio is unlikely to cough up more money for a substitute in the meantime. So when veteran showrunners are saddled with an ineffective staffer, they will try to maximize whatever assets that writer might possess until their time is up.

Once you've made the decision to let a writer's option lapse, you need to be sensitive about how to break the news. We all want to be liked, and letting someone go is unlikely to engender warm feelings. But your job as a leader is to earn respect, not affection, necessarily—which means delivering bad news in person. Some showrunners absolutely refuse to do this, hiding in their office while the writer gets the bad news from their agent. Don't be that person.

The process is made easier if you've talked with the writer throughout the season so that the hammer doesn't fall out of the blue. Good showrunners will let struggling writers know when they're falling short, why, and how to improve. This is beneficial not only to the writer but also to your own peace of mind should you need to let the writer go; at least you did what you could.

Firing a writer in these situations doesn't have to involve a long conversation—and usually won't. The writer will often suspect what's coming—in fact, their agent may call as the option date approaches, advancing your timetable. When the writer appears in your office, courtesy and concision are all that's required. I express appreciation for the writer's talent, then cut to the chase: I won't be renewing their option. I remind them of the difficulties we've discussed to that point, acknowledging that the failings might have been as much mine as theirs, that this is painful for both of us, though clearly more for the writer; in the end, it just wasn't a good fit. I wish them luck with their next job and, if warranted, tell them I'd be happy to serve as a reference. The writer is usually content to let things end there. On occasion, a writer might protest, but if an ineffective staffer doesn't acknowledge the heavy amount of rewriting their work has required and the warning signs you've provided, it's further evidence of their unsuitability.

After meeting with the writer, I notify their agent. A good agent will appreciate the call, asking for input on how to help their client improve moving forward. Alerting the studio is also in order. The studio has a role in hiring writers, but firing tends to be your call, as you're the one who has to deal with writers. Execs are unlikely to object when you tell them someone didn't work out. In doing so, however, be mindful of the writer's reputation. Whatever you tell the studio is going to be repeated to other execs, so choose your words carefully.

"Didn't work out" is different than "He stinks" or "She can't do the job." Be similarly circumspect when a showrunner calls to ask about a writer you've released. You want to be truthful but you don't want to blackball anyone—unless they deserve it. The trick I employ is to imagine the writer standing behind me; I don't say anything I'd mind the writer overhearing. The writer might not like what I have to say, but couldn't consider it inaccurate or hostile. "Terrific guy, team player; his sensibility just wasn't the right fit for the show." Translation: "He may work out for you, but I'm not sure of his writing chops." (You'll note I didn't say he's a terrific writer.) Another example: "I can't comment on whether she's ready to be a coproducer; that's not a position she had on our show." Translation: Thumbs down. By contrast, it's a pleasure to endorse a writer you've worked with in the past and believe in: "I love her. She's a terrific writer who's ready to take on more responsibility." That's a big thumbs up.

Firing the Misbehaving Writer

Although most showrunners employ the "no-asshole rule," offenders occasionally fall through the cracks (pun intended). Unprofessional conduct by writers comes in two categories: yellow card offenses and red card offenses. Soccer enthusiasts will understand the analogy. A yellow card is a warning, but the player is allowed to stay in the game. A red card results in immediate ejection. Red card offenses on a writing staff include racist, sexist, xenophobic, and similarly hateful behavior; bullying; efforts to undermine your authority and arrogate power; dishonesty; and other breaches of basic integrity. An unfortunate reality is that red card offenders are often among your most accomplished writers, which isn't a coincidence; their misconduct is often fueled by the arrogant belief that they're too talented to be fired. Wrong. Sometimes you have to amputate a limb to save the patient. Although red cards are rare, you'll know when to pull one from your pocket. Your next step is to immediately send the writer home, then contact the studio to discuss subsequent actions, which will likely involve termination for cause.

Yellow card offenses are more common and more nuanced than red card offenses, requiring tact and patience. The red card offender is relatively easy to deal with—once they've committed a grievous foul, they're gone. The goal with a yellow card offender, however, is to redeem the writer. That said, you need to handle things on an escalating basis so that, should there be repeat offenses, you don't have to fire the writer because the writer essentially will have fired themselves. The key is to follow consistent procedures and keep contemporaneous records.

My advice: After an initial offense, call the writer into your office. Don't start with an accusation, which puts the writer on the defensive, but with a question: "Are you aware that you've been talking over Tanya every time she says something in the room?" or "Remember my rule about no texting during room time?" This allows the writer to save face. The offender may not realize what they've done. More likely, they're fully aware of their transgression(s) but will appreciate the opportunity to act surprised. In either case, the writer needs to accept responsibility for what they did and agree not to repeat it.

When the meeting's over, I write a concise description of what took place and email it to myself to provide a time stamp. This record not only becomes a baseline for future conversations, should they be necessary, but provides a potential backstop for legal purposes. In extreme cases, you may want to send a copy to a studio exec, but this shouldn't be necessary with most first meetings.

If the offender denies wrongdoing in this initial meeting, you might have to gather more information. If you're sure of your evidence, next steps would involve contacting the studio and the writer's representatives—dishonesty is a red card offense in my book; if you don't trust a writer, you can't keep them around. Most often, however, the writer will own up.

Should there be a second offense, you follow the same procedure, but with a firmer tone, getting the writer to acknowledge that you've talked about this before, the writer agreed to reform, yet here we are again. You conclude with a clear message: this won't be tolerated any further. Afterward, you once again make notes and email them to yourself. The studio now likely needs to be informed so that they can advise on how to handle a potential termination. The writer's reps also need to know so that they can do what they can to help turn the writer around.

If there's a third offense, all that remains is to show the writer the door. If you've followed the process to this juncture, the studio can fire the writer for cause, meaning they'll be sent home without further salary. In any case, they'll be sent home. Happily, this rarely happens. Most writers won't require a second meeting if you handle the first one well. As with much of showrunning, prepare for the worst and hope for the best.

37

"WE HAVE A FEW NOTES . . ."

EXECUTIVES

Into the life of every script, a little rain must fall—a lot of rain, actually, in the form of notes: notes on outlines; notes on scripts; notes on casting, wardrobe, and dailies; notes on editing, music, and visual effects. There would be unending notes were it not for the need to eventually meet air dates. If you detect some exasperation here, it's not because notes are bad, necessarily; most, in fact, are reasonably intelligent, some are quite useful, and few do active harm. The problem is that there are so many of them. Knowing how to deal with the ceaseless onslaught of notes is a vitally important aspect of showrunning. Which means knowing how to deal with executives.

Despite the temptation to think of executives as soulless bureaucrats whose sole purpose in life is to fill yours with misery, executives are not the enemy. This attitude is not only unproductive but also inaccurate. Most execs are articulate individuals who love the business and—believe it or not—want to help you succeed. Many began their careers with dreams of writing or directing or acting. One Amazon exec I know began as part of a writing team with a film school classmate but soon came to realize that his partner was the one with the writing talent. "I just gave him advice," he says. "I didn't realize that was a job."

This doesn't mean execs won't drive you crazy at times. They will, particularly when reversing course on stories they've already approved without owning up to their prior enthusiasm or acknowledging the headaches they've now created by demanding changes so late in the game. But given proper respect and sympathy, they can be crucially important allies. Here are some tips to nurture the collaboration.

Know the Food Chain

As showrunner, you will encounter layers of executives, so it's important to know just how the tiers intersect and where they potentially conflict. If you've created a series from scratch, you possibly began the sales process with a management firm or POD, whose execs will have accompanied you on pitches. Once a studio buys your project, you then acquire a set of studio development execs—likely the people you pitched to—whose job is to further shape your project for sale to a platform. These development execs are in direct touch with the head of the studio, whom you might meet, but might not. When a platform commits to your series, their own development execs become part of the mix. After the series is successfully launched, the development execs at both places hand off their batons to current execs, who oversee the series for the duration of its run.

This describes a typical broadcast or basic cable situation when the number of execs is clearly regimented. Other business models might use fewer execs; some might use more. Should you take over an existing show, you'll likely deal only with current execs.

Regarding hierarchy, power normally descends from the top, which means the platform (which is the ultimate buyer) gets last word. Sometimes, however, the studio and platform butt heads, even if they're working under the same corporate roof. If a POD (a company with a "production overall deal") is involved, their execs may disappear once the show is underway—or not. It can be bewildering. You might get conflicting responses and not know whose notes to take, in which case your reps might possibly clarify matters, but don't count on it. It's largely up to you to sort things out; that ability must become part of your skill set.

Go to Lunch

It's easy to disregard the execs who give you notes each week, treating them more as unavoidable irritations than sensitive colleagues. Don't. Take them to lunch, ask how they got into the business, make them feel like part of the team. Not only is this a nice thing to do, but it also will pay dividends down the line.

Listen

More than anything, execs want to be heard—not obeyed, necessarily, or merely tolerated, but genuinely heard. And they deserve to be. As my first boss, Michael Gleason, taught me, "It doesn't cost you anything to listen." Don't reflexively parry, dismiss, or be defensive about everything that comes out of an executive's mouth. Hear what's being said and thoughtfully choose how to respond.

Do Not Fight Every Note

Not only is it impossible to win every battle in a notes session, it's also not smart. Give and take is part of the game. It's hard to believe an entire notes session can go by without at least one opportunity to say, "Good idea, we can do that."

Do Not Take Every Note

This is as bad as fighting every note—maybe worse, because it implies a lack of vision and/or confidence. Pushing back when appropriate demonstrates you know what your show is about; it has a spine and so do you. "We don't expect you to take all of our notes," a Warner Bros. exec told members of the WGA Showrunner Training Program: "Nothing terrifies me more than a writer saying, 'What do you want?' or 'Just tell me what you want,' because I don't know how to do what you guys do." Another exec put it more bluntly: "Don't say, 'It's whatever you want.' Am I the showrunner? Do I get the check?"

Look for the Note behind the Note

Bad notes come in a variety of guises but can often be transformed through a bit of alchemy known as "the note behind the note." Execs are your first audience. Understanding their experience of an outline or script or cut can be an enormous help—you want to know what grabbed them and what bumped them. A good exec will offer honest observations, leaving you to adjust as you see fit. A mediocre exec will lead with suggestions: "What if we make the boy a dog?" Rather than going ballistic at such moments, veteran showrunners are more likely to say, "Interesting. What makes you say that?" The exec then explains they didn't find the lead character sympathetic, but if she had an adorable puppy rather than a bratty six-year-old daughter, maybe the audience would like her more. Ah, now you get it. The exec doesn't like the mom. You've found the note behind the note.

Use the Writer's Best Delaying Tactic as Needed

"Let me think about that" are the five most commonly used words by showrunners during notes calls. Employed properly, they buy time to respond. Dispensed indiscriminately, they become a not-so-subtle smokescreen for "Fuck you, I am never taking that note." Execs know the difference. The fact is that you often do need time to consider how to accommodate a note or find a diplomatically acceptable way to reject it. (Some showrunners make it known in advance they'd rather not respond to notes during a meeting, but will get back to the execs later.) If you use, "Let me think about that," however, the key is to follow through. Should you end up incorporating the note, that speaks for itself (although a brief email to the relevant exec couldn't hurt). If you don't take the note, then an email or phone call explaining your decision is more warranted—and appreciated. How you handle kicking back notes is a matter of personal style. Scott Rosenberg once told a Showtime exec, "I tried your note. I'm just not a good enough writer to pull it off." I don't think the exec bought it, but he did smile.

Be Open to Good Notes

The only thing worse than a bad note is a good note. Because now you actually have to do something about it. You might, in fact, have to do a lot about it. Ultimately, you'll be grateful, but, in the short term, your response is more likely to be, *Shit, there goes my weekend*. Keep the big picture in mind—and be sure to thank the responsible executive for helping you make a better show.

Observe the "Drunk Rule"

It's generally accepted that if one person at a party says you're drunk, you're allowed to disagree. If two people say you're drunk, sit down. I apply the same rule to notes. If I hear a note I don't agree with, I'm inclined to ignore it. If I hear two separate comments on the same area, even if the details differ, I pay attention.

Mind the Creaky Floorboards

This is a corollary to the drunk rule. When you finish a draft, there may be something that's always bothered you, something that lingers in your subconscious like a creaky floorboard. Did you really hear that, or was it just your imagination? You sense there's dry rot underneath—in fact you know it, but you think maybe you can get away with it. A good exec always hears the creak. Like a stern building inspector with a metal clipboard, they'll march right up to the soft spot and frown. Damn. Now you've got to tear up the woodwork—like you knew you should.

Finish on a Positive Note (Pun Intended)

One showrunner I know concludes lengthy notes sessions by saying, "Let me recap," then walks down the notes she's agreed to take and the notes she's going to think about. It's a constructive way to ensure you and the execs are on the same page.

Dam the Flood (If You Can)

At the beginning of a project, you may be fielding three or more separate sets of notes—from a POD, studio, platform, and possibly others. Emphasizing the virtues of concision, you might ask the various parties to combine notes, at least on some occasions. They'll probably refuse—turf is important to execs—but you can try. If at first you don't succeed, keep asking at regular intervals as your series continues. Wear 'em down.

Avoid Loose Lips

In Hollywood, there are more people listening to your phone calls than you're aware of. This applies not only to calls with executives, but with agents and managers as well. Assistants and other "unofficial" personnel routinely camp out on calls to make notes—and gather gossip to be repeated elsewhere—so be careful what you say. Discovering this was highly offensive to my Midwestern sensibilities. but as Dorothy learned, we're not in Kansas anymore.

Never Send an Email in Anger

You'll regret it. Write it if you must, but don't address it, for fear of accidentally hitting "send." Let it cool, then render it into diplomatically neutral language. What are you trying to accomplish other than vent? You may find you don't need to send it at all.

Beware the Overmounted, the Ignorant, and the Entitled

One consequence of Peak TV has been the elevation of underqualified executives—the equivalent of the good, the bad, and the ugly. Much as what happens when professional sports leagues expand, the explosive growth of content providers has thinned the ranks of first-rate executives, creating a vacuum in which some deserving players have gotten the chance to shine while others have been promoted beyond their ability. The latter is particularly true at premium entities with deep pockets, although it can apply with equal misfortune at the lower end of the economic spectrum. The common characteristic is an inverse relationship between knowledge and arrogance. I've often discovered that the more ignorant the exec, the more entitled the behavior. A showrunner at a premium subscription platform told me she received postproduction notes from an exec who admitted he'd never seen a rough cut before. The situation will likely improve over time, but, in the short term, if you encounter exasperatingly mediocre executives, your only solace may be knowing that you're not alone.

Keep Execs Out of the Black Box

Many execs say they want showrunners to consider them friends. I believe them. I just don't trust them, and it's not because they're untrustworthy people; it's because I don't believe it's possible—or healthy—for a showrunner to be friends with an executive any more than I think it's advisable for a showrunner to be friends with actors, directors, or writers they're actively working with. You have to maintain a professional distance with those you supervise because the time will come when you have to make a decision they won't like. Friendships disintegrate under such friction, often taking professional respect with it. Furthermore, execs will disappoint you if you take them at their word and turn to them for help outside their normal sphere of authority. This is illustrated by what I call "the black box theory" of TV production.

To explain: I took the first half of an AP Biology course during my senior year of high school; I didn't take the second half because of something called the Krebs Cycle. The Krebs Cycle is a component of cellular respiration in which our bodies convert potential energy into kinetic energy. Confused? So was I. The textbook used a black box to illustrate the process. Glucose and oxygen go in one end, carbon dioxide and water come out the other. What goes on inside the box? I knew it had something to do with semipermeable membranes and gas exchange, but I didn't care. The fact that it worked was good enough for me. It was not good enough for my biology teacher; I took a theater directing course the second semester in place of AP Biology.

TV execs have a similar attitude regarding television production. Money goes in one end, finished shows come out the other. What happens in between? Most don't know and most don't care; that's why they pay you the big bucks. Their job is to give notes; yours is to convert them into television episodes. Should you have a serious problem behind the scenes and call your friendly studio exec for help, you'll find not only are they ill-equipped to provide solutions, but they're also disappointed that you couldn't handle it yourself. Execs want to feel you're always in control. You're the genie inside the black box. Don't give them reason to believe anything else.

38

THE MONEY PART

BUDGETS

Nothing strikes more fear in the hearts of first-time showrunners than the word "budget." The common perception is that it takes an MBA degree to comprehend the budget process. It doesn't. In fact, most of your budget discussions won't involve forensic accounting so much as common sense: you can't have everything you want, so you have to make choices. Just like at home.

Sure, budgets can be complicated if your goal is to understand every line item—and some showrunners want to do just that. I'm not one of them. I only want to understand the money I get to play with from episode to episode, which is a surprisingly small slice of the pie. Out of a $4.5 million episodic budget for a broadcast series, say, only a few hundred thousand will be discretionary, under your direct control. The rest is essentially out of your hands.

If you should ever reach the level of success where you're directly involved in financing your own shows and/or have equity in them, then it might be advisable to scrutinize every line item with a microscope. For most showrunners, however, the primary focus is on the levers you can push and pull each week. And for that you need a good line producer to be your guide.

Your education should start at the beginning of your series (or at the beginning of a new season on a returning show you've been called in to run). The studio will provide an overall budget number, which is generally fixed (you can ask for more, certainly, but it's unlikely you'll get it). Within that rigid number, however, you have some flexibility in how to allocate your portion of it.

The studio will have plugged standard assumptions into the line items under your control, so ask your line producer to walk you through those items to see if the assumptions are realistic. If not, the two of you need to figure out how to reallocate the money so that you can make the show you have in mind. For example, if you plan on using a lot of popular music in a typical episode, does your music budget provide enough money for that? If your show is heavy on visual effects, are a VFX supervisor and related expenses provided for? Maybe there's more money allocated to guest cast than you plan to use on a weekly basis, so some of that money could be transferred to other areas where the needs are more critical.

Be curious. Ask questions. Lots of questions. You can't be expected to know all the ins and outs of series budgets the first time—or even the fifth time—through the process. Don't assume and don't relent until you get answers you understand, because once you formally sign off on the budget, which you'll be asked to do, it's hard to change. To repeat: you don't have to understand everything in the voluminous budget document that will land on your desk with an intimidating thud, you just need to understand "your" money.

And that's it, really. Things are a bit more complicated in operation, but your line producer should be with you every step of the way to help you through. For a deeper dive into budget, see appendix A. For the moment, however, let's move on to how budget discussions usually go.

39

HORSE-TRADING

PREPRODUCTION

One truth holds universal for all series: you will never have enough resources to shoot everything you want. Which is why a call from the line producer on a broadcast or basic cable show often starts like this: "Love the new script, but we're one day and three hundred thousand over." Streaming and premium cable may not be as wedded to pattern budgets and shooting schedules, but the same principles apply. Every script will undergo a metamorphosis from idealized vision to practical reality.

Before becoming a showrunner, when you finished a script, you likely felt the heavy lifting was over; all that remained was to shoot the damn thing. Well, "shooting the damn thing" is a long, complex journey; as showrunner, you can't afford the ignorance you enjoyed as a staffer. You're in charge of a cast and crew whose job is to turn pages into finished episodes. To supervise this alchemy, you need to understand the hard work behind the magic.

It begins with preproduction, which starts when a fresh script hits the line producer's desk and is immediately given to a first assistant director to generate a tentative shooting schedule. In the old days, this was done by hand: scene information was written onto narrow cardboard strips that were fitted into an oversized triptych folder known as "the board." Today it's all done via laptop, but the process is still called "boarding." In our example—"one day and three hundred thousand over"—the first assistant director came up with nine days of shooting, one over the eight allotted to an episode in our hypothetical series. (Broadcast and basic cable typically use eight- or nine-day schedules.) Simultaneously, the line producer tallied the estimated costs submitted by all HODs, which came to $300,000 over pattern. This means you now have to hunker down with the line producer to determine which scenes will be shot as written, which will be rewritten to reduce costs and shooting time, and which may be dropped altogether.

Such horse-trading is the essence of prep. To insist on shooting everything when over budget and over schedule is not only ignorant but suicidal, as you'll discover when the studio steps in to make changes without you. Your part in prep starts with gathering information. Where are we over, and why? A good line producer will supply answers with their initial assessment, which will not only put you on the road to revision but add to your knowledge of how to get the most from your budget. Overages can usually be attributed to a familiar set of factors under your creative control.

Days In/Days Out

The pattern budget for most broadcast shows is based on a fixed number of "days in" (shot on the studio lot) and "days out" (shot on practical locations). On an eight-day schedule, five in and three out is a typical pattern. Days out are considerably more expensive, as they involve transportation, trailers, location rentals, catering, security, and a host of other additional costs. Days out also burn more time, as lighting must be rigged and a thousand other things done before cameras can roll.

By contrast, days in maximize assets the studio has already paid for. Standing sets are the obvious example. On a cop show, standing sets might include the precinct house and a corner bar. On a medical show, an entire hospital interior could be constructed on the lot with preset lighting. Days in also utilize "swing stages," used for temporary sets. It might be more efficient to build a swing set for a guest character's apartment rather than rent and prepare a practical location. The studio might also own some useful exteriors to be used on days in. Though most Hollywood backlots were sold off years ago, a few studios still have standing exteriors like a city street or small park.

If the AD's board shows three days in and five out when your pattern calls for the opposite, you can understand why you're going to be over budget on Teamster (transportation union) costs alone. There may be ways to minimize this—it could be that three of the five days out are at the same location, so you can economize by leaving equipment and catering tents set up. But usually, to make things work, you'll have to lose scenes, combine scenes, and/or rewrite scenes so that they can be shot back at the studio.

Number of Sets

Obviously, the more sets you write into a script, the more sets have to be found or constructed. Presumably, some of your interior scenes will be written for standing sets. Some, however, will likely require practical locations, which must be scouted and rented. Sometimes adjusting the specific nature of a set will make the board work. For example, say your initial draft has scenes set at a church and a restaurant. The location manager has found a great church that has a coffee shop next to it. Could the restaurant become a coffee shop? That would save a separate company move and help eliminate a day from the schedule. Now, it could be there's a good reason to keep the scene in a restaurant, but if not, such adjacencies make for easy fixes.

Number of Locations

This is related to the number of sets but is not necessarily the same. You can have multiple sets at the same location, such as the coffee shop next to a church. Similarly, a high school story line might involve scenes in a gymnasium, classroom, science lab, and principal's office, all shot within the same building. That's quite different from a script requiring a hockey rink, marina, warehouse, and prison yard.

Number of Scenes

This is yet another variation on the same theme. You might have a reasonable number of sets and locations, but too many scenes can add an extra day to the schedule. Why? Because lighting, wardrobe, and other conditions can change from scene to scene on the same set. And directors will want to block and rehearse the actors separately for each scene, designing unique ins and outs, all of which adds time. This is why one three-page scene is usually more efficient to shoot than three one-page scenes on the same set.

Guest Cast and Extras

Your pattern will allow for a limited number of guest cast and extras for each episode, so it shouldn't come as a shock to discover that if an episode features a family reunion with eight prominent guest stars or a police funeral calling for a hundred uniformed cops, you're over budget.

Number of Characters within a Scene

This is a different problem than too many characters overall. Adequate coverage of a scene requires exponentially more shots with each character you add. For example, while it's possible to capture a two-person scene with a "oner" (a seamless shot covering the entire scene), full coverage would typically include a master, two singles, and two overs (a view of one character over the shoulder of the other). Adding one more person to the same pattern could bump it to a master, three singles, and six overs. You don't often need all those angles, but you get the point—the more characters, the more time. Which is why your director may not be as thrilled as you are with the emotional "six-hander" (a scene with six actors) you've just written into the latest script. Courtroom sequences come with a host of challenges: attorneys, the accuser(s), the accused, the judge, jurors, media, and spectators. There may be little you can to do to reduce the number of players within a particular scene, but be aware that directors have only twelve hours to make their day.

Night Work

Night exteriors take time to light, often requiring cranes, light towers, generators, and yards of electrical cable, all of which have to be set up in advance of filming and taken down after. This is particularly irksome in summer, when days are long and nights short. The early darkness of winter favors more night work, but it will always be costly.

Action

Action comes in a variety of forms—car chases, explosions, fistfights, shootouts—each with its own requirements. The common denominator is the need for safety. And safety takes time. Everything about an action sequence must be scrupulously rehearsed and planned. Beyond that, it might surprise you to learn which actions are relatively easy to pull off on your show and which are hard. Take explosions. You may think blowing up a car or anything else you choose to obliterate would be a big deal. Well, yes and no. It takes time to rig charges, ensure safety, place multiple cameras, and so forth, but, once the director calls action, that's it. When the dust settles, it's on to the next scene. Compare that to a shootout, which gets covered from multiple angles and requires multiple takes. Between takes you have to rearm the weapons, rerig the electronically activated squibs for characters who take a hit, and replace bullet-riddled wardrobe. Even a fistfight requires plenty of coverage.

Writers love car chases. Heck, it's only a page. How hard can it be? Well, on a TV schedule and budget, it's often impossible. You need camera cars, stunt drivers, and permits to use public streets. The nine-minute-and-forty-two-second car chase in *Bullitt,* the 1968 Steve McQueen classic, took three weeks to film. In the TV world, a line producer is likely to suggest a foot chase instead.

SFX/VFX

Special effects are practical effects like bullet hits or explosions that are filmed in real time during a scene. Visual effects are effects added in postproduction. Once associated strictly with science fiction, VFX are now used widely to create a host of "invisible assets"—from set extensions (making it appear a scene was shot somewhere it wasn't) to depicting massive armies on the march to blood trickling down a victim's face. On *Designated Survivor,* we were able to convince viewers we shot exteriors in Washington, DC, even though filming was done in Toronto. In fact, we had to tweak footage once because the digitally inserted Washington Monument appeared to be stalking our characters as they moved from scene to scene.

A promising trend in VFX is "virtual production," technology that eliminates the need for much location shooting altogether, utilizing LED sets and sophisticated camera engines originally designed to drive video games. Disney's *The Mandalorian* is a notable pioneer in this area; more productions will follow as costs come down and expertise spreads.

Because VFX are expensive and require significant lead time, they can become an economic sinkhole if you're disorganized or indecisive. Trying to rush VFX will burn through your budget and lead to compromised results—if results can be had at all. It's a great tool, but you need to control it, not let it control you.

Water Scenes

When you watch a film crew on location, you'll see concentric circles of people, beginning with actors at the center, rippling out to include director, crew, and dozens of others needed to shoot a scene. Director-producer Craig Siebels points out that when you film on water, you've just added a moat around the actors, complicating everything from director's notes to adjusting makeup and wardrobe. Additionally, if you put an actor in the water, you have to include special safety precautions. If there's a moving element in the shot, like a boat, it has to be reset after every take. When I was a journalist in 1978 covering the set of *Jaws 2* in Navarre Beach, Florida, the crew hung a sign on the camera boat: "Some days you eat the shark. Some days the shark eats you." Not much has changed since. I wouldn't say, "Don't go near the water," but do think twice before jumping in.

Specifics

Specificity in narrative descriptions adds richness, but it can have unintended consequences. For example, say your script opens with a character driving up in a yellow Lamborghini. Unless directed otherwise, your transportation department is going to bypass red Lamborghinis and yellow Maseratis to find that exact vehicle, when all you really meant was a cool sports car. The solution isn't to lose specificity but to let your line producer know when it literally matters and when it doesn't. Communicate early to save money and goodwill.

Children and Animals

Regardless of whether W. C. Fields actually said, "Never work with children and animals," you have good reason to heed the advice. I happen to love children and animals, but they lead to expenses and headaches. Labor laws limit working hours for children; that's a good thing, but it can have a dramatic impact on your shooting schedule. For example, infants under six months can be on set for only two hours a day and can be filmed for only twenty minutes max. A child of two to six years old may be on set for up to six hours a day and actually work for three hours. The conditions are calibrated up the line all the way to age eighteen. Because of the limited time allowed with the youngest children, such parts are often cast with identical twins, which adds cost. And when you hire a child actor, you're also hiring their parents or guardian and often an on-set teacher as well.

Animals don't come with parents, but they do come with wranglers, who will promise the moon but often deliver far less—after fifteen takes. Sometimes scenes have to be modified to accommodate what a particular animal will and won't do on the day. Working with horses and other large animals provides unique hurdles, including cleanup. Shit happens. Literally. That said, we used children and animals liberally in *Army Wives*. My advice: go in with your eyes open.

Montage

"Montage" or "series of shots" might take a mere moment to write but can consume hours, even days, of production time. "Atlanta burns" is the classic example, but "the parade passes by" will do. Montages are deceptive in their apparent brevity. Like many writers, I shamelessly used them at the beginning of my career to reduce page count. The line producer wasn't fooled. As showrunner, you shouldn't be, either. Use them judiciously.

Needle Drops

Needle drops are recorded music, most often pop songs, inserted into an episode's soundtrack. The price of needle drops can range from $5,000 for an unknown to $40,000 and up for top acts. The cost for rights is divided into two parts: sync license and master license. Sync buys you use of the song itself; master buys you the original recording. The fees are usually the same, so a $40,000 total price tag would represent $20,000 for the sync license and $20,000 for the master license. There are times when the combined cost is too high, so a show will purchase only the sync rights and hire a soundalike group to make a recording. If your show is predicated on a lot of needle drops, your budget should reflect that. If you don't need well-known artists, your music coordinator can suggest an abundance of talented singer-songwriters out of Nashville, LA, and elsewhere whose needle drops will be a bargain. But should you decide the original recording of "Yesterday" would make a nice ending to an episode, expect a call from your line producer.

Anything Out of a Show's Wheelhouse

Every show develops areas of production expertise. When you stay within those parameters, you get maximum bang for your buck. When you stray, you're going to spend more money for less satisfying results. For example, as Craig Siebels tells members of the SRTP, *Glee* excelled at choreographed music numbers and *24* led the pack in high-tension action sequences, but the *Glee* team likely would have been as thrown by a car chase as the producers of *24* would have been by a high school musical. It's not that you can't color outside the lines, but know what you're asking for.

TMZ

Not the tabloid digital site, but the "thirty-mile zone," an imaginary circle with a thirty-mile radius drawn around Hollywood used to determine whether production is local or on location, a factor that will significantly affect your costs. If your production is based in Los Angeles, know that staying local is cheaper than shooting outside the zone. If you don't know, your line producer will certainly inform you should you stray.

* * * * * * * *

Having identified the most common levers you get to push and pull, what follows is some advice on how to use them.

Forget Everything

Not really; just set it aside while writing. Not only is it no fun to self-censor, but you'll also outsmart yourself. I'm often surprised to learn that things I thought would be difficult to shoot are a breeze and things I thought would be easy are a nightmare. Don't assume. Write what you want—within reason—and let the line producer point out the problems.

Communicate as Early as Possible

Share ideas with the line producer as early as you can. I instruct the writers' assistant to send the daily room notes to both the line producer and the director-producer, which allows them to comment on an episode well in advance of prep. That can be a great help. As noted earlier, with advance notice, you pay wholesale; with short notice, you pay retail; with late notice, you pay a ton—if you can pay at all. On *Army Wives*, for example, the US military let us use Charleston Air Force Base in South Carolina for occasional filming but required six weeks' notice to set aside a day.

The stark facts of production are graphically illustrated by "the production triangle," shown below.

Good, fast, cheap—pick two. If you want it good and fast, it won't be cheap. If you want good and cheap, it won't be fast. If want it fast and cheap, it won't be good.

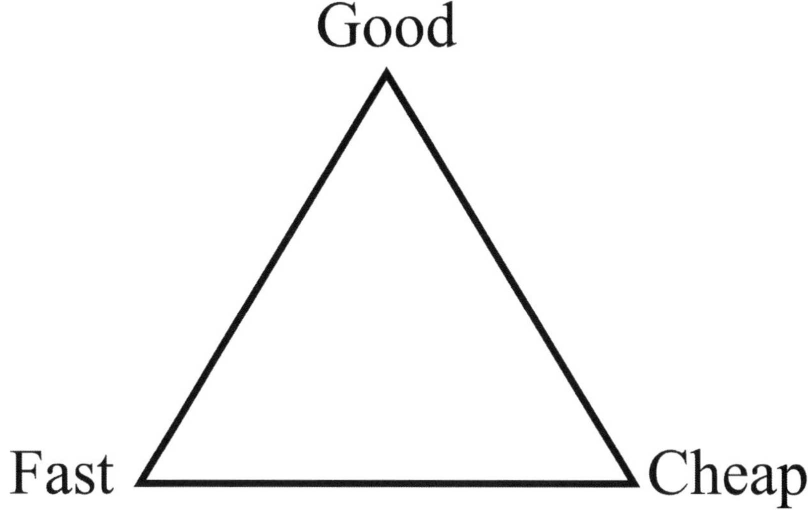

Credit: Author

Find the Essential

If a scene is problematic to film, finding the essential elements while eliminating the rest may make it shootable. For example, Craig Siebels recalls a script on *Burn Notice* that called for characters to run through snow-covered woods at night, a tall order for a spy show shot on location in Miami. Craig asked showrunner Matt Nix to rank what was most important to the scene: the running, the woods, the snow, or night. It turned out that the running was least important. By dropping that, they could shoot the scene on a sound stage.

Watch Your Deficit

Years ago in broadcast, you were allowed to go over budget on individual episodes if you could convince the studio that you'd make up the aggregated deficit over time. Today, the reins have been tightened at many places. There are notable exceptions, particularly at the high end of the food chain, where fiscal discipline often appears less of a priority. But you need to know your studio's policy because it will determine just how much wiggle room you have from episode to episode.

Trust Your Line Producer's Sleight of Hand

You don't need to know where and how, but be assured that your line producer has some money tucked away for a rainy day. TV budgets typically don't include a line item for contingencies, so line producers are forced to create their own contingency account, surreptitiously scattered among various departments. One trick some line producers employ is to give each production department a budget number slightly below the actual number provided by the studio, creating a reserve. Other funds might be hidden in the camera package or other densely detailed departments where the money can sit well disguised. Whatever legerdemain is involved, trust that the line producer is doing all they can to make the show you want, so when they tell you there's a money problem, believe them; they've already pulled all rabbits from available hats.

Be Wary of Bottle Shows

Should you face mounting deficits, someone is bound to suggest a "bottle show" to save money. Strictly defined, a bottle show is an episode that's shot exclusively on your standing sets and backlot—no days out, hence no Teamsters or location rentals or catering and so forth; you're making a ship in a bottle. It sounds good, but bottle shows rarely pay off as well as expected. Why? Because to compensate for the inherent limitations, showrunners often come up with exotic storylines that ratchet up costs—a catastrophic flood traps your main characters; a fire threatens the hospital; a terrorist group holds your lead attorney hostage with the jury (that's twelve extra speaking roles carried across all of production). Whatever you come up with, there's bound to be something to make it cost more than you thought.

Be Skeptical of Silver Bullets

A savvy line producer I know says if you want to cut $100,000 or more from a budget, there's one surefire way to guarantee it: cut a day from your shooting schedule. The logic is impeccable. By dropping a day, it's almost impossible not to save six figures. The only problem is, I've never heard of anyone actually doing it. I certainly haven't. Even if you could, I'd think the logistical challenges of rearranging a season's shooting to accommodate the change would be overwhelming. Such silver bullets often prove more elusive than real. But go for it.

40

SHOW AND TELL

DIRECTORS

When I began working in broadcast, directors fell into two categories: pilot directors and episodic directors. Pilot directors were innovators who set the style of a new series, often having a strong say in principal casting as well. Episodic directors were viewed primarily as skilled custodians expected to maintain standards established in the pilot. But these roles have evolved and blurred in recent years, particularly with the advent of premium cable and streaming. Shorter seasons, deeper budgets, evolving technology, and the elimination of commercial breaks on newer platforms have allowed both pilot and episodic directors to approach a growing number of series with the creativity and resources historically associated with movies, not television. When *House of Cards* debuted on Netflix in 2013, it wasn't just showrunner Beau Willimon who got the accolades, but feature director David Fincher as well. Similarly, in 2014 writer Nic Pizzolatto shared laurels with director Cary Joji Fukunaga for the first season of HBO's *True Detective.* And in 2020 Scott Frank directed all seven episodes he wrote for *The Queen's Gambit*, the limited series he cocreated for Netflix.

Like so much else in television today, one size hardly fits all. At the premium end, some episodic directors wield authority equal to or greater than that held by showrunners. Most television directors, however, are freelancers who remain subordinate to the showrunner. This chapter is about them: the hardworking professionals who go from series to series, platform to platform, using their talents to get the most from your show on a limited schedule and budget. To work effectively with episodic directors requires an understanding of what they do and how they do it.

Director Prep

This is a checklist used by veteran director John Kretchmer to prepare for a new directing assignment.

"Pre"-Preproduction

- Read at least five scripts of the show.
- Ask to view the five best episodes.
- Talk to other directors who've worked on the show.

Day One (of Eight-day Prep)

- Travel to location.
- Make notes on script for concept meeting.

Day Two

- Meet the line producer, director-producer, production designer, first assistant director.
- Review location photos prescreened by production designer.
- Tour set with production designer and first AD.
- Attend concept meeting with showrunner, writer, and all HODs (heads of department).
- Go on preliminary location scout.
- Meet director of photography and cast on set to get a sense of the mood.
- Reread script.

Day Three

- Location scout.
- Conduct props meeting.
- Conduct wardrobe meeting.
- Conduct makeup/hair meeting.
- Conduct casting session/review casting tapes; give showrunner three choices for each guest role.
- Begin making shot lists.

Day Four

- Go on location scout.
- Conduct visual effects/art department meeting.
- Conduct stunts/special effects meeting.
- Continue casting, including sensitivity meeting with affected cast as necessary (reviewing potentially uncomfortable sequences involving physical intimacy and related concerns should they appear in the script).
- Continue making shot lists.

Day Five

- Go on final location scout.
- Revisit key locations with first AD and DP if necessary/possible.
- Finish whatever casting needs to be done.
- Finish shot lists.

Day Six

- Go on tech scout with all HODs (except makeup/wardrobe) to discuss location requirements.
- Reread script.

Day Seven

- Attend production meeting with showrunner, writer, and all HODs.
- Conduct cast read-through, if possible.
- Attend budget/schedule meeting with line producer, director-producer, production manager, DP, and first AD. Major purpose: Can we make each day?

Day Eight

- Attend tone meeting with showrunner (sometimes held earlier in prep).
- Review final prep with first AD and DP, if necessary.
- Conduct props show-and-tell.
- Meet with lead actors individually (fifteen minutes per actor).
- Reread script.
- Get a decent night's sleep.

I get exhausted just reading this. Of course, different directors take different approaches, but all must cover the essential tasks outlined above. This checklist not only provides a concise summary of a director's responsibilities, but also serves as a useful overview of the entire preproduction process itself, underscoring the relatively limited role the showrunner has to play—when things are going well. Normally, as showrunner you have two meetings with the director that bookend prep: the concept meeting and the tone meeting. You may also choose to attend the production meeting, but that can be delegated to a subordinate once your series is well under way.

The Concept Meeting

The first day of prep for directors is often spent traveling to location because so many shows are now filmed outside of Hollywood. Even when a series is shot in LA, however, the first day for directors is often spent absorbing the script—assuming there is one—and making notes for the concept meeting on day two. That meeting is attended by the director, the first AD, the showrunner, the writer (on most shows), the line producer, and all HODs. The AD leads the group through the script page by page, but the director drives the meeting. The focus is on identifying what's needed to make the episode work. I view it as the showrunner's opportunity to listen, clarify, and adjust as necessary.

For example, let's say the opening scene of the script being prepped takes place in a coffee shop. Questions immediately come from all quarters: is that a build or practical location? How large a coffee shop? How many extras? It says a writer is working on an Apple laptop in the background. Does it have to be an Apple? Is the writer wearing earbuds? These can be important considerations—and we haven't even gotten to the opening dialogue. In a later scene, a character's forehead gets cut on a doorframe; the wound bleeds throughout the following action. Do we need a stunt double? Is the blood practical or added later with VFX? If practical, does the blood get on the character's wardrobe? If so, how many extra outfits will be needed?

When the concept meeting's done, the director and the production team should depart with a clear sense of direction. You'll continue to supervise casting, script revisions, and other creative matters, but you've effectively handed the production reins over to the director. If the director has creative ideas or concerns about a script, the beginning of prep is the time to make them known; the tone meeting comes too late to make serious revisions. Rather than offer suggestions, experienced directors will often ask questions, which can prompt adjustments. When you've already spent weeks on a script that's gone through rounds of notes, you hope a director won't spot something requiring wholesale revision, but if so, that director has done you an invaluable favor.

The Tone Meeting

I view the concept meeting principally as the showrunner's opportunity to listen to the director; the tone meeting is the director's opportunity to listen to the showrunner. There's overlap, of course, but that's my rough characterization. The tone meeting is scheduled for the end of prep to accommodate whatever script changes might have been made for production and creative purposes. If there's been a read-through, that also becomes part of the discussion. The showrunner drives the tone meeting, leading the director, first AD, writer, and editor through the script from front to back. (The editor is there to get a sense of what you're looking for.) Because the goal is to talk about the intent and nuance of every scene, tone meetings can run several hours.

In addition to purely creative concerns, this is your chance to point out any personnel issues the director should be aware of: your male lead tends to cry during emotional scenes—don't let him; your two leads have been dating in real life but recently broke up, so things are tense. Paris Barclay, past president of the Directors Guild of America, advises: "Don't tell me what's in the script. Tell me what's not in the script, what I really need to know." Once the tone meeting's over, if all is going well, you wish the director good luck and move on to a thousand other tasks awaiting you.

Know the Rules

The Directors Guild of America publishes the *Creative Rights Handbook*, available as a free download on the DGA website. The work rules in it have been negotiated with the Alliance of Motion Picture and Television Producers, so, as a WGA member, you're expected to follow them. Some highlights:

- *Scripts:* Directors must get a script one day ahead of their official prep date. If not, your show can be "grieved" by the DGA. This isn't done often, but if you're a habitual offender, the studio might be forced to pay fines.
- *Casting:* Directors have the right to participate in all casting decisions related to their episodes. You don't have to take their recommendations, but their input has to be invited.

- *Editor's cut:* Although you can view dailies as much as you want, you can't look at edited footage during shooting without the director's permission. Which is fine—you're too busy most of the time to want to look at edited footage while a show is shooting. The only exception is if the editor flags a possible problem. In such instances, you can ask the director for permission to take a look at the edited footage. Invariably, they'll grant it because if there's a problem, they want the opportunity to fix it while doing principal photography. Which brings up a related issue . . .
- *Reshoots:* Unless the episode director is unavailable, they are entitled to do all reshoots and additional scenes that may be required beyond principal photography on their episode. This is another reason to promptly determine whether reshoots are required while the director is still on location and sets and actors readily available. To fly a director back to a remote location and possibly have to rebuild sets and reengage actors is expensive. And annoying.
- *Replacing directors:* Essentially, forget it. It's so difficult procedurally that you're better off muddling through with the assigned director unless the problem is physical incapacity or inherent danger to cast and crew. In those rare instances when directors are simply overwhelmed, a director-producer can often shepherd the episode to the finish line.
- *Director's cut:* For a one-hour show, the director is guaranteed four days to work on the director's cut before turning it over. You can't do any editing before receiving the director's cut.
- *Postproduction:* Directors are permitted to attend postproduction meetings and playback sessions and should be informed of all relevant dates and times. In broadcast and basic cable, directors will rarely ask to be included (because they're too busy with other work and/or know they have limited influence), but you should be aware of the provision.

Tips for Effective Collaboration with Directors

- If you're on set, let the director work through a rehearsal and even shoot a take or two before making comments. It's a common mistake to step in prematurely. Directors often need time to work out a scene with actors.
- All comments to the director should be made privately. If the director openly invites your reaction after a take, that's one thing. But if not, find the opportunity to communicate discreetly. Huddled conversations at video village (the area where camera monitors are stationed) can undermine the director's authority and disturb the actors' sense of security; actors are keenly aware of dissonance on set.
- A common solution to actor disputes over dramatic interpretation is to shoot a scene two ways: one the actor's way and one the way it's written.
- Director Paris Barclay reminds members of the WGA Showrunner Training Program to give the director some love. If an episode turns out well, directors rarely receive more than passing credit. If an episode is deemed mediocre, however, it's the director who often gets thrown under the bus. An encouraging email or phone call during shooting means a lot.
- On a similar note, let the director win at least some of the time. One area where this is particularly pertinent is casting. For guest roles, you'll often get three choices from the director, with their preference indicated. It's easy to override the director's selection, particularly on remote-location shows when you're in LA and they're somewhere else. Give in when you can. It's a small concession that can relieve potential "us against them" anxieties.
- Alert the director to any imminent changes in the script as early as possible. Not only is this specified in the DGA's *Creative Rights Handbook*, it's common courtesy and common sense.

* * * * * * * *

As suggested earlier, episodic directors used to be viewed as little more than traffic cops by industry insiders. My first boss, Michael Gleason, told us to write scripts that were "director-proof." It was said tongue-in-cheek, but the subtext was clear: directors don't have much to add to the creative mix, but have the potential to screw things up, so spell things out. A lot has changed in the intervening years. Treat directors with the respect they deserve and you'll benefit in many ways, on-screen and off.

41

"I'M NOT SAYING THAT"

ACTORS

Yes, everything you've heard is true. If you're looking for the most boorish behavior on the planet, you can find it among Hollywood actors—a few Hollywood actors. Very few; in fact, hardly any. The great majority of actors I've worked with are dedicated professionals who pursue their craft as diligently as you do yours. Unlike you, however, they put their emotional lives on the line every time they come to work. If you've never acted before, I encourage you to take some acting classes, which will not only expose you to how difficult it is but also make you painfully aware of how a word of encouragement can make your day while the mildest criticism can send you into paroxysms of despair.

Because vulnerability is an actor's stock-in-trade and acting is a form of play, managing actors requires the heightened sensitivity of a parent (one of the "Twelve P's" of showrunning listed in chapter 27). If you created a series, you're literally the parent of the characters; if you've assumed leadership of a show you didn't create, you're still the head of the household, but as a stepparent. In either case, the cast will be looking to you for the reassurance, patience, consistency, and compassion of a good parent. To do their best work, actors have to trust you. And you establish that trust from your first contact.

Casting

If you're running a new show, your first encounter with actors will likely be at a casting session. You'll have looked at a lot of taped auditions to begin the process, but ultimately, you'll see the top candidates in person. Typically, this takes place in a small room with the actors performing just a few feet away from you, reading opposite the casting director or a casting assistant, whose function is to feed cues, not necessarily "act" or emotionally engage with the actor. It's a setup designed to create stress.

Immediately before their audition, it's likely the actor will have been sitting in a waiting room among other actors waiting their turn. Because they're often up for the same parts, many will acknowledge one another with polite smiles. It's a brutal business, so whatever courtesies you can extend are always appreciated. Do what you can to put actors at ease. Ask if they have questions before reading. While they're performing, give them your complete attention—no eating, drinking, whispering, or passing notes. (You'd be appalled at some of the bad behavior that goes on.) Once the actor is done, you might ask for an adjustment, which they can do on the spot, or they might request a few moments to prepare. When the audition's over, don't start talking with the casting director until the actor has left the room and the door has been closed. Discuss your impressions with the casting director, who will be familiar with an actor's work and might occasionally want to ask them to come back, believing they can do better. I'm always happy to go along, which has resulted in some choices I wouldn't have made otherwise.

Naturally, your execs at the studio and platform will have a lot to say about casting a pilot—and the director will be involved as well. Even at the episodic level, you may not have carte blanche to cast certain roles. But you can always control how you treat actors, so treat them well.

Due Diligence

Before casting a major role, ask around about an actor's conduct on other shows. If reliable sources tell you that an actor is a nightmare, believe them. Do not cast such actors; they will not change. You will not transform them; they will transform you—into a wreck. A toxic actor belongs in the "life's too short" category. This tag applies to very few cases, but if you encounter one, flee.

Offer Only

When actors achieve a certain level of success, they become "offer only." That means they don't read for a part; you have to offer it to them. Offer only can be a mixed blessing. While it's potentially exciting to sign a proven actor, you're flying blind. Even though you need to meet the actor to assess their interest and compatibility, you won't have the chance to hear your words coming out of their mouth. Furthermore, should the actor sign, you inherently begin from a compromised position, the subtext being that you needed them more than they needed you. This doesn't mean the actor won't turn out to be a treasured collaborator, but you've ceded at least a little of your initial authority.

Set Expectations

A healthy working relationship with actors begins with a good talk. I start by telling actors how thrilled I am to be working with them and ask if they have questions about their character, the series, how I run a show, anything. I want to know what their experience has been on other shows, what they're most looking forward to, and what are their biggest concerns. Then I get into expectations—theirs and mine. From me, they can expect a positive working environment, an open door, and scripts on time. In return, I expect them to come to the set prepared, to treat fellow actors and crew members with respect, and to obey the "twenty-four-hour rule"—they can get back to me with script issues up to twenty-four hours before a scene is shot. After that, no changes will be made because there won't be enough time for me to fairly consider revisions. Many showrunners use this rule (or variations of it), and most actors respect it; those that don't might require firm reminders. Your talk should leave cast members with a solid sense of your organization and thoughtfulness, which helps build confidence moving forward, setting the stage for a productive partnership.

Praise Widely and Often

On many shows, actors hear from the showrunner only when there's a problem. Don't let that happen to you. Spread praise liberally and often. Let actors know you like what they're doing; it costs nothing and pays plenty. This applies to guest cast, not just principals. I recall a veteran character actor on *Army Wives* who played the mother of a series regular. Though she made only a few appearances, she was always terrific, so when her arc was done, I called to tell her so. She choked up: "In all my years in the business," she said, "this is the first time I've ever gotten a call like this." You can make a difference.

Do Not Overshare

It's tempting, but do not tell actors about upcoming storylines—and don't let your writers do it, either. Scripts often change over the course of development, and you don't want your lead actor dreaming of an Emmy when you have to tell them a few weeks later that their character is not going to lose a leg to diabetes after all. Discuss character arcs as you see fit, but don't commit to specifics until you're sure they're going to happen.

Maintain Distance

No matter how much you may love your cast, you have to maintain professional distance. One showrunner told members of the WGA Showrunner Training Program (SRTP): "Do not make actors your friends. You'll regret it when you start getting phone calls at 3 a.m. to hear about their miserable love lives." Most actors won't come to you with such problems. If they do, however, be compassionate but set boundaries. Depending on the situation—I'm thinking particularly about addiction and mental health issues—you may need to get the studio and the actor's reps involved. Don't become ensnared in something you're not qualified or expected to handle.

Number One on the Call Sheet

Number one on the call sheet is your series lead, your star. Your number two (and numbers three and four) may be equally important to the show, but by definition there can be only one alpha. And that position has impact. If your star is punctual, comes prepared, and is respectful of colleagues, their example will mold the culture of your set. If, on the other hand, your number one is late, rude, and acts irresponsibly, that will also influence your set. Be proactive: let your star know that you're counting on their leadership to create a professional environment.

Number One as Executive Producer

Years ago, few stars were executive producers on their own shows, and when they were, it was largely a vanity credit, reflecting little actual influence. Today, many stars with executive producer titles expect a more active voice, which often means an additional set of notes on outlines and scripts, usually delivered verbally rather than by email. Whether this is a good thing or a bad thing is irrelevant; it's a thing—and a thing you should embrace, because only by wrapping your arms around it will you stay in front of it. To encourage collegiality, you might invite the star into the writers room for a day; many actors will appreciate the offer—and after seeing how difficult the work is, might never wish to return. Regardless, the experience should deepen their understanding of what goes into the writing of an episode. One showrunner I know makes a point of criticizing his own ideas when his number one is in the room. He'll suggest something and then say, "Forget it, that sucks," showing that everyone's pitches are fair game. The hope is that your star will absorb the lesson.

To maintain your equilibrium when fielding notes from your star, it helps to assume they want what's best for the show, not merely for them. And sometimes it's true—at least, they'll think it is. Accommodate as best you can. What you want to avoid is open conflict: you versus them. If that happens, you're locked in a death spiral from which only one of you is going to come out alive—and it's not going to be you.

Single Lead versus Ensemble

For a showrunner, the obvious advantage of an ensemble show over a single-lead show is that you can't be held hostage by an individual actor; should a cast member misbehave, you can send them home and distribute their material to others. If you're in charge of a single-lead or dual-lead series, solutions can be more challenging.

Of course, even successful ensemble shows present problems over time. As the old adage about television actors goes, "The first year, they work for you; the second year, you work together; the third year, you work for them." The trick is to stay at stage two for as long as possible.

On-Set Protocol

The set belongs to the director. This was drilled into me by Barbara Patterson, my high school drama teacher, and nothing has altered my thinking since. This means that notes come through the director, not from you or other writers who might be on set. This discipline makes it easier on everyone, particularly the actors. Only if there has been a serious breakdown in protocols should you have to address actor problems on the day of shooting.

"I'm Not Saying That"

Actors are going to have notes—not all your actors and not all the time, but when they do, it's your obligation to deal with them thoughtfully. Listen and adjust where you can. In my experience, most actors are rarely disruptive with their comments. They often are just looking for an explanation of a line or scene. Should they become truculent, the key is to remain calm. On my first showrunning job, deep into the season, one of the stars came into my office to complain about his role; apparently, a friend had given him an earful about how his character had changed, so now he was giving it to me. He wasn't terribly articulate, but he certainly was loud. This was a feature actor my dad's age, someone I'd admired for years, yelling at me from across the desk. And all that was running through my mind was a calm voice repeating, "You're the adult here, you're the adult here." Where that voice came from, I don't know, but I owe it a lot. After the actor's eruption had played out, I told him I was sorry he felt that way; I respectfully disagreed, but I'd do what I could do to address his concerns moving forward. That was it. After he left, we never had another problem—at least that I'm aware of.

When confronted by an upset actor, I've found that their emotional level often dwarfs the actual complaint. Once you've discerned the problem, it often can be fixed with a simple tweak. A typical exchange might go like this:

> Actor (angrily waving script): "I'm not saying that."
>
> You: "Okay. Why not?"
>
> Actor: "Because it's stupid."
>
> You: "Why is it stupid?"
>
> Actor: "Because I wouldn't say that. I wouldn't call my sister 'attractive.'"
>
> You: "Why not?"
>
> Actor: "Because it's disgusting."

You: "Hmm . . . It wasn't intended that way. You're describing your sister to a friend who has to pick her up at the airport. How do you think your character would put it?"

Actor: "I don't know . . . 'She's a pretty redhead.'"

You: "Great. Let's make the change."

Actor: "Okay . . . cool."

Problem solved. There's no need to determine whether the change is actually better; it's so lateral, it doesn't matter. Nor does it matter why the original line touched a nerve. Once the issue emerged, it was easy to let the actor solve it.

Some showrunners have limited patience with actors' notes. I know one prominent showrunner of an HBO show who blew up when an actor said, "My character wouldn't say that." The showrunner shouted back, "Yes, your character would say that, because I created your fucking character and I wrote that fucking line and you're going to say it the way it's fucking written!" Which the cowed actor did. Different strokes. As showrunner, you have to be comfortable in your own skin.

Do Not Expect Gratitude

I worked with a talented actor on *Army Wives* who insisted on talking to me about changes on every script. Her notes were usually minor dialogue choices rather than story content—"The words just don't want to come out of my mouth that way." She was relentless, but because she did a great job on camera and respected the twenty-four-hour rule, I always made time for her. The director-producer thought I was overly indulgent, but it was a concession I was willing to make.

Toward the end of the run, however, I got an email from her requesting changes on a scene that was shooting that day. Not only was this a violation of the twenty-four-hour rule, I didn't agree with her suggestions, so I sent back an email respectfully declining to rewrite anything. I immediately received a blistering response in my inbox, railing about how she knew her character better than I did and couldn't believe I turned her down. The director-producer, who'd been copied, was outraged on my behalf. I told him I was disappointed but not surprised. Returning to the parent analogy, you don't expect children to thank you for being a good parent until years after they've left the house, if then. Despite her flaming email, this actor played the scene as written—and well. Yes, she could be a pain, but if the right part came along, I'd gladly work with her again—although we'd have a talk first.

Disasters

Question: how do you make an actor unhappy? Answer: hire them.

This old joke applies to a very small percentage of actors, but it only takes one to threaten the success of your show and your sanity. Should you find yourself stuck with such an unhappy soul, your salvation will lie in following a rational course of action with escalating consequences. If this sounds like basic parenting advice, it's no coincidence—be firm, explain consequences, follow through.

Take a classic example—an actor refuses to come out of their trailer. You knock on the door and ask why. If you get a coherent answer, you respond accordingly, but under no circumstances should you concede anything while the actor remains sequestered. You explain this isn't the way to handle disputes, that it's costing the company time and money, and if the actor doesn't emerge, you'll have to notify the studio and the actor's reps that the actor is in breach of contract. Even if the door opens at this point and the actor agrees to do the day's work, there has to be follow-up. The bad behavior must be noted and acknowledged, with the actor agreeing not to repeat it and the studio and actor's reps fully informed.

What if the door doesn't open? You explain that what happens next is in the actor's hands, not yours. You then get the studio on the line and explain that you've done all you can, but the actor refuses to cooperate. You might also contact the actor's agent or manager, although the studio could also do that. Your immediate concern is to keep the cameras turning. Can the actor be written out of the upcoming scene? If not, can you switch the day's shooting schedule to accommodate other scenes? If not, after consultation with the line producer and the studio, you might have to send everyone home. It depends on how the studio, the actor's reps, and the barricaded actor respond.

If you anticipate a problem is brewing with an actor, you can prepare for it with "backup pages," alternate versions of the day's scenes with the actor omitted. It's extra work for you, but it can pay dividends. A first-time showrunner heard about this gambit while a member of the SRTP and took it to heart when she assumed the reins of a successful show with a notoriously difficult star. On the showrunner's first day, the star pulled a major stunt, showing up on set with the wrong hairstyle, totally inappropriate for her character. When the showrunner insisted that the hair be changed, the actress stormed into her trailer and refused to come out. The showrunner sent another producer to talk to her. He emerged with the report that, amid tears, the actress had said, "Fuck you." Armed with backup pages, the showrunner said, "Fine, that's her decision. Tell her she can go home; we won't need her today." Within minutes, the actor came out and changed her hair. Shooting resumed. The showrunner told the class: "That never happened again. It wasn't about the hair. It was about me being new and who's the boss of the set. Well, that got settled." It got settled because the showrunner was smart and tough. She knew the studio would be judging her by her ability to keep a successful show running; she wasn't about to let an irrational actor jeopardize that.

Grace Note

For the typical viewer, it's the actors—not you or your writing—that make or break a series. You may have imagined the characters, but the actors become them. It's a remarkable art, and if those who practice it sometimes require an extra measure of patience, it's worth remembering that the greatest special effect ever invented will always be the human face.

42

FINAL REWRITE

EDITING AND POSTPRODUCTION

There's a moment in *Apollo 13* when the astronauts on that ill-fated moon mission face carbon dioxide poisoning because they don't have the proper air filter replacement for the lunar module, where they've been forced to take refuge. A team of NASA engineers on the ground are tasked with improvising a substitute solely from raw materials available in the module. After dumping a box of odds and ends on a table, the lead engineer holds up a square filter in one hand and a round filter in the other and says, "We've got to find a way to make this fit into the hole for this, using nothing but that." That's often the way it feels in the edit bay. You've got to make the best episode you can from the footage you have. Unlike *Apollo 13*, however, no one dies if you don't succeed—only careers.

Why the need for such improvisation? Because directors' cuts, much like writers' first drafts, usually need a lot of work—and this will be true even with the finest directors. This isn't because they did a poor job. They likely did an excellent job. The episode simply needs more time to realize its full potential. It needs the final rewrite.

As showrunner, when you look at a cut, you have to take off your writer's hat and put on your editor's hat. Rather than focus on what the script said—or what you thought it said—you now must ask: What's the footage telling me? Where does it want to go?

"There are two types of showrunners," a veteran producer once told me, "those who see what's there and those who see what they'd like to believe is there." Your job is to see what's there—and make it work. If a sequence strays from your preconceptions, can you wrench it back to its original intentions? Is there a compromise? Or does the footage take you someplace different, possibly someplace better? Every episode provides its own journey, and I've found making that trip with a skilled postproduction team is one of the joys of showrunning.

The Postproduction Team

- *Coproducer (Associate Producer):* Your contact for all things post, who helps hire editors, interacts with various studio and network execs you'll never meet, and supervises the workflow through the post supervisor, post coordinator, and production assistants. Unlike titles on the writers' side of things, the titles in post carry consistent meaning.
- *Editor:* Your partner in the final rewrite, who sits in with you for the tone meeting with the director, creates an editor's cut from dailies, works with the director on the director's cut, then works with you the rest of the way, including music and sound spotting, often sitting in on the final mix as well. Each editor has an assistant editor, responsible for inputting all media and keeping the edit bay up and running. Assistant editors are often given the opportunity to cut scenes as part of their apprenticeship and deserve your respect and support.
- *Sound Supervisor:* Oversees every element that goes into the sound mix.
- *Composer:* Responsible for original score. Working alongside the composer is a music editor, an expert in Pro Tools and other music software, who coordinates recording. The music editor can make on-the-spot revisions at the final mix should you want to tweak or replace a cue.
- *Music Supervisor:* Responsible for all music not created by the composer, most commonly "needle drops," which can

range from hits by well-known performers to inexpensive originals by unknowns.

- *VFX Supervisor:* Needed depending on the number of visual effects on your show. In the old days, one effects house typically handled all VFX work, but with today's demands for increasingly sophisticated effects, several companies are often required, each with specific tasks and areas of expertise. Costs and delivery schedules can quickly spiral out of control without a VFX supervisor to coordinate the work.
- *Mix-Stage Personnel:* Masters of the mix stage, the final step in the process, where all audio elements are added to the locked picture. A mix stage resembles something out of mission control at NASA and is typically manned by three mixers, one responsible for dialogue, one for sound effects, one for music.

Workflow

You won't have time (or need) to be involved in every phase of post, but you should be familiar with the process. The term "post" is actually a bit misleading, as some of its functions begin before shooting—like deciding on camera packages, coordinating with effects houses, and having editors sit in on tone meetings with directors.

- *VFX:* It may seem odd to list visual effects at the head of workflow, but because VFX requires careful planning and budgeting, it's essential to determine what's needed for a particular episode well in advance of shooting. As indicated earlier, VFX today applies to far more than intergalactic space battles. Digital mattes can augment real-world backgrounds, digital crowds can supplement or replace extras, digital blood can be added to injuries. These are but a few examples. Each usage affects budget and shooting.
- *Shooting:* What is filmed and recorded to make the episode. Film and audiotape were replaced years ago on most

shoots by digital image and audio files, created separately by the camera crew and the sound crew.

- *Telecine:* The term for marrying image and audio files into a format editors can work with. Telecine originally referred to converting motion picture film into videotape. Now it covers any conversion of image and audio files.
- *Offline Editing:* The editing process from dailies to locked picture. The editing is "offline" because it's nonlinear; scenes are edited and repositioned until the network signs off on the final cut. As a cost-saving measure, the digital files used for offline editing are more compressed than the finished product, requiring less storage space.
- *Temp Sound and Music:* Temporary sound effects and music in a cut. The director will play with these elements before you get your own shot. Temp sound and music are critically important when showing cuts to execs.
- *Cuts:* On most series, work proceeds from editor's cut to director's cut to producer's (showrunner's) cut to studio cut to network cut, which leads to locked picture, the final cut. There can be intermediate cuts. For example, two or three network cuts may be required before lock. You oversee all this work, incorporating notes. Traditionally, the showrunner has final cut, though this can change at the premium end of the spectrum, where directors and studios might exert more influence.
- *Spotting:* Once a picture is locked, the time code becomes fixed, which allows you to "spot" music and additional sound elements, picking the exact moments where an effect or cue should begin and end. Some shows use a single spotting session for both music and sound. I split them up, handling the music myself and delegating the sound spotting.
- *ADR:* This stands for automated dialogue replacement (or additional dialogue replacement, depending on whom you talk to). It's the process of rerecording actors to either add dialogue or replace dialogue that got messed up during production. Audio glitches can happen for a variety of reasons: equipment problems, background noise

(airplanes are frequent offenders), overlapping dialogue. Sometimes, you'll want a different line reading from an actor. Some cast members bristle at that, which is why the post supervisor (who conducts ADR sessions) might blame other factors when trying to coax an alternate interpretation from an actor. When ADR is used to add dialogue, it's most often to provide exposition or help the pace of a scene. For example, you can add a line while the camera is on an actor's back or insert entire exchanges over a shot of a car driving down a road. A visit to an ADR session should be part of your education.

- *Loop Group or Walla Group:* A team of improvisational actors who provide ambient background dialogue and other bits of speech needed to fill out a scene. If a sequence takes place in a busy restaurant, for example, during filming you'll see plenty of diners apparently talking, but they're actually miming to avoid creating background noise. This trick allows you to edit different takes with seamless background levels. Once the picture is locked, the loop group (or walla group—from the "walla, walla, walla" allegedly mumbled to create crowd noise) is brought in to provide all background dialogue. Loop groups are highly versatile and can supply everything from foreign accents to airport flight announcements to police radio bulletins.
- *Foley:* Named for sound effects pioneer Jack Foley, Foley is an invaluable part of the postproduction process. Practically every sound created by action on-screen, from a door closing to a purse being zipped to a character being slapped, is re-created by a Foley artist. This bag of tricks allows sound mixers to have options on the mix stage. For example, if an actor's dialogue on the production track is marred by a door closing in the background, ADR will rerecord the actor and Foley will supply a variety of door closings that can be mixed into the picture without stepping on the dialogue. Or say the action calls for the door to creak more than it did on set; Foley will supply several varieties of creak that match the action. You should visit a Foley stage to appreciate the imaginative range of materials

and techniques used to make your show sound good. It's like dropping in on the old days of radio.

- *Sound Effects:* Just about everything not covered to this point—from gunfire to car squeals to explosions—falls into the category of sound effects. Sound effects experts have vast libraries of sounds and are always looking to add to their inventory. Don't like that ship's whistle? Here are a dozen more.
- *Music Editorial:* While the composer is creating an original score, the music supervisor is finding needle drops and handling license fees.
- *Online Editing:* Once the picture is locked, the offline becomes the online edit, assembled in linear form at full resolution. There are still technical tasks to be performed on the picture, but most of this work, like color correction and laying in titles, rarely requires your input.
- *Mixing:* When the music and sound elements are ready, they're combined and balanced on the mix stage. On most broadcast and basic cable shows, the mix team has two days to do their work. When they're ready, you're brought in to watch final playback with the coproducer, sound supervisor, and post supervisor. The editor and writer of the episode are often there as well—the editor for input, the writer largely for education. The director is invited as part of the DGA agreement but in broadcast and basic cable rarely attends (as explained in chapter 40); customs are different in situations where directors have more authority. At playback, the episode is run without a break from beginning to end. You scribble notes on a legal pad (you're in the dark and things are moving too fast for use of a laptop), noting the time code when problems arise, which can range from unintelligible dialogue to dissatisfaction with music to background elements. Sound mixers, particularly on episodes that aren't terribly challenging, will often throw in background elements to augment a scene. These extra touches are often subtle and effective, but occasionally, the mixers have to be saved from themselves. Watch out for barking dogs and lonely freight trains.

- *Layback, Dubs, and Delivery of Masters:* This covers everything that happens to an episode after the mix through distribution. Constantly evolving standards have put pressure on post to deliver episodes weeks earlier than in the past, particularly on streaming platforms that require subtitles or dubbing for international consumption. Fortunately, none of this normally requires your active participation; some of it, however, might affect your writing schedule.

The Art of Editing

Editing a television episode is an art form with discrete stages; like an artist creating an oil painting, you don't do it all at once. You stand back from the canvas, assess, move in, make changes, stand back, make more changes. And you don't start with your finest horsehair brush, but with a palette knife to move big chunks of paint around. Only after you're satisfied with the overall composition do you start refining details, and even then, you don't do the actual brushwork yourself—you empower the editor to use their skills.

To save time, much of your initial communication with an editor can be through written notes. Streaming technology makes it possible to view cuts from anywhere at any time, allowing you to do other things during office hours. I typically view cuts at home at night so that the editor can wake up to my comments. The latest software allows you to embed notes directly into the cut, which saves time for both you and the editor—you don't have to write out time code, and the editor doesn't have to read it; the note is right there.

You can deliver initial notes in person, of course, but if you do, leave the edit bay immediately afterward; do not sit down to "help." Editing is where showrunners go to hide. It's dark and quiet and peaceful, making it easy to forget about the thousand other things you should be doing. And the editor doesn't need your help in the early going. Looking at the episode together should be the last step of your process in most cases, not the first.

Your initial notes should focus on structure: Is the story working? Do you need to shuffle scenes? On ensemble shows with multiple storylines, the script will often present scenes in an alternating pattern. Because we use colored note cards in the writers room, it's what I call "the rainbow effect": red, blue, green, yellow, red, blue, green, yellow. Not only is this aesthetically pleasing on the bulletin board, but execs like the symmetry. There may be slight variations to accommodate a longer "A" story, but execs tend to get nervous if you mix things up too radically in an outline or script.

But reading is not viewing. What might have seemed like a logical balance on the page can become tedious or even confusing on-screen. Some storylines may require more immediate continuity, while others can wait. This is particularly true on series that employ act breaks. Because execs are often quick to criticize outlines that don't include at least one scene from every story in each act, I've made concessions on paper that I knew I'd change in editing—and when I did, I heard no complaints, because the new structure worked. Some episodes end up well-rounded, others well-lopsided. It all depends on what the film's telling you.

A side note: although directors have the right to rearrange and omit scenes, most won't because they recognize that's treading on your turf. If an editor tells me a director has dropped scenes or played with the order, I ask for the footage to be restored before I view it. It could be the director made a good call, but I have a firm sense of the shooting script embedded in my mind and need to see the original structure to determine whether I think the director's changes are warranted.

On shows with a fixed running time, your first pass may also need to address length. Ideally, on a show with a forty-two-and-a-half-minute limit, a director's cut will come in three to five minutes over, providing enough room to edit without dropping scenes. Omitting some scenes is inevitable over the course of a season, but deleting too many is costly—and wasteful.

Virtually any director's cut can benefit from tightening, so if it comes in short, your hands are correspondingly tied. (This is assuming that all scenes have been included in the director's cut.) Though it's easy to blame a short director's cut on the director, the fault often lies with the script, whose running time may have been overestimated—it's an imprecise science. When the editor's cut is being assembled during shooting, you may get an early warning that the episode is running short, which may allow you to pad scenes or even add scenes remaining to be filmed, but it's often too late to make meaningful changes. And because it's impractical on most broadcast and basic cable series to shoot additional scenes after principal filming is done, you usually have to make the best of a short cut, letting some sequences limp along to fill out the time.

Once you've attacked the big picture—structure and length—your next level of notes should focus on execution. The temptation is to give specific shot instructions: "At 2:12:02, let's be on Ava, not Catherine." But not only are such notes time-consuming for you to deliver, they also deny the editor the opportunity to work their magic. I start with general instructions: "Right now, this scene is about Catherine. Let's make it more about Ava." Let the editor interpret that for the next pass.

In broadcast, you've usually got four days from director's cut to producer's cut. If you have a disaster on your hands, you might have to sit down immediately with the editor to run the episode—or at least problematic sequences—but in most cases, for the first two days, it's more efficient to communicate through written notes. You'll sense when you've reached the point where it's more practical to sit in. When you do, you engage the editor in continuous conversation: "Is that the best shot we have?" "That moment has always bothered me; what can we do about it?" "Is there a better performance?" The editor will present specific options or explain why alternatives don't exist. You're largely tweaking at this stage, adding final brushstrokes and dashes of color. (For basic editing terms, see appendix B.)

There may be one or two challenging sequences that require the editor to rack up the gallery of relevant dailies so that you can hunt for solutions together. In such cases, you may end up literally rewriting a scene by inverting the order of dialogue or employing other tricks to make it work.

Under the broadcast and basic cable model, once you've delivered the producer's cut, the studio usually has two days to get back to you with notes. Having seen the dailies, a savvy exec will offer more questions than criticisms: "I assume that's the best shot of Jack we have?" "Is there a reason we don't have a wide shot of the house?" Mediocre execs will be more demanding and less understanding. Once you've incorporated the studio's notes, you go through the same drill with the network. You might have to generate two or more network cuts before being given the go-ahead to lock picture. At that point, the visual editing is done. Though additional effects may remain to be inserted, they'll be added within the locked time code. Your next level of involvement is with sound and music spotting.

Sound Spotting

I deputize a writer to oversee whatever ADR, sound effects, and other elements may be needed for an episode, reviewing concerns beforehand. You might ask a staffer to write some specific background elements (like a TV newscaster who didn't appear in the shooting script), but if such matters are insignificant, they can be left to the loop group.

Music Spotting

I love sitting down with the composer and music editor to discuss where music goes and what it should say. On a typical episode, I've already put in the temp score, which provides a template, and we bat it around from there. You don't need specific musical knowledge to communicate with a composer, just a sense of what you think is needed within a scene: "I want to feel Sonia's loneliness here" or "I want the audience to feel proud of what she's accomplished." Being an amateur musician, I can get specific at times—"How about solo piano here?" or "What about a pedal point with strings?" I think it amuses the composers more than irritates them—at least, I hope so.

Tricks of the Trade

Editors have an impressive array of wizardry at their fingertips, which can enhance or even salvage sequences, as needed. A few examples:

- *Transitions:* Most transitions are simple dissolves or hard cuts, but there are other effects "in the box" that you can evaluate instantly. It's amazing, particularly for those of us old enough to have worked in the days of film, when a simple dissolve required the editor to mark the "A" and "B" sides of the work print with a grease pencil, then wait three days for the results to come back from the lab—and you couldn't change it once it was done. But be wary: misuse of fancy transitions can make your episode look more like a proud parent's home movie of their three-year-old than an episode of quality television.
- *Enlargement:* Blowing up shots digitally to achieve a closer angle or eliminate unwanted background elements. It's generally advised to stay under 20 percent enlargement, but depending on the footage, you can go further without losing quality—as much as 200 percent for a quick insert, I've been told. What's especially useful is the ability to create a subtle push-in or pull-out for dramatic effect.
- *Changing Speed:* Slowing things down or speeding things up digitally. The higher the degree, the greater risk of degrading the image, but it can be useful.
- *Rotoscoping/Painting:* Removing unwanted images and altering on-screen elements through digital masks and brushes. One common use is "painting out" wires used to fly characters and objects, but all sorts of situations arise, both planned and unplanned, that may require this magic.

Edit Bay Protocol

- Do not snap fingers to indicate where to cut. "Right there! (*Snap!*)." It's a natural impulse. I used to do it all the time. Editors hate it.
- Ask why a certain shot is in a cut before asking the editor to remove or replace it. It could be that there are no decent alternatives.
- Similarly, ask the editor's opinion about a problematic sequence before tearing it apart. The editor may have a better version in their cut. As a rule, editors do not throw directors under the bus, but if questioned about an unfortunate sequence, they may respond, "Would you like to see my cut?"—which is a polite way of saying they think their cut was better before the director "improved" it.

Realities of Editing

- There's no such thing as a perfect cut. Corollary: you will never have all the performances or coverage you want. Before a script is written, everything's possible. When it's written, less is possible. When it's shot, still less is possible. The edit bay is the final reality. If you've spent time on a TV set, you know how challenging it is for directors to make their days. The footage you end up with is the best they could deliver under the circumstances. Any director worth their salt will have a litany of shots they wish they could add or redo on every episode. But as is said, perfect is the enemy of good.
- We see as much with our ears as with our eyes. I learned this on my first showrunning job on *Picket Fences*. CBS had come up with a promotional gimmick known as "tornado week." Every show in the prime-time lineup had to feature a tornado. (There's a reason broadcast lost its empire.) On *Picket*, we had a scene set inside a store while a storm was brewing outside. During filming, big off-screen fans blew stuff past the windows, but when I watched the scene with

the editor, it didn't register at all. I despaired. "Wait," the editor said, then turned a few knobs to bring up the sound of howling wind and rattling windows. In the blink of an eye, I saw everything. My ears directed my eyes to what was going on in the background. It was amazing. Sound can make viewers believe there's more happening onscreen than what literally exists.

- No exec knows how to look at a rough cut. They'll tell you they do, but they don't. This was true even before the current glut of newly minted executives flooded the market. When execs watch a cut—any cut—they expect a finished picture with full visual effects, sound effects, ADR, and music. The moral: provide the most complete viewing experience you can. And be prepared. The editor will put a title over a scene that reads, "Eiffel Tower to be added in background," but when you get your notes call, the exec will say, "Hey, what happened to the Eiffel Tower?" Exhale. All will be well.

Director Deficits

I sympathize with directors, but they're often their own worst enemies in the edit bay. In broadcast, they have only four days to edit their episodes, they don't have final cut, and they're typically giving edit notes while prepping for an episode on another series. Some common problems that result:

- Directors may use too much coverage in their cuts. This might seem an odd criticism, but it's a function of directors needing to please many masters. Knowing they must give the showrunner and executives choices for every scene if they want to keep working, episodic directors strive to provide maximum coverage of every scene, which is great. But having done so, they often feel a corresponding need to utilize every bit of it, which isn't necessarily great. Certain scenes benefit by using fewer shots of longer duration. I remember a director being astonished when in my cut I stayed in his initial master of a scene until forced to cut away to maintain continuity. Though he had given me plenty of options, the master told the story elegantly.

- Directors can be too "democratic" with coverage. In dialogue scenes between two characters, directors tend to favor the speaker. It's logical, but the practice can diminish the effectiveness of a scene depending on what's being said. Sometimes it's more important to register the reaction of the listener.
- Directors may confuse speed with pace. Pace is not simply a matter of tempo, but also of rhythm and dynamics. To keep things moving, some directors race through their cuts, using a profusion of short shots. Not only can relentless speed become monotonous, it can also inhibit comprehension. Sometimes you need to slow things down to speed things up.
- Directors often misuse music. They start it too early and use temp music that telegraphs a scene rather than supports it. This is such a common problem that I often ask editors to show me directors' cuts "dry," without music. Someone told me that Steven Spielberg once said it helps to look at a cut without any sound at all to see if the story's being told effectively. Even if he never said it, I get it.

Pilots

Pilots present special challenges. If a pilot represents the first time you've been intimately involved with a cut, you're in for an intense ride because the director and executives will exercise significantly greater control than they would with a conventional episode. Once past the pilot, things should loosen up. (I'm referring to broadcast and basic cable; directors and executives in newer platforms may wield considerable influence throughout the life of a series.) Although you'll still have a steep learning curve ahead, the process will become more familiar and your confidence will grow.

Confession

At the risk of being considered a heretic, I have a confession: I don't watch dailies. To clarify, I don't watch dailies once a series has achieved a certain level of stability. This saves time and allows me to view the director's cut with fresh eyes. I assign the writer of the episode—or deputize someone on staff if the episode was written by a freelancer—to write a dailies report, circulated to the entire writing staff, summarizing the previous day's shooting and highlighting anything particularly good or bad. I make cautionary or congratulatory phone calls accordingly. For the most part, however, when I view a director's cut, I'm seeing the footage for the first time.

Two arguments in my defense: First, unless you're willing to look at every minute of dailies, the most you're going to watch is a take or two before fast-forwarding to the next setup, which adds little to your ultimate ability to edit the episode but subtracts precious minutes from your day. Second, dailies can be deceptive. "Good" dailies—dailies that make writers laugh and cheer—don't necessarily make a good episode, and "bad" dailies—footage that seems routine—can result in a terrific episode. So even if you should make time to watch everything, you won't know if an episode really works until you've seen it put together. It's all part of the art—and mystery—of what we do.

43

TWO SUITCASES

WORK-LIFE BALANCE

Showrunning exacts such a heavy toll on personal lives that many writers ask if it's even possible to have one. I say yes, but not without conscious effort—otherwise, like Homer's Lotus Eaters, you may forget you even have a home. Not only is work-life balance possible, but I believe it's essential for a long career. I liken it to walking through an airport with two heavy suitcases. (I'm referring to the days before suitcases had wheels—yes, there was such a time.) If you carried a single suitcase, you tended to keel over; carrying a second bag kept you upright and moving—if you didn't collapse. That was the key: not collapsing. The same can be said for showrunning. The first suitcase is the job, the second is everything else that makes you a healthy human being. How do you manage both?

Check in with Yourself

One of the more pernicious myths about Hollywood success is that it will somehow make you a happier person. It can certainly make you a wealthier person and a more famous person, but the one thing it can't do is shield you from yourself. "The job just makes you more of who you were," is the way one showrunner put it. As was said earlier, showrunning is a heat-seeking missile that will find the holes in your psyche and blow them wide open should you be caught unprepared. The best defense is knowing yourself, and for that, some therapy may be in order.

I believe everyone can benefit from therapy before entering a high-stress situation. If you haven't taken a look under your hood in a while—or ever—I encourage you to do so. Review your checklist of personal priorities. Success is a moving target. What you wanted at twenty won't necessarily be the same as what you want at thirty or forty or fifty. What are you working toward, and why? The goalposts may have shifted without you realizing it. Balance begins with you.

Take Care of Yourself

It's not just your mind and soul that need tending, but your body as well. "Let me sleep on it" is more than a cliché; it's a prescription for clear thinking, good relationships, and constructive work. You need to get a good night's sleep. Exercise and diet are additional components. Even if you only take a ten-minute walk a few times a day, you need to use a muscle other than your brain. Writers rooms are notorious bastions of bad food, so watch those carbs. And see your doctor on a regular basis. As showrunner, it's easy to convince yourself that you're too busy or important to keep regular medical appointments. That's just stupid. Do all you can to protect your health, because without it, you're no good to anyone—especially yourself.

Set Boundaries

To maintain balance, you need to set a line between where work begins and ends and where you begin and end. As showrunner, you could live at the office 24/7 and always have more to do. Consequently, you don't go home because your work is done; you go home because you choose to. Set reasonable work hours. It's an open secret that ideas don't suddenly improve after 9 p.m.

You only convince yourself they do. Releasing your staff in time for dinner not only boosts morale, it also results in better episodes. There may be times when you have to burn the midnight oil, but make those the exception, not the rule. And be sure that when you're home, you're home. One of the lessons from the COVID-19 pandemic is that working from home can actually increase stress, not reduce it. As one colleague put it: "I wasn't working from home; I was sleeping at work." Setting boundaries isn't an excuse for doing less than your best; it's a means of producing your best.

Communicate

There's no way to anticipate how the job is going to disrupt your personal relationships, so it's important to communicate as openly and often as you can with those you care about. It's easy to fall into a bunker mentality, believing no one outside your immediate circle of coworkers can understand what you're going through. It reminds me of something a cop told me years ago when I was a reporter: "There are only two people I trust in this world, my partner and my wife. And I'm not too sure about my wife." The pressures of the job can create bonds under stress that are difficult to explain to someone who's not part of it. What's more, your significant other (should you have one) might display limited interest in your difficulties while dealing with difficulties of their own. Although your personal conversations may not be as catchy as what's in your scripts, keep a genuine dialogue going with those near and dear to you. Express what's important and listen to what they have to say to you.

Look Up

Find a way to regularly remind yourself that there's a higher power at work in the universe than studio execs and network metrics. Whether your spiritual side takes the form of religion, yoga, meditation, music, or the outdoors, anything that feeds the soul should be encouraged. Recreation helps, too. I coached my sons' soccer teams from when they were eight until they were out of middle school. Because I was also chief coach for the region, I was in charge of the practice schedule and assigned myself Friday afternoons, which allowed me to get back to the office if necessary when practice was over. Nothing will take you out of your own troubles faster than dealing with a bunch of young soccer players—and their parents. I figured if I couldn't afford to take the last two hours of the work week away from my office every fall, I was doing something wrong. No regrets.

Beware the Beast

In the course of running your show, it's likely you'll reach a point where you don't know how you're going to make it through the next day, never mind the rest of the season. You're exhausted, at your lowest, which is when everything you're up against—the schedule, the stress, the incipient panic—metamorphoses into a monster with giant claws and razor teeth. The Beast from Hell, who's coming after you—fast. You could be working eighteen-hour days seven days a week. The Beast doesn't care. It just wants pages. It devours pages. It will kill for pages. You'll think your executives are trying to kill you, too. No, they're only shoving you in front to keep the Beast from eating *them*.

The Beast may be a fiction, but the dilemma is real. You're trapped in a nightmare, seemingly with no way out. Successful showrunners employ different strategies to keep the Beast at bay. One colleague I know closes the door to her office and crawls beneath her desk for a little "me" time. Literally. She emerges a few minutes later, ready to calmly carry on—not dissimilar to the effect of the "squeeze box" that animal behaviorist Temple Grandin built to control her anxieties, as depicted so movingly by Claire Danes in the eponymous HBO movie.

Some showrunners keep a bottle of Valium or other antianxiety medication close by; having it within reach is often enough to keep them from needing to use it. Dependence on any drug is to be strictly avoided, of course, but the pressures of the job can make judicious use of proper medication beneficial on occasion. I've been known to keep a bottle of Kentucky's finest in my bottom drawer; on the rare occasion, the bottle will emerge during daylight hours to fortify a cup of coffee with just a big enough dose to take the edge off a difficult moment.

At times, the most effective way to tame the Beast is to call someone who knows what you're going through. I turn to my oldest friend in the business to say, "Look, I know I'm going to get through this, but I need to hear you tell me I'm going to get through this." When he does, my heart rate goes down, my breathing returns to normal, and we talk through the crisis. And all's well. Until next time.

Side note: whatever your method, don't let your fellow workers see you at your worst. They expect you to be always in control, so do your coping in private.

Know When to Leave

Your goal is to stay in the job, hang in there. Quitting may give you a reputation that can be difficult to overcome. The only exception—and it's crucial—is when your emotional, psychological, or physical well-being is at risk. If you feel like you're losing control, literally asking yourself, "What's happening to me?"—then you need to stop and get help, at least for a moment, consequences be damned. Thankfully, most showrunners never reach this point. Even when things are darkest, events don't threaten their sense of self. When that line gets crossed, however, when you no longer trust yourself, then it's time to take a step back and possibly step away. Your first obligation is to yourself and your family. No work is more important than your health. As related earlier, I walked away from *Hill Street Blues* for a week when I felt I couldn't go on. With the help of family and friends, I regained my grip on that second suitcase. And it got me through.

44

FADE OUT

THE ROAD AHEAD

It's been said that we never finish scripts in Hollywood, we just abandon them. I feel that way about this book, reluctant to let go because there will be more to say tomorrow about this rapidly changing business. Within these pages I've tried to concentrate on those aspects of writing and showrunning that won't change with the latest technology or trend in consumer behavior. Nevertheless, it's inevitable that future disruptions will have unforeseen consequences. Recognizing that, I'll close with a few observations, rather than predictions.

To me, the most astounding development in mass entertainment over the past twenty-five years has been the blurring of the line between movies and television. As I'm fond of telling students, there's a new word for independent film today; it's called television. My college classmate Richard Peña, a professor of film at Columbia and longtime program director of the New York Film Festival, recently told me, "My students nowadays tend to be much more close-minded about cinema than they were in the 1990s. Their frame of reference is TV. Rather than referring to a Bergman film, for example, they'll say, 'It's like that episode of *The Wire*.'" It's an ironic comment on how far the circle has revolved since Richard and I graduated in 1975. Back then, cinema was king; television was crap. Now television is seen as the cutting-edge creative force in scripted drama.

Compounding matters, the COVID-19 pandemic crippled movie attendance while boosting television viewing. The long-term impact of the crisis has yet to be determined, but it appears doubtful that moviegoing will return to prepandemic levels any time soon, if at all.

Other ironies abound. When I was earning my stripes in broadcast, I thought the promise of emerging technologies was that television writers would be able to find select audiences to support original material. And that has largely come true—though with unintended consequences. The rise of niche programming and narrowcasting has promoted levels of polarization and intolerance in this country not seen since the late 1960s. Television is no longer the public square; it's an endless prairie in which viewers never have to leave their private silos, marinating in their fixed values and beliefs. Although I marvel at the variety of voices and visions now available on television, we no longer watch it as a community, and I wonder how we can regain a sense of mutual understanding without the benefit of mutual experience.

Another less lofty, more focused area of concern to me is the status of television writers in general and showrunners in particular. The rise of subscription cable and streaming has led to unprecedented freedom for television writers, but through the proliferation of short-order series and mini-rooms, this ascendance has also contributed to the erosion of job security and professional apprenticeships. The new platforms also have taken money out of writers' pockets through business practices that conceal audience numbers, preventing writers from using such data as leverage in negotiations. At platforms like Netflix, series creators don't have equity in their own series; the platform owns the shows, which makes most creators and showrunners more employees than partners.

What disturbs me most are threats to the showrunner's authority. Here, too, the danger comes principally from subscription cable and streaming, but broadcast and basic cable may feel compelled to follow their lead in the mistaken belief that it will keep them more competitive. To the degree that studios and platforms treat television more as an extension of the movies and less as a unique medium of its own, the influence of directors and executives will grow at the expense of writers and showrunners. So, even as my friend Richard laments the loss of cinema's status among students, the movies may be having something of a last laugh—or at least a prolonged chuckle.

Of course, it's hardly a black-and-white situation; there are far too many platforms for one business model to dominate—and there are signs that Netflix and others may have to adjust their protocols to remain competitive themselves. Despite Peak TV's astounding refusal to die in the face of continual expansion, some contraction of platforms is inevitable. The leviathans will eventually swallow smaller rivals or drive them out of business. What effect this will have on writers and showrunners is an open question, but fewer companies exercising greater control has rarely been good for labor in any field.

But I didn't come this far to end on a note of dejection. By virtually any standard, there's never been a better time to write for television. What problems exist are minor compared to the opportunities available to writers with the vision and boldness to seize them. Ultimately, the best defense against today's challenges for writers is to do what writers have always done: write. And not write merely well, but outstandingly well, so that when a studio or platform wants to do business with you, they have to do it on your terms. It's like the moment in *The Road Warrior* when Mad Max addresses the besieged encampment: "You wanna git outta here, you talk to me." It's this bravado—and the skill to back it up—that led to the rise of the showrunner, and it's this same combination that will keep the showrunner in demand. Your writing gives you the leverage; your managerial skills keep you at the head of the table. You wanna git outta here, you talk to me.

BUDGETING 101

For those wanting a deeper dive into budgets, here's a brief analysis of a simplified budget.

This is the top sheet of a pattern budget for a broadcast or basic cable series of ten episodes with eight weeks of preproduction. The "pattern" refers to the budget that applies equally to every episode in your order. ("Locked Pattern Budget" means it's the final version, hence "locked.") The amounts for each line item are supported by many pages of supplementary line items with hierarchical subcategory designations, allowing you to trace every penny that goes into the top-sheet totals.

You'll note the budget is divided into two overall categories, above-the-line and below-the-line. "The line" refers to the distinction between creative and production costs: creative costs go above, production costs below. Though hardly a perfect filter, it's a useful frame of reference to determine how your production is fiscally balanced. For example, if you're working with a relatively unknown cast on an effects-heavy show, you'd expect your above-the-line to be relatively small and your below-the-line to be relatively large. If working with a star-studded cast and a big-name director, you'd expect the above-the-line to consume a greater portion of the budget. This illustration features a typical ratio of nearly three-to-one in below-the-line costs to above-the-line costs.

LOCKED PATTERN BUDGET - LOS ANGELES

DIRECTOR:
EXEC PRODUCERS:
CO-EXEC PRODUCERS:
LINE PRODUCER:
NOTES:
Holidays:(2)During Shoot; Memorial Day, July 4th

Acct#	Category Description	Page	Orig	Total	Var
111-00	STORY RIGHTS	1	$52,787	$52,787	$0
112-00	SCENARIO	1	$200,065	$200,065	$0
113-00	PRODUCER	3	$153,628	$153,628	$0
114-00	DIRECTOR	4	$60,861	$60,861	$0
115-00	PRINCIPAL CAST	5	$523,376	$523,376	$0
116-00	SUPPORTING CAST	7	$200,230	$200,230	$0
117-00	STUNTS	7	$28,108	$28,108	$0
	TOTAL ABOVE-THE-LINE		**$1,219,055**	**$1,219,055**	**$0**
121-00	EXTRAS	9	$78,388	$78,388	$0
122-00	PRODUCTION	9	$167,930	$167,930	$0
123-00	ART DEPARTMENT	13	$48,454	$48,454	$0
124-00	SET CONSTRUCTION	15	$121,873	$121,873	$0
126-00	GRIP / SET OPERATIONS	16	$160,900	$160,900	$0
127-00	SPECIAL EFFECTS	19	$29,871	$29,871	$0
128-00	SET DRESSING	20	$119,224	$119,224	$0
129-00	PROPERTY	22	$47,819	$47,819	$0
130-00	PICTURE VEHICLES/ANIMALS	22	$11,034	$11,034	$0
131-00	SET LIGHTING	23	$142,999	$142,999	$0
132-00	CAMERA	24	$167,325	$167,325	$0
133-00	SOUND	26	$53,286	$53,286	$0
134-00	WARDROBE	27	$100,145	$100,145	$0
135-00	MAKEUP & HAIR	30	$80,478	$80,478	$0
136-00	TRANSPORTATION	31	$352,041	$352,041	$0
137-00	LOCATION EXPENSES	37	$369,721	$369,721	$0
	TOTAL PRODUCTION		**$2,051,488**	**$2,051,488**	**$0**
211-00	EDITORIAL	40	$69,822	$69,822	$0
212-00	MUSIC	40	$57,014	$57,014	$0
213-00	SOUND EDITORIAL	41	$46,338	$46,338	$0
214-00	TITLES	41	$3,980	$3,980	$0
215-00	POST PROD FILM & LAB	41	$97,000	$97,000	$0
	TOTAL POST PRODUCTION		**$274,153**	**$274,153**	**$0**
311-00	AMORTIZED SERIES COSTS	43	$790,220	$790,220	$0
	TOTAL OTHER		**$790,220**	**$790,220**	**$0**
	Total Above-The-Line		**$1,219,055**	**$1,219,055**	**$0**
	Total Below-The-Line		**$3,115,861**	**$3,115,861**	**$0**
	Total Above and Below-The-Line		**$4,334,916**	**$4,334,916**	**$0**
	Grand Total		**$4,334,916**	**$4,334,916**	**$0**

Series Pattern/10 Eps/8 wks Prod Prep (incl Writers)

Credit: Craig Siebels

LOCKED AMORT

DIRECTOR: VARIOUS
EXEC PRODUCERS:
CO-EXEC PRODUCERS:
LINE PRODUCER:
NOTES: LOCKED VERSION
Holidays:(2)During Shoot; Memorial Day, July 4th

Acct#	Category Description	Page	Orig	Total	Var
112-00	SCENARIO		$315,746	$315,746	$0
113-00	PRODUCER		$135,931	$135,931	$0
114-00	DIRECTOR		$25,897	$25,897	$0
115-00	PRINCIPAL CAST		$9,231	$9,231	$0
	TOTAL ABOVE-THE-LINE		$486,805	$486,805	$0
121-00	EXTRAS		$4,459	$4,459	$0
122-00	PRODUCTION		$493,696	$493,696	$0
123-00	ART DEPARTMENT		$176,797	$176,797	$0
124-00	SET CONSTRUCTION		$1,143,723	$1,143,723	$0
125-00	SET STRIKE		$127,711	$127,711	$0
126-00	GRIP / SET OPERATIONS		$313,800	$313,800	$0
127-00	SPECIAL EFFECTS		$5,274	$5,274	$0
128-00	SET DRESSING		$624,991	$624,991	$0
129-00	PROPERTY		$55,000	$55,000	$0
130-00	PICTURE VEHICLES		$7,420	$7,420	$0
131-00	SET LIGHTING		$782,766	$782,766	$0
132-00	CAMERA		$59,612	$59,612	$0
133-00	SOUND		$8,447	$8,447	$0
134-00	WARDROBE		$255,733	$255,733	$0
135-00	MAKEUP & HAIR		$33,600	$33,600	$0
136-00	TRANSPORTATION		$410,874	$410,874	$0
137-00	LOCATION EXPENSES		$93,738	$93,738	$0
138-00	GENERAL EXPENSES		$702,252	$702,252	$0
139-00	TESTS		$15,000	$15,000	$0
140-00	SECOND UNIT		$250,000	$250,000	$0
141-00	STAGE & BACKLOT RENTAL		$971,380	$971,380	$0
	TOTAL PRODUCTION		$6,536,275	$6,536,275	$0
211-00	EDITORIAL		$367,675	$367,675	$0
212-00	MUSIC		$17,500	$17,500	$0
214-00	TITLES		$43,950	$43,950	$0
216-00	STOCK SHOTS		$50,000	$50,000	$0
	TOTAL POST PRODUCTION		$479,125	$479,125	$0
411-00	PROD FEES/INSURANCE/LEGAL		$399,995	$399,995	$0
	TOTAL OTHER		$399,995	$399,995	$0
	Total Above-The-Line		$486,805	$486,805	$0
	Total Below-The-Line		$7,415,395	$7,415,395	$0
	Total Above and Below-The-Line		$7,902,200	$7,902,200	$0
	Grand Total		$7,902,200	$7,902,200	$0

Amort/10 Eps/8 wks Prod Prep (incl Writers)

Page# 1

Credit: Craig Siebels

And that's it, really: your bare-bones intro to what a pattern budget is all about. From here, you can continue down the rabbit hole through increasing layers of detail to your heart's content.

Actually, I lied; there is one line item in the pattern that requires additional explanation: 311-00, "Amortized Series Costs." This number involves a separate document, the amortization budget, known as "the amort," which is an accounting device that distributes certain costs evenly across the entire season. This sub-budget results in a single line item inserted into the pattern budget. Sounds complicated—and it is, a little, but it's easier to understand when you take a look.

This is the top sheet of our sample amort budget. You'll see that most of the categories are the same as in the pattern budget, but the allocations have specific reasons for being entered in this document rather than in the pattern. For example, category 112-00, "Scenario," includes writers and related office staff. The figure of $315,746 accounts for eight weeks of writing and related administrative work before shooting begins. Such costs can't be assigned to specific episodes; the work it pays for will be reflected in every episode. Because the series order is for ten episodes, the cost is divided distributed among all ten.

Similarly, 124-00, "Set Construction," represents the cost of standing sets to be used throughout the season, so that hefty total of $1,143,723 should also be shared by all episodes. When all the amort items are added up, the total comes to $7,902,200. Divided by ten episodes, that rounds out to $790,220, which then becomes line item 311-00, inserted into the pattern budget. So while you might find the rationale behind specific amort items mystifying, the overall principle is relatively easy to grasp.

* * * * * * * *

No matter how well you prepare, once shooting begins, you'll discover certain budget assumptions don't play out as predicted. You'll go over in some areas and under in others. It's like taking a ship out for sea trials: you don't know what you've got until you put the vessel through its paces. Subsequently, you and your line producer will be forced to adjust as best you can. But that's part of the fun. At least it helps to look at it that way.

THE VOCABULARY OF EDITING

OR, HOW TO SOUND REASONABLY SMART IN THE EDIT BAY

Mark Twain once said, "The difference between the almost right word and the right word is really a large matter—'tis the difference between the lightning bug and the lightning." That's particularly true in postproduction. Being conversant in the vocabulary of editing will help you communicate with the editor more efficiently, effectively, and enjoyably.

Shots

- *Coverage:* The sum of all shots used to film a scene. This refers to both the variety of shots and the number of individual takes (often invoked in negative terms, as in, "That's all the coverage we have?").
- *Master:* A shot including all actors and action in a scene.
- *Single:* A shot featuring one actor.
- *Two-shot:* A shot featuring two actors.
- *Three-shot:* A shot featuring three actors. And so forth up the line.
- *Three-quarters:* Referring to an actor's face; includes both eyes.

- *Profile:* An actor viewed from the side. When two actors are profiled facing each other, it's sometimes referred to as a "fifty-fifty shot."
- *Raking:* An angled shot of two or more actors; a driver and passenger in a car is a good example. The angle is raked to include both performers.
- *Over-the-shoulder:* In a scene between two actors, the camera shoots over the shoulder of Actor A to show Actor B. If only a small portion of Actor A is shown, it can be referred to as a "dirty single."
- *Clean:* Using above example, Actor B is shown in a single from Actor A's perspective, but without Actor A in frame. Over-the-shoulder shots establish the eyelines of the actors, which is important for continuity when cutting to singles. Clean shots are most often used for intimacy and impact.
- *French over:* Shot from behind, as in capturing two actors on a park bench, seeing only part of their faces. Originally developed as a cheap way to cover two actors in a car with the camera operator in the backseat, French overs can be used to convey atmosphere, particularly mystery or tension.
- *Dutch angle:* While we're on foreign names, a Dutch angle is deliberately tilted off axis, yielding a slanted horizon. Used for all kinds of dramatic effects. The term apparently didn't come from Holland, but from expressionist German films; "Dutch" is thought to be a corruption of "Deutsch."
- *Tracking shot:* The camera moves on a dolly mounted on actual tracks, most often moving alongside the subject. The Steadicam has replaced dollies in many cases, but tracks are still laid when a camera is needed to move smoothly and consistently over uneven or challenging terrain.
- *Dolly shot:* The camera is mounted on a dolly that's pushed or pulled by a dolly grip over a flat surface without tracks. A dolly shot is like a tracking shot but is more versatile because the dolly is free to move in multiple directions.
- *Steadicam:* Invented in 1975, the Steadicam is a camera-stabilization mount that allows the camera operator to

move anywhere while the camera remains steady. The Steadicam revolutionized filmmaking by facilitating all sorts of moving shots that wouldn't have been possible or would have been prohibitively time-consuming in the past.

- *Handheld (verité):* The camera is held by the operator without stabilization, creating the shaky feel of old-time documentaries, known as cinema verité.
- *Leading:* A moving shot in which the camera is in front of the subjects, looking back at them as they move forward.
- *Following:* The opposite of leading; a moving shot in which the camera follows the subjects from behind
- *Subjective:* The camera moves from the perspective of an actor or, occasionally, an object—like an arrow or guided missile.
- *A Camera/B Camera/C Camera:* When two or more cameras shoot a scene from different angles simultaneously, each camera receives a separate designation.
- *Push In/Push Out:* The camera is physically moved in or out, usually on a dolly.
- *Zoom In/Zoom Out:* The camera remains fixed, but a zoom lens is used. Generally considered more of a cliché than pushing in or pulling out but still has its uses.
- *Rack focus (focus pull):* Changing the focus from foreground element to background element or vice versa.
- *Tilt up/tilt down:* The camera tilts on its axis up or down from a fixed position, as opposed to the camera actually moving as in a crane shot.
- *Pan left/pan right:* The camera swivels on its axis left or right from a fixed position.
- *Insert shot:* A close-up of some detail in the scene, often shot separately from principal photography—for example, a character looking at a text message may require an insert of a cell phone.
- *Slow-mo:* Slow motion created by the camera shooting at a faster rate than the usual twenty-four frames per second. Although slow-mo can be created in post, it's not as elegant as shooting at a higher frame rate, which captures more detail.

- *Oner (pronounced "won-er"):* A scene covered in one continuous take. Oners can be highly efficient in a shooting schedule or consume significant time to set up depending on the requirements (Martin Scorsese's three-minute oner in *Wise Guys* is a classic example). While oners can be very effective, they handcuff the editor because there's nothing to cut away to.
- *Long shot:* A shot taken a considerable distance away from a subject.
- *Wide shot:* A shot covering the broadest range of a scene.
- *Medium shot:* A less wide shot.
- *Cowboy:* A variety of medium shot in which an actor is shown from the hips up, as in a shot of a cowboy holding a six-gun.
- *Extreme close-up:* A pair of eyes, for example, as opposed to an entire face.
- *Overhead shot (bird's-eye view):* An angle looking directly down on a scene.
- *Establishing shot:* Usually, an exterior without principal players in it to establish where a scene takes place—a helicopter shot of New York City, a hospital, a suburban home.
- *Crane shot:* A shot with the camera mounted on a moving platform that can move up and down; some cranes include room for a camera operator, others are remote-controlled. Drones are replacing cranes in many instances, as they can often perform similar functions with less setup and lower cost.
- *Helicopter (drone) shot:* An overhead shot, usually a moving shot, with the camera mounted on helicopter or drone. Helicopters are expensive; drones have become inexpensive, versatile substitutes in many instances.
- *VFX (visual effects):* Special effects are effects created live while shooting. VFX are added in post. In rough cuts, the editor will add titles to indicate where a VFX shot is intended to go.

Editing Terms

Some shorthand to make communication with an editor easier and more efficient.

- *Scroll:* Moving a cut continuously forward or back, as in, "Let's scroll to the point that Jill crosses the room."
- *Head:* The beginning of a shot or sequence.
- *Tail:* The end of a shot or sequence.
- *Trim:* Cut frames: "Let's trim the pause before Joan starts speaking."
- *Extend:* Add frames: "Can we extend the look on Steve's face?"
- *Open up:* If a scene seems too compressed, you can ask the editor to open it up, which generally means letting the scene breathe, giving it more air. This often translates into creating pauses, not being in such a hurry.
- *Tighten:* The opposite of opening up. If a scene is sluggish, you can ask the editor to take out air, which involves shortening or removing pauses, pulling up dialogue while on the speaker's back, and other tricks.
- *"A" side/"B" side:* If you want to add time to the opening of a shot and tighten the end of the next shot, you might say, "Let's extend head on the 'A' side and trim tail on the 'B' side." Similarly, you can refer to transitions between scenes as the "A" side and "B" side: "Let the siren decay over the 'B' side of the cut."
- *Roll the cut:* A convenient way to say you want to change the cut point between two shots without altering the overall length of a sequence; particularly useful in dialogue exchanges: "Let's roll the cut so we stay on Rick for both of his lines before going to Dave." This tells the editor to add tail to Rick and trim a corresponding amount of head from Dave.
- *Reverse angle:* Used to describe the other half of a camera setup: "After Clint pulls into town on his horse, let's go to the reverse and show what he sees"; "When Catherine's talking to Kim, I'd like to go to the reverse earlier."

- *Intercut:* To alternate shots from one or more scenes within the same sequence. A telephone call between two characters is a common example. Intercuts can be used for clarity, pace, and dramatic effect: "While the killer's stalking the banker, let's intercut the detective's car speeding through the city."
- *Double cut:* Used to return to a shot. Louise has just insulted Tom, who stammers a response, but you want to see Louise enjoying Tom's unease before he speaks: "Let's double cut to Louise before Tom replies."
- *Hard cut:* A direct cut between two scenes without any dissolve.
- *Smash cut:* An abrupt form of hard cut, often going from something tranquil to something dramatic or vice versa, leaving the "A" side or joining the "B" side in midaction, hence the "smash." Used mostly for dramatic effect, though it can be employed comedically, as well.
- *Dissolve/cross-fade:* A transition between scenes in which the "A" side fades into the "B" side. Can be long or short. Some people use cross-fade exclusively to describe an audio transition, but the terms are often synonymous.
- *Fade in/Fade out:* Like a dissolve, but the picture goes to black in a fade-out and comes up from black with a fade-in.
- *Pull up:* Applied to dialogue; trimming a pause before an actor speaks: "Let's pull up Joe's response."
- *Pre-lap:* A pre-lap begins dialogue or other sounds from the next scene before cutting to the location in which the pre-lap is actually taking place: "Let's pre-lap the classroom bell while on the school bus, then cut to the kids walking down the corridor."
- *Ramp in/Fade up:* To dial up the dialogue, sound, or music, as opposed to starting it at the ultimate level: "Let's ramp in the music on the cut"; "Let's fade up the crowd noise on the establishing shot of the church."
- *Decay/bleed over:* To dial down dialogue, sound, or music, letting it fade away: "Let the bugle decay over the beginning of the next scene"; "Let the applause bleed over the transition."

- *Hard out:* When you want the soundtrack on a scene to stop completely before the next scene.
- *Ring out:* Often used for music cues before act outs in broadcast and basic cable, ring out means to let the sound carry over into black.
- *Dry:* Without musical score. Because directors can overload their cuts with music, I often ask to see a director's cut dry.
- *Crossing the line:* This phrase throws a lot of writers but is relatively easy to understand. To maintain the proper physical relationship between actors on-screen from shot to shot, the camera has to observe a basic rule of perspective. A simple way to think of it: when two actors are talking, draw an invisible line between their noses; while they remain in that relative position, the camera has to stay on one side of that line or the other. If the camera "crosses the line," the actors' relative positions will appear to have flipped on-screen. The major reason you need to know this is to understand why you're occasionally missing certain coverage. You: "Don't we have a tighter shot of Dwayne?" Editor: "Yeah, we do, but they crossed the line"—meaning you can't use it. Too bad. It doesn't happen often, but it happens.

ACKNOWLEDGMENTS

Years ago, after pestering renowned writer-producer Richard Levinson (*Murder, She Wrote*; *Columbo*) for advice on showrunning, he shook his head: "Melvoin, you're like Diogenes with his lamp, searching for one perfectly run show." He was right. I *was* searching—and still am. Of course, what I've learned since (and what Richard was archly insinuating) is that there's no such thing as a perfectly run show. But there have been plenty of well-run shows, led by showrunners who have elevated the practice and inspired others through their example. I've tried to capture their collective wisdom in these pages and offer my sincere thanks to all.

I am personally indebted to my first boss in the business, Michael Gleason, showrunner of *Remington Steele*, for taking a chance on a young journalist in 1983 and letting him grow in the job. My thanks to David E. Kelley for entrusting his first series to me in 1995 when he stepped away from *Picket Fences*. Showrunner John Wirth, who started with me on *Remington Steele*, kick-started my educational writing in 1999 by suggesting that we coedit a WGA booklet on writing for episodic television. "It'll take a year," he said. It took five. (Thanks, John.) That effort led me to propose the Showrunner Training Program in 2005. John Wells was president of the WGA West, at the time. He got behind the idea and pitched it with me to the Alliance of

Motion Picture and Television Producers for funding, becoming a valued colleague and adviser in the process.

The hundreds of class members and scores of instructors who've participated in the Showrunner Training Program since its inception in 2006 have been invaluable to my own showrunning and to this book. I thank them for their candor and humor in sharing their stories. I particularly thank Carole Kirschner, the SRTP's professional director, who not only has been a steadfast collaborator from the program's start, but has provided many teaching opportunities for me around the world and encouraged me to write this book. Thanks, also, to showrunner Yvette Lee Bowser, my inspiring half-hour counterpart in the SRTP. I couldn't have asked for a better partner.

I've benefited from a number of excellent teachers over the years, but two bear special mention: Barbara June Patterson, my drama teacher at Highland Park High School in Highland Park, Illinois, and the playwright, screenwriter, and novelist Robert Anderson, who taught a writing seminar during my senior year at Harvard. I simply couldn't have gotten where I did without their talent and generosity.

Thanks to the many students, fellow instructors, and colleagues I've encountered at the places I've taught—particularly the Peter Stark Producing Program at the USC School of Cinematic Arts, the Film Institute of Cologne, UCLA, the Sundance Institute, and Harvard University, all of whom helped shape this book directly and indirectly. A special thanks to Jack Megan, director of the Office for the Arts at Harvard, who in 2007 encouraged me to create an undergraduate seminar on scriptwriting for the college, which continues to inform my teaching and showrunning. For almost twenty years, Katrina Wood, founder and CEO of the media consultancy group MediaXchange, has invited me to talk to writers and producers at her international forums, which have sharpened my insights into what we do well here in the States and what we can learn from others making television around the globe. My thanks to her.

My gratitude again to John Wells, this time for granting permission to reproduce his writers' schedule for *The West Wing*; to Audrey Gelb, vice president, production, at ABC Studios and

Dan Gilgore, vice president at Walt Disney Television, for securing permission to use the *Lost* and *Army Wives* outlines; to J. J. Abrams, Damon Lindelof, Eddie Kitsis, and Adam Horowitz for their additional authorization for the *Lost* outline; to Shawn Ryan for use of his *Prep/Shoot/Post Etiquette* guide; to Craig Siebels for his help on the chapters dealing with production, including his mock budget illustrations; to John Kretchmer for supplying his episodic director's agenda; and to Charissa Sanjarernsuithikul and Richard Winnie for their guidance on the postproduction chapter and appendix. Thanks, too, to Matt Nix, SRTP alum and instructor, for recommending Keith Sawyer's book *Group Genius* to me.

The first "nonfamily" reader of this book was historian David Reynolds, emeritus professor of international history at Cambridge University, whose initial advice ("Reread your introduction; I don't think it describes the book you're writing"), subsequent insights, and unflagging support were of immeasurable help. The last reader before submission to my agent was novelist and lifelong friend David Fuller, who supplied the tough love and blue pencil necessary to cut the manuscript down to size.

In between were a platoon of colleagues and friends who commented on intermediate drafts: T. J. Brady, Sarah Chricton, Andy Cohen, Peter Cohen, Daisy Dennerline, Rodes Fishburn, Deb Fordham, Joan Grayson, David Grinsfelder, Keshni Kashyap, Carole Kirschner, Katri Maninnen, Karen Maser, William MacDonald, Kevin McNulty, Andrew Nunnelly, Sonya Sones, Ava Tramer, Bennett Tramer, Jordan Reddout Wilhoit, Robb Weller, Richard Winnie, Kim Winther, Tom Wright, and John Yorke. Thanks, everyone. You're all in there somewhere. Author Robert Masello never quite got around to reading any drafts, but his steady advice on how to navigate the publishing world more than made up for it.

Special thanks to my book agent, Deborah Schneider, for her belief in me and the book, which helped me keep the faith on the manuscript's journey to its proper home at Applause. Thanks also to Cathy Gleason of Gelfman, Schneider Literary Agents for her friendly help throughout.

Acquisitions editor John Cerullo of Applause Books has my eternal gratitude for seeing the book's potential. My appreciation extends to the entire Applause team, particularly Melissa McClellan, Barbara Claire, and Laurel Myers.

Journalist, editor, and grammatical fussbudget Martha Groves generously gave the manuscript her own copyediting pass before I formally submitted it, which led to many spirited discussions. The book is far better as a result. That said, I confess to a certain devilish delight in pointing out that I began this paragraph with an Oxford comma, a choice that Martha, a stickler for the *Associated Press Stylebook*, would heartily disapprove of. My book, my comma.

Any acknowledgment must include my parents, Hugo and Lois Melvoin, who not only instilled in their children a profound love of the arts, but also let me leave the dinner table early on Tuesday nights when I was six years old so I could watch *Sea Hunt*, starring Lloyd Bridges.

My older son, Nick, and I enjoyed three weeks of peace and quiet (and fly fishing) together in the early summer of 2014 in Last Chance, Idaho, where he studied for the California Bar Exam while I began to make notes for what would become this book, so I consider Nick part of its DNA. My younger son, Charlie, read an early draft and offered prompt, sincere encouragement, which was—and remains—deeply appreciated. Finally, my wife, Martha, patiently pored over numerous drafts, always offering gentle advice, which wasn't always so gently received but invariably appeared in the next draft. My family makes the world a wonderful place to wake up in regardless of whatever else may be going on. My greatest thanks—first, last, and always—goes to them.

INDEX